REELING
THROUGH
LIFE

REELING THROUGH LIFE

HOW I LEARNED TO LIVE, LOVE, AND DIE AT THE MOVIES

TARA ISON

Soft Skull Press | Berkeley | An Imprint of Counterpoint Press

Library of Congress Cataloging-in-Publication Data

Ison, Tara.
Reeling through life : how I learned to live, love, and die at the movies / Tara Ison.
pages cm
Includes bibliographical references and index.
ISBN 978-1-61902-481-6
1. Ison, Tara. 2. Authors, American—20th century—Biography. 3. Screenwriters—United States—Biography. 4. Motion pictures—Influence. I. Title.
PS3559.S66Z46 2015
818'.5403—dc23
[B]
2014033792

Cover design by Kelly Winton
Interior design by Neuwirth & Associates

Soft Skull Press
An Imprint of COUNTERPOINT
2560 Ninth Street, Suite 318
Berkeley, CA 94710
www.softskull.com

Printed in the United States of America
Distributed by Publishers Group West

10 9 8 7 6 5 4 3 2 1

To my mother and father, who said it was a gift

CONTENTS

REELING THROUGH LIFE

INTRODUCTION

A friend of mine with two children, ages three and six, won't let them watch movies. She lives out in the country, on a heavenly rural estate with an organic garden, roaming peacocks, a buzzing apiary, a small pond . . . and a lavish home movie theatre in the basement, tricked out with a five-by-nine-foot screen, an overhead projector, a digital-everything system, and a split-level viewing area of a dozen roomy Barcaloungers upholstered in rich celadon velvet. This state-of-the-art retreat was a concession to her husband, who likes to watch Charlie Chaplin pictures and documentaries on Winston Churchill in the wee hours of the night; I'm not sure her kids even know it's there. The first time I ever saw it, I could feel my pupils dilate and the Pavlovian mouth-watering for popcorn and M&M's kick in. Who wanted a tour of the arbor, or to visit the sheep, pick blueberries, swim in the pond? All I wanted was to curl up in sweatpants and all that plushy velvet and lock myself in that endless glowing pleasure dome of cinema for days.

I'm a child of the movies, a movie freak, a film junkie, a cineaste. It's a lifelong addiction, the activity for which I happily forsake all else. I don't believe it's wholly a craving for escape—my passion for watching movies is more engaged than that. It is a proactive desire to enter into and inhabit other realities, other lives. To slip into someone else's clothes, trod along in their shoes, try out their actions, accents, and attitudes. To imagine myself as an Other, and to layer that Other's experience onto my own. It's a desire for more layers—and a desire to learn from those layers, to figure out who I am and how to be in the world. Movies have gotten under my skin, formed my perceptions, influenced the choices I've made. I've learned how to live *at* the movies, *from* the movies; I am who I am because of movies, and, to some degree, all the other movie freaks out there are, too.

And for me, it's not a very discriminating desire; I've never formally studied film or film history, and despite seven years working as a screenwriter, I rarely analyze a movie in which I'm wholly engrossed with an eye toward structure, technological achievement, character development, and so on. As a moviegoer, I want to be dazzled by the smoke and mirrors and enflamed roar of the Great Oz—I have no wish to pull aside the curtain and see the frantic machinations of humble Professor Marvel. There's a time for examination, and a time for immersion. The lingering impact of a movie often has nothing to do with artistic merit; a forgettably wretched movie might sear one indelible image into my brain. If one scene set in contemporary Manhattan or nineteenth-century Venice, or a line of dialogue about the tender mercies of life, or a nonverbal moment of romantic love . . . if any such moments get to me, they usually do so through some idiosyncratic and subjective portal in my consciousness. The images that hit a nerve for me this way might not be those that electrify someone else—and the movies I discuss, from the relatively obscure to the blockbuster hits, from multiple-Oscar winners to critical and commercial bombs, are not necessarily those on anyone else's roster of personal film favorites. But all of us who love to watch movies experience those universal points of connection; we all have our own subjective, idiosyncratic collection of indelible cinematic moments.

And sometimes those remembered images aren't even accurate; in revisiting some of the movies I discuss here, I've been surprised to realize that what I remember about a particular movie moment, the influential lesson that has stayed with me—how to kiss in the rain, what to say to my shell-shocked parents about their divorce, where in the linen closet to hide the liquor—sometimes doesn't actually exist in the film. It's a trick of memory, the mix of my emotional and intellectual state of being and the circumstances of my life when I first saw the movie. Or, looking back, I've realized my younger self's misunderstanding of, or lack of appreciation for, certain subtleties of character or story or theme. But even so, at the time, the impression was made, the image formed, the lesson learned. Sometimes the mere mention of a movie title is my Proustian *madeleine*, hurtling me back to that memory-dimension like a time-machine traveler. In discussing these movies, I'm tapping back into that original moment of absorption and immersion, and not always or necessarily my perspective now, reflecting with a more analytical eye.

I especially love movies based on books. Sometimes I've read the book before rushing out to the movie; other times I've seen the movie first, then hurried to pick up the book. Either way, more layers. I'm a reader and a writer as well as a moviegoer, and books are as crucial to me as movies—but the book is *not* always better, not always more stimulating, engaging, formative. Whether I read the book or saw the movie first, and regardless of how powerful an impression the book may have made, in the case of adaptations I'm choosing here to stay within the experience and feeling of the film.

Going to the Movies has always been, as far back as I can remember, both an event and a way of life, the deliberate exit from my own mundane living room—with its twenty-inch TV screen, a mediocre seascape, and a macramé creeping charlie plant hanging over it, people's quotidian grumblings interrupting the far-more-fascinating conversations on-screen—in order to fully enter some exotic Other World. You go to the movie theatre, you cross the threshold to a sacred space dedicated wholly to that experience, smelling of popcorn in hot oil, strangers and their unfamiliar toiletries, and dry, stale velvet. Your sneakers stick to the black floor as you grope your way among the pews to the unexpected feel of a flap-bottomed seat, and sit at full attention in the dark, before an expansive altar of flickering images that shows you intimacies of other people, accompanied by arousing lilts and swells of music and sounds. The experience demands you abandon your own body, exit your own mind, leave your real life and real self at the door, and give your willing, spongelike consciousness over to it, ready to both absorb and be absorbed.

The rites and rituals were so clear. As a kid you went with your mom or dad or sitter or older brother to animated Disney flicks and watched morality plays of romance, loyalty, and familial bonding featuring anthropomorphic singing animals. Or, if no sitter could be found, your parents (mine, at least) sometimes took you with them to entirely inappropriate R-rated fare and hoped or assumed you wouldn't really pay attention . . . where, squirming in your seat, you'd see the gross-out scenes from *The Exorcist* or perhaps some romantic sex romp that flashed a naked buttock or breast, bodily contortions both thrilling and terrifying. At eleven or twelve years old you convinced your parents to drop you and a friend off for an entire Saturday afternoon of freedom at a place like *Theee* Movies of Tarzana!—part cineplex and part arcade, loud, shiny, and plastic— where you loaded up on soda and Reese's Peanut Butter Cups, played jittery games of *Pong* or *Pac-Man*, and sat through an eighty-minute movie starring bratty, precocious adolescents outsmarting dim adults. After that, if you were feeling lucky and bold, you'd try to slip past the usher and go all by yourselves into the R-rated movie playing down the hall, until someone's mom swung by to pick you up outside.

In your so-mature midteens you went in the late Sunday afternoon to a sedate, arcade-free theatre with your parents for a more sophisticated *Annie Hall* or a *Kramer vs. Kramer*, where you sipped a Diet Coke, picked at Junior Mints, and tried to puzzle out adult relationships and why they always seemed to fail. At seventeen you drove yourself with girlfriends to Westwood for the big Saturday night out, hoping to flirt with UCLA guys on the street; you were able to buy your own thrilling ticket to those R-rated movies, *Atlantic City* or *Body Heat*, and afterward went for coffee to discuss the flirtatious use of lemons and the hot sex in a tub of ice cubes (hoping to be overheard by UCLA guys in the next booth). At eighteen, nineteen, and twenty, you went quite late at night, during the week, with your college boyfriend to the Nuart or the Beverly Cinema, the rundown and funky revival/foreign film theatres, to watch Montgomery Clift or James Dean feeling misunderstood and tortured, or perplexing Godard films you pretended to understand, or the midnight showing of *Rocky Horror*. This was when you had arrived, when Going to the Movies was the synthesis of social ritual, cultural rite of passage, intellectual and artistic stimulation and challenge, and the ultimate behavioral expression of being cool. By now the movies were fully in your system; you'd absorbed the education of a lifetime.

The grandmother of my friend with the country estate and pleasure-dome home movie theatre recently suggested she rent *Fly Away Home*, a very charming family movie about a girl and a gaggle of motherless geese, that the kids might enjoy that one. But my friend won't do it—it isn't any concern about violence or sex in film, she explains to me; it's because image shapes experience, actually *creates* it. Her children can take a walk in the woods or along the river and see *actual* geese; she wants their later memories to be of their authentic experience, she wants them to remember the realities of their lives, not the manufactured versions offered to us by a mainstream corporate culture. Later, she says, with a foundation of real experience in place, the kids can watch all the movies they like.

I admire her philosophy, the integrity of her vision. And she's right; I've often questioned just how impressionable I was—and still am. I've wondered about the influence of film on my own authenticity. But don't we all, to some degree, project ourselves onto the screen, cast ourselves as the main character in the imagined "remake" of every movie we see? And I didn't grow up in the country, with wild geese around, so if the closest to wild geese I might come is watching *Fly Away Home*, at least I'll always have that—those abandoned baby geese, for an hour and a half, aren't a secondhand experience; they become real babies for me to mother, too, and that's a lesson I'll happily learn.

So, for better or worse, whether it's due to subliminal absorption or conscious emulation, my identity has been as shaped by the movies I've seen as by anything else in real life. The very thing that concerns my friend is unalterably, inextricably part of my reality: Movies have created entire aspects of my self. They've given me definition. They've taught me how to light Sabbath candles, how to seduce someone with strawberries. Bulldoze my way past writer's block. Go a little crazy. Characters are my role models, my teachers; the movie theatre has been a classroom. The blur has happened, and I often catch myself thinking: Did I actually *do* that? *Say* that?

Or did I just see it in a movie?

HOW TO
GO
CRAZY

ELECTROSHOCK, BEAUTIFUL MINDS, AND THAT NASTY PIT OF SNAKES

One Flew Over the Cuckoo's Nest

Frances

Suddenly, Last Summer

The Snake Pit

An Angel at My Table

Planet of the Apes

Girl, Interrupted

A Beautiful Mind

had my first experience with electroshock therapy when I was eleven.

It was 1975, the year I started seventh grade, and boys my age were strutting their Crazy Jack Nicholson imitations from *One Flew Over the Cuckoo's Nest* all over school.[1] I know I saw the R-rated *Cuckoo's Nest* when it opened in a theatre, and I know some adult must have accompanied me—my parents, or an indifferent babysitter, although why would anyone take an eleven-year-old girl to see such a movie?—because I was too timid and well-behaved to sneak into verboten theatres on my own. I didn't break rules; I was scared Something Bad would happen, that vague threat if you somehow sullied your permanent record by misbehaving, by acting out.

In *Cuckoo's Nest*, Randle P. McMurphy, a.k.a. Crazy Jack, is a charismatic petty criminal who tries to evade prison by feigning craziness, which he thinks will earn him some easy time in a mental ward. Doesn't work out to his benefit, in the end. The film was shot in the real Oregon State Hospital in Salem, and looks it—some of the zombielike extras with deformed craniums seem too creepily real. Lots of metal doors clanging, chains clanking, images of leather restraints installed on cots, and stooped men with shaking hands. Orderlies are incongruously dressed in white button-up shirts and black bowties and look just like diner soda jerks from the 1950s. It all haunts. At eleven, I feel haunted and creeped out even as I watch from the safe distance of my theatre seat, even as I tell myself *it's only a movie*; when the dazed and confused patients line up to get their little Dixie cups of pills and water, I can almost smell that thin wet-paper smell as they swallow.

Bad-behaving McMurphy comes up against Nurse Ratched, the white-stocking'd, sexually repressed, modulated-voice, emasculating image of the Bitch in Charge; when McMurphy boasts to an orderly

---

1 *One Flew Over the Cuckoo's Nest* (United Artists, 1975): screenplay by Lawrence Hauben and Bo Goldman, based on the novel by Ken Kesey and the play by Dale Wasserman; directed by Milos Forman; with Jack Nicholson and Louise Fletcher

that he'll be getting the hell out soon, and the orderly grinningly tells him, "You're going to stay with us until we let you go," McMurphy, for the first time, realizes he's trapped—that Nurse Ratched is truly in control of his destiny, his body, his mind.

But what haunts me the most, then and now, is the scene where McMurphy, after inciting a near riot during one of Nurse Ratched's therapy sessions, is given electroshock therapy. He isn't wheeled into the small white procedure room, strapped to a gurney—no, he strolls in, with that cocky Nicholson bounce and grin teenage boys love to emulate, oblivious to what's in store. When he's asked to lie down on a table, he cheerfully complies. My heart starts racing around here—I know what is coming, I believe, but I don't know how I know, I just know in my belly it is the punishment coming, the Something Bad. I am too old to look away, to seek the comforting glance or hand of an indifferent adult. McMurphy's shoes are removed, conductive gel is smeared on his temples, and I feel the pasty chill of that on my own face. He obligingly takes into his mouth a rubber guard that looks exactly like the dental plate my orthodontist uses to take impressions of my teeth for braces. Attendants place padded white tongs on either side of his head and grip him under his chin, a flip is switched, and there's a brief, brief buzz that isn't the worst of it—it's the seizing up and sudden clench of McMurphy's body, the whine from the back of his throat, the convulsive shaking and straining he does for long moments after the shock itself has ceased, the way everyone has to struggle to hold him down. I watch that with my pulse racing, my fingers gripping the armrests hard, my own body in some kind of mimetic, rigid seize. McMurphy is eventually lobotomized at the end of the movie, but it's off-screen and not nearly as memorable.

Earlier in the film, at McMurphy's admissions interview, the weak, emasculated man in charge, Dr. Spivey, tells him that prison officials, in fact, suspect he might be faking his craziness, and they want an evaluation to determine whether or not he's really mentally ill. The evidence he's nuts: He's "belligerent, talked when unauthorized, been resentful in attitude toward work in general," and that he's "lazy."

You hear that when you're eleven years old, you see where Breaking Rules can get you.

An Italian neuropsychiatrist in the 1930s, Ugo Cerletti, was studying the link between epilepsy and schizophrenia, and that research, combined with a slaughterhouse visit where he watched panicked pigs electrocuted to docility just before getting their throats cut, sparked the idea of electroshock therapy as a form of psychiatric treatment. He killed a lot of dogs, first, by placing electrodes at each end of the animal; he eventually learned to put them on either side of the head, which allowed the current to bypass the heart. He moved on to humans in 1938 and had positive results with an itinerant, jibbering man from Milan, whom he zapped back to a productive lucidity. By 1940 electroshock was in use in the United States, the new Holy Grail of convulsive therapy, viewed as more humane than Metrazol shock or insulin coma, more progressive and civilized than the "treatment" of dumping the straitjacketed or shackled "insane" in hellish asylums for life, and, despite subsequent memory loss or disorientation or broken bones or spinal injuries from the severe spasming (or from being restrained), more effective.

Electroshock reached a zenith in the early 1950s (see: Sylvia Plath), then began a slow tapering downward during the development of antipsychotic drugs. The practice hit its nadir in the mid to late '70s, but a 1985 conference of the National Institutes of Health acknowledged its efficacy, and electroshock—now referred to as ECT, electroconvulsive therapy—is back on an upswing; the National Mental Health Association has reported roughly one hundred thousand people a year are receiving it, primarily as a treatment for depression. Advocates say most of the kinks have been worked out—the equipment is upgraded, the appropriate voltage standardized; anesthesia and muscle relaxants are administered to prevent the bodily convulsions; the current is applied unilaterally rather than bilaterally, for fewer side effects.

But whichever side you're looking for, whichever side you're on, it's tough to find an article or book on electroshock therapy written after 1975 that doesn't reference *One Flew Over the Cuckoo's Nest*. That image smacked both culture and science hard. Some attribute that one depiction of electroshock to the overall decline of the practice in the United States; others claim ECT was already on the wane, and the movie simply heightened awareness or hastened its fall from grace.

They weave discussion of Randle P. McMurphy in among actual case histories of real people and words like *hypothalamus*, *the temporal cortex*, *neuroendocrine hypotheses*, *cognitive dysfunction*, *neurotransmitters*, and *joules*.

But for me, at eleven, it isn't a cultural phenomenon; it's the most brutal, cautionary thing I have ever seen. It's the iconic electric chair that bursts a prisoner's head into smoke and flames. It's the cop's stun gun shocking the belligerent perp; it's the blue fluorescent bug zapper that fries any creature that stings. It's bang, bang, Maxwell's Silver Hammer coming down upon your head, it's the throbbing cartoon thunderbolt of agony stabbing the brain in aspirin commercials. It will be the time, later, when I am fifteen and working in a bakery, that one of the older guys in back tells me to *Put your hand, here*, on the metal side of a dough-mixing machine, and *Okay, now grab on to this post*, and I do, and I hear the *burr* as all my marrow jerks up hot and vibrating, my jaw snaps, the roots of my teeth begin to burn, and every thought I have ever had of owning myself is for a flash seared away. It's the imagined whiff of cerebral scorch. It's the image of cocky, swaggering, feral Jack Nicholson reduced to an electrode-wired animal in a cage and temporarily made meek. It's the terror of that one day happening to me, if I ever step out of line, ever become *belligerent*, ever talk when *unauthorized*, ever appear *resentful* in attitude to work in general, ever become *lazy*.

Because most of all, I learn, it's something people in power can do to punish you.

- - - - - - - - - -

I had a blind Aunt Edith, one of my grandmother's six siblings. As I child I saw her on holidays and the odd family occasion when we'd all go out to a formal Chinese restaurant. I remember her as pleasant and smiling and dull, a well-groomed aging lady in a boxy suit and careful bouffant who smelled of Aqua Net and fruit Life Savers and gave crisp $5 bills as presents. Most of the time she would be perched on the couch next to my grandmother, who brought her miniature quiches and cocktail dogs on a napkin; it was my job to escort her to the bathroom once or twice during an evening, where, always forgetting, I would lean in to turn on the bathroom light for her and then be embarrassed at the light switch's *click*.

My mother and I would visit Aunt Edith at her Miracle Mile apartment, and I was amazed at how tidy it was, every knickknack in place. Once I remember Aunt Edith talking about a book she was writing, the story of her life, and she waved a thick sheaf of neatly typewritten pages at us. She had big, big plans for it. I remember an unusual spark in Aunt Edith that day, an off-kilter excitement that seemed unusual for her. A simmer that somehow made me uncomfortable.

Edith was born sighted, but lost the sight in one eye from a bout of babyhood measles, and a few years later had the incredible bad luck of losing the sight in the other after a schoolyard accident. Each of her six brothers and sisters took on defined family roles: the Beauty, the Businessman, and so on. Edith, in addition to being the Blind One, was also considered the Bright One. My grandmother Ethel, the second youngest, was the Party Girl, the classic '20s flapper, but she was also, always, Edith's Caretaker, even after she married my grandfather at nineteen.

In her early twenties, Edith married a man named Everett, who was partially sighted and a genius with electronics; they started a successful business together, and she became more independent of my grandmother for many years. But when the marriage ended, it seemed to trigger an alarming change in Edith—now she became the Crazy One. She began showing signs of manic depression; during wild upswings of energy she'd get angry and mean or ramble about the big, big plans she had for her life. She'd also hit the bars at night, picking up men and having a lot of sex. She was still relatively independent—living on her own, getting by on savings and disability, getting around in cabs—but she'd make incoherent and frenzied phone calls to my grandmother in the middle of the night. She was robbed and beaten up at least once; she might have been raped. Then she'd crash and disappear for a while, to my grandmother's despair and panic and perhaps my grandfather's relief. She'd return, apologetic, brushing off concerns, picking up her life, and all would be fine. Then the mania would start again, the upswing of frenzied partying and sex, the shrieking, volatile phone calls—my grandmother was terrified Edith would get herself killed, and my grandfather became increasingly resentful at being Edith's Caretaker, the role he inherited when he married my grandmother. It was during one of these manic periods that my grandfather decided to commit Edith to the mental institution at Camarillo State Mental Hospital.

Mondays through Fridays, everyday at 3:00, my local ABC station used to run "The Afternoon Movie." I'd come home from junior high and heat up a Stouffer's Tuna Noodle Cassarole, open my algebra or history book, and watch classic old movies with Bette Davis or Audrey Hepburn. I see *Suddenly, Last Summer* this way, with Elizabeth Taylor; her character, Catherine, has been committed to Lion's View State Asylum by her rich evil spider of an Aunt Violet, who pressures caring psychiatrist Dr. Cukrowicz (Montgomery Clift) to perform surgery on her rambling, babbling, violent, and promiscuous niece.[2] Dr. Cukrowicz is a lobotomy specialist, who calls the procedure "the sharp knife in the mind that kills the devil in the soul." Aunt Violet says she wants the surgery to help her niece, but in truth she wants snipped out and away an unpleasant and scandalous memory of Catherine's dead cousin, Violet's son. The aunt wields absolute control over the family, using her power and money to convince Catherine's feckless mother to sign the authorization for it, and this Ratched-like supremacy is unnerving to me; it's clear that Catherine isn't crazy: She's inconvenient. Beautiful Catherine convinces Dr. Cukrowicz to get her out of the ward of crazy, shrieking women; she gets her hair done and gets out of the surgery at the end, too, and I expect to feel relieved, but I still feel a sense of personal, familial threat hovering in my own living room. That evening I take pains to do an extra good and industrious job on my homework. I tidy up my room. I offer to do chores.

I also watch *The Snake Pit*, with Olivia de Havilland as another going-crazy woman, this time committed by her caring husband to Juniper Hill State Mental Hospital after she's exhibited uncomfortably

---

2 *Suddenly, Last Summer* (Columbia Pictures, 1959): screenplay by Gore Vidal, adapted from the play by Tennessee Williams; directed by Joseph L. Mankiewicz, with Elizabeth Taylor, Katharine Hepburn, and Montgomery Clift

odd behavior: blankness, confusion, inexplicable hostility.[3] There is a nasty montage of hospital-gowned Olivia undergoing shock treatments—menacing shiny black machine, padded tongs, conductive gel scooped from what looks like a pot of marmalade—but the zapping itself is off-screen, save for the moans. I give the quickest glances to the jerking feet, the naked legs that try to thrash. But I'm drawn back in later when Olivia, a wannabe writer, is given a typewriter and permission to write one hour a day; she feels stronger, more assertive, is looking to reclaim some control over her self, and makes the mistake of asking the sadistic, vengeful Nurse for the privilege of some privacy.

NURSE

Look, you, being a writer is nothing to be so excited about. It doesn't set you above the other ladies, you know . . . all you have is an exalted view of your own importance!

And as punishment, Olivia is immediately thrust into a ward with the craziest of the crazies. She stands in the throng of ranting and raving women, the camera swoops up, fast, and the ward visually transforms into a huge craggy pit, Olivia lost in the swarm. We next see her, now calm, polite, and well on her way to recovery, telling her caring doctor what she remembers reading once about "the snake pit"—how, in the past, they threw insane people into a pit of snakes in the hope of shocking them back to normality. Because, the theory goes, what might drive a normal person insane might well drive an insane person normal. It seems to work for Olivia—but the movie ends the day she wins release from the asylum, and who knows what happens to her after she gets to go home with her caring husband. Who put her there in the first place. Because her "odd" behavior made him . . . uncomfortable.

I still have Crazy Jack in my mind, but Olivia and Catherine become my images of Crazy Women, and they unnerve me because of their

---

3 *The Snake Pit* (20th Century Fox, 1948): screenplay by Frank Partos and Millen Brand; directed by Anatole Litvak; with Olivia de Havilland

helplessness. There is an aunt or a husband in full charge of them; one is vindictive and one is loving, but both have the power to hand a family member over to someone with the even greater power to strap them down, use a sharp knife to kill the devil in their souls—or just an awkward bit of memory—or toss them into a pit of snakes.

Forget it, I tell myself, they're just a couple of old, outdated movies. I empty the dishwasher, I Windex the glass coffee table in the living room, I bury my nose in whatever I'm supposed to be studying, my x-plus-y calculations or review of the Marshall Plan; no resentful attitude against work, no laziness, no bad behavior here.

Camarillo State Mental Hospital, in Camarillo, California, was once the largest mental institution in the western United States. Now a college campus, the grounds are still considered a "Historic Asylum." Charlie Parker wrote "Relaxin' at Camarillo" in 1947 after a six-month stay there for a nervous breakdown. Rumor has it the Eagles wrote "Hotel California" in its honor. After its closing, an editorial in the *Ventura County Star* bemoaned the loss of their local hospital, "which for six decades provided a humane and tranquil refuge for the mentally ill. . . . For some, the well-tended grounds and Mission-style buildings were the only real home they'd ever known, and the caring staff had become as close as family."

As a kid, I never realized I had a famous mental institution practically in my neighborhood, the we're-getting-closer point en route from Los Angeles to Santa Barbara along a highway lined with gentle eucalyptus trees. My Aunt Edith's multiple commitments there happened long before my time and my experience of her; vague references to Aunt Edith's "craziness" usually went over my head, and I didn't connect her with lockups in a Camarillo asylum, or with Olivia de Havilland and Elizabeth Taylor, with their shapeless smocks and Medusa hair, staggering around the bottom of a snake pit and screaming to get out, until I was older and my mother told me more of the story, and I realized that my memory's version of the pleasant lady with the crisp-folded $5 bills didn't, perhaps, really exist.

Watching *Frances* in 1982, when I am eighteen, I spend much of the first half of the movie amazed the lead actress is the same insipid girl from the Jeff Bridges *King Kong*.[4] This time Jessica Lange is 1930s movie star Frances Farmer, who goes to Hollywood, refuses to conform, leaves after she can't get along with anybody, gets used and abused in a love affair with Clifford Odets, returns to Hollywood, and continues to piss people off—from that point it's pretty much a sad downhill, as the ruling figure in her life, her mother, Lillian, keeps terming her ornery willfulness as mental illness and commits her to a series of progressively worse insane asylums.

The movie initially tries, I think, to make the point that strong, passionate women get punished, but what, exactly, Frances is so strong or passionate *about* isn't especially clear. Her politics are imprecise to me, and early in the movie it seems she gets into trouble or antagonizes people for foolish, bring-it-on-yourself reasons: Bad behavior such as driving drunk and then assaulting the cop who pulled her over, or showing up three hours late for shooting, which has nothing to do with integrity or the courage of one's convictions and is all about being egotistical and rude. Even the journalist who adores her from start to finish tells her she ought to pick her battles better and fight the ones that count. She does a lot of shrieking, and it seems unprovoked. The hysteria just hangs there. But once she's in the hands of people with power, once she's placed in that very first "convalescent home," the shrieking becomes rooted, substantial. It finally makes sense. As the movie goes on, shrieking becomes all she can do, all she has left— until the end, when even the power of outburst and outrage is taken from her.

I see the movie with my mother. Early on, Lillian Farmer applauds her teenage daughter for winning an essay contest, clearly a vicarious thrill for her, and my mother and I both feel warm and happy and identifying at that; I am a high-achieving, well-adjusted teen—a role at which I excel—and she is my biggest, most voluble fan. But when the movie shifts, when Frances starts acting out and her mother's devoted and concerned maternal signature on papers becomes a warrant, a weapon, a threat, my old discomfort returns, increases.

---

4 *Frances* (Universal, 1982): screenplay by Eric Bergren, Christopher De Vore, and Nicholas Kazan; directed by Graeme Clifford; with Jessica Lange, Kim Stanley, and Sam Shepard

Lillian sends Frances to Meadowbrook Hospital for some rest—but we hear the real reason from the Man in Charge: That in her "present excited state," her "mother is unable to control her." At Frances's intake interview, the Director of Meadowbrook reassures her that "for creative people under stress, erratic behavior is not uncommon," but Frances already hears alarm bells:

                    FRANCES
    I don't want to be what you want to make me . . .
    dull, average, normal!

Cut to a syringe plunged into her thigh like a meat thermometer into a roast, and a rubber guard thrust in her mouth, for her own protection during an induced bout of insulin shock. Frances tries to make nice and polite after that, soon telling the Director how much the treatment at Meadowbrook has helped her, how excited she is to return to her exciting movie star life. Good, he tells her—"Your mother has such big plans for you!" But he also tells her she still has obvious feelings of "anxiety, hostility, and guilt"—and that she isn't going anywhere.

                    FRANCES
    You're trying to rearrange what's going on in my
    head. You're trying to drive me crazy!

She escapes and rushes to Mother, telling her she's finally figured out the *why* of her messy life: The actress biz doesn't work for her, she plans to buy a country house and have a vegetable garden instead: "I've realized the only responsibility I have is to myself." She isn't going to be a movie star again, but that flips Mother out—"You selfish, selfish child!"—and Frances is next dragged shrieking, shrieking, shrieking, down a hallway in a straightjacket.

We're back to electroshock. It's the now-familiar scene: Several people hold the patient down, the conductive gel is smeared on, a rolled towel is shoved in her mouth, the dial turned, that brief and innocuous buzz, and then the convulsions, the jerking, the straining against restraint. She's thrown in a snake pit of a ward with other wacko women—unlike McMurphy's relatively placid wardmates, these gals are underworld Gothic in their excessive, whooping, drooling craziness, they're Olivia de Havilland's freakish snakes, and Frances practices her next Good Girl speech on them, rehearsing her next pleas to be released. She dooms herself when she commits the ultimate sin; Frances tells her Mother—she *shrieks* it, in fact—that she *doesn't love her*. That's it.

Cut to a procedure room, where a White-Coated Doctor describes the beauty of what happens when a slender instrument is slid up under a person's eyelid to sever the nerves of the temporal lobe, the nerves that "deliver emotional energy to ideas." Electroshock first, to sedate the patient, helps, of course. That way, you can do ten an hour. Frances, bruised and covered with sores, is wheeled in, strapped to a gurney, while the White-Coated Doctor caresses something like an ice pick.

> **WHITE-COATED DOCTOR**
> With the cure comes a loss of affect, a kind of emotional flattening, with diminished creativity and imagination. After all, it is their imaginations and emotions that are disturbed.

The White-Coated Doctor then holds up a hammer the shape of a small mallet, and, just out of frame, thank God, thank God, positions the pick, takes aim, and there's a gentle but definitive *tap*. End shrieking. Cut to black, then the final shell of Frances, years later, autopiloting her way through a 1958 episode of *This Is Your Life*, then zombie-ing off alone down a dark Hollywood street.

Feelings of anxiety, hostility, guilt, a daughter blurting out *I don't love you* and a mother's accusatory *You selfish, selfish child!*—is that really all it takes?

I'm excessively sweet to my mother for the rest of the day.

My first therapist, when I was around fifteen, was a lovely man in sweaters named Steve, with an unthreatening office in velours and earth tones and macramé'd hanging plants. I saw him once a week and I remember he insisted I pay $15 toward each session—my mother was paying the rest—in order for me to feel more responsible and involved in my own treatment.

Treatment for what? Many of my friends went to therapists, and most of our parents certainly had. It was the late 1970s, it was Marriage Encounter and EST, it was the San Fernando Valley. It was an expected coming-of-age ritual, like nose jobs, a status symbol, even, a casual qualification for club membership. Annie Hall, an Unmarried Woman, and Ordinary People all went to shrinks. My parents had divorced a few years earlier, but that was expected, too, and, in comparison with other parents' divorces—in comparison with other parents' *marriages*, even—it seemed relatively bumpless, untraumatic, everything done by the book. I was by the book as well, a good kid, trouble-free and achieving, good grades, good friends, never cause for worry, a sweet-natured, self-reliant daughter who had learned to make zero demands on the self-absorbed, physically and emotionally absent father, on whom the divorce-traumatized, needy mess of a mother could lean, depend, the one who didn't need any taking care of herself, no problem at all, a good good girl, a fucking Good Girl.

My mother behaved as if my visits to a shrink were perfectly ordinary, like going for a haircut—and yet, paradoxically, she seemed bewildered by it, taken aback that her perfect daughter was showing any kind of crack. I had asked, tentatively, vaguely, not wanting to alarm or disturb, if I could "talk to someone"; there was something hot and coiling inside of me, a simmer that terrified me with its threat of mess, like tomato sauce in a pot on the stove, little bubbles exploding to spatter the range with orange grease. There was no room in the house for my mess. I remember, at the first visit, numbly asking Therapist Steve if he wanted to hear my dreams. He said sure, because the process of discussing them could open stuff up. I don't remember what they opened up, but I know I started to cry, loudly, and then I tried to stop crying, because crying leads to wailing and wailing leads to shrieking, and if I began to shriek and explode that way, I thought I might not be able to stop. It isn't good to be a shrieking Afternoon Movie Woman; people who say they care will do anything to get you to stop. And who knows what else might blurt out of you, along with the shrieks?

But everything was *fine*, really, perfect, I kept insisting in between choked sobs, so what *was* there to sit on a brown velour couch and complain of, what was there to cry or shriek about? I was ashamed of my distress, aware of my privileged life—what was I making such a spattery fuss for? Why be anxious, hostile, guilty? Therapist Steve seemed so nice, caring, but you never know; I apologized and smiled a lot, trying to assert myself as unanxious and already meek. But for fifty minutes, once a week: An explosion of choking, convulsive sobs without reason or source, of gasping for air.

I stopped seeing Therapist Steve not long after I started driving. My indulgent grandfather bought me a car for my sixteenth birthday and I was abruptly empowered; you can drive *yourself* places, escape to and away from, you're an adult, autonomous, and it worked on me, somehow, that new ability to navigate the Ventura Freeway meant the magical ability to control myself and my destiny, even just a few miles of it. In the confined safe space of a Honda Civic, I could breathe. I was incredibly relieved; no more encroaching threat of orderlies in white shirts or shiny black machines, no more inexplicable crying, not for me.

"You know, your Aunt Edith was in a mental institution," my mother told me as we drove home from *Frances*. I hadn't known that, but now it made an awful kind of sense. Edith had died of cancer by then, a year or two earlier, and my mother told me about all the commitments—how Edith would go too far, go too nuts, my grandfather would say they had no choice, my grandmother would protest, but my grandfather would sign the papers and off Edith would go, to Unit 45 at Camarillo. Afterward she'd tell my mother about the electroshock treatments, how she hated and feared them.

"They shuddered her," my mother said. This all happened in the late 1940s, when my mother was in her early teens. (And the same era as *The Snake Pit*, now suddenly far too close to home.) "But your grandfather said it helped. It calmed her down. She'd go home and everything would be fine for a while. She would just be . . . normal depressed, not crazy. She wouldn't be a problem for anybody. Then it started up again. And she'd beg your grandparents not to send her back there." Pause. "But your grandfather said it was the right thing to do. It was for her own safety. And it was his decision. And she was never a problem after that."

When Frances is wheeled off to her first round of electroshock, we see the ceiling from her point of view, the stained tiles running past overhead, and I tried to imagine my Aunt Edith being wheeled off in the blind dark; she wouldn't have known where she was headed, the first time, she wouldn't have seen the menacing black machine. But she would have felt the cold gel on her temples, gagged on the rubber forced in her mouth, suffered everyone holding her down. I wonder if she shrieked, the second time they came for her. Or the next time she found out my grandfather had signed those papers again and found herself on her way back to Camarillo, or the third, the fourth. I have this version of her in my mind now, shrieking, locked away with Frances and Catherine and Olivia and wondering what hideous thing she has done to deserve such a punishment as this.

Because this is the real terror of *Frances*, *The Snake Pit*, and *Suddenly, Last Summer*, the chilling thing beyond the electroshock and the ice pick and that conclusive, tender *tap*: That familial signature on the commitment form. There is a thin, shaky line between being *crazy* and being *inconvenient*, and this is the penetrating moral of these stories: Keep on being a good girl, don't piss people off. Don't go too crazy, don't say the wrong thing, don't become a problem, a mess, don't start shrieking, don't lose control. Be sweet to your mother; be nice to your father. Look what a caring family member is capable of.

I thought about all this again a few years later, when my grandfather, whom I adored and still do, and who was a man of impressively catalogued lifelong angers and resentments, had disowned my mother, who also adored him, ostensibly for a single wrong thing she'd said to him one night at dinner, a careless and inappropriately disrespectful remark that got blurted out and triggered an enragement. But I believe it was my aging, lonely grandfather's last bid at a vindictive kind of control, his wielding of a bolstering power against the only vulnerable person he had left: It was a Ratched-esque, Aunt Violet–like, Lillian Farmer–style bid for authoritative command. He was unable to control my emotionally extravagant and exhausting mother, and at the same time he resented her childlike dependence on him—he couldn't cut out part of her brain, but he could cut her out of his life. He refused to ever speak to her again, and he died that way. It was an agony for her, a shock to her system she never fully recovered from; it kept her in an emotional straightjacket, made her a little crazy and a little terrified of the people who loved her. And I'll always believe he wanted to drive my mother a little crazy *because* he cared about her enormously; otherwise, that act of commitment would have been meaningless.

The story of my Aunt Edith is interwoven with the story of my mother and her father, a story of power, of control and self-control and the loss of those things, a story of the agonies a person who cares can inflict. But I'll never know my aunt's real story, or at least *her* version of the real story, because all those pages she wrote, what I think of now as a written shriek, a brave and futile attempt at going on record, have disappeared forever.

I had a grand mal seizure once. Just one, once. My own little electroshock. Some minor synaptic wackiness. I was twenty-two, in my last year at college, and in line with a friend to see *Down and Out in Beverly Hills*; we were seated on the ground eating M&M's, waiting for the doors to open. I remember standing up to go in and closing my eyes—and when I opened my eyes again what to me was a second later but in real time was about forty-five minutes, I was flattened out on the ground, my head in my friend's lap, disoriented and sort of pissy about missing the movie. I heard later I did convulse and jerk, I did foam at the mouth a little, and in the ER we made seizure jokes about Rex Harrison in *Cleopatra*, Laurence Olivier in *Othello*. But the actual experience of it, for me, was a big nothing. No electric chair, no burning cartoon thunderbolt. It was just being briefly blotted out, an anticlimax. After multiple misdiagnoses, the doctors never really found out what caused it, and it never happened again. After six months of observation and tests, they told me to just go on back to my regular life, to be happy and grateful and fine.

Prior to the arrival of the seizure, I'd been slipping back into the cryings again, the baffling kind of impotent and enraged sobs that would spring up in me out of nowhere and hang around to stymie and drain. I'd been trying to stay calm (*dull, average, normal*), go to school, hang with friends. But for a while the activity of being sick (Is it epilepsy? Brain tumor? Bizarre neurological quirk?) was a terrific focus, an external, tangible, blameless source of drama. There had been talk of brain surgery for a while, and I'd thought about that slender instrument rooting around in my mind, I could hear the *tap*, could hear *with the cure comes a loss of affect, a kind of emotional flattening, with diminished creativity and imagination*, and I wondered if that would happen, if they would indeed wind up snipping out the devil in my soul, leaving me diminished and flat. But when they decided I was perfectly fine, and took all that that away (Go back to your happy life, you're *fine*!), I plunged.

The medication didn't help matters. I was on Tegretol, which prevents seizures, sure, but there's a reason it's also used to treat bipolar and psychotic disorders—this is your brain coated in Pepto-Bismol, this is your brain wearing two condoms, this is your banana slice of a brain suspended in Jell-O. I couldn't function; I couldn't go to class. I also wasn't allowed to drive, an infantilizing, demoralizing condition in Los Angeles, and I spent six months in a trapped and paralyzed splay on my couch, too numb, this time around, to even cry. Is it time for the big guns, a psychiatrist? That petrified me: First the pills, then comes the caring signature on a form, maybe, and a meat-thermometer syringe, the leather restraints. . . . I'd just been given a Second Chance at life, and I should be overjoyed, energized, buoyant. But if there *is* nothing empirically wrong, say, a tumor—well, that means something else *is* actually going on wrong inside your brain, doesn't it? That means *crazy*. That means mental illness. It is in the family, after all. It is in my blood. Camarillo was just down the street. Waiting for me, like Olivia's Juniper Hill, Catherine's Lion's View, Frances's Meadowbrook. I couldn't let that happen. "High-achieving" = "well-*performing*," I reminded myself, = you know how to perform = you are a good actress, yes, are good at playing that role. Fake it till you make it. I threw away the pills; I got in my car and drove myself alone to the beach through treacherous, windy, and steep Topanga Canyon; I went back to college and studied and graduated, had dinners and movies with friends and said all the right things, kept busy, bootstrapped and faked it all just enough that everything circumstantial gradually took over to hold me up, distract, carry me along and aloft until faking it became the new normal, became real. No plummet into the snake pit, not for me.

- - - - - - - - - -

My brave spirit!
Who was so firm, so constant, that this coil
Would not infect his reason?

> —Prospero to Ariel, from Shakespeare's
> *The Tempest*—and popping up on-screen in
> *An Angel at My Table*

I didn't want to see *An Angel at My Table* in 1991.[5] I'd heard it was about a woman going crazy, and I was done with women-going-crazy movies. I'd learned those lessons. But no, I'm told, it's really about a New Zealand writer from the 1930s and '40s, so I go. And it *is* all about a writer, at first; Janet Frame is a painfully introverted and awkward young woman, with rotting teeth and Little Orphan Annie hair, who wins people over with her brilliantly obtuse poems and short fiction, and this long initial writer part is lovely to aspiring-writer me. But then her professor compares her, ominously, to Virginia Woolf and van Gogh. By this he means he thinks she's crazy as well as brilliant, and suddenly strange men show up to convince her she needs to go someplace for a nice rest. Janet agrees, but when she sees PSYCHIATRIC WARD on the door (*Run*, I want to yell), she starts to question what is going on—she doesn't belong here, does she? It's a good question: There's been no shrieking, no belligerence, no laziness. No erratic behavior, no manic fits. There isn't even anyone looking to punish her for something or wanting her out of the way. She's just a little shy, that's all, has some anxiety, sure. But she's diagnosed with schizophrenia. To me this seems almost worse than someone consciously seeking control or revenge—it's an arbitrary label, too casually and unaccountably slapped on, an almost clerical error of judgment.

---

5 *An Angel at My Table* (ABC/Television New Zealand/Sharmill Films, 1991): screenplay by Laura Jones, based on the autobiographies of Janet Frame; directed by Jane Campion; with Kerry Fox

However, Janet seems pleased by the diagnosis, as if, finally, she has an identity. Until, sure enough, we cut to the shrieks. An assembly line of crazy women are getting communal electroshock; Janet, watching and listening, is terrified. "Close your eyes," she's told, her temples swabbed, the rolled towel shoved in her mouth, the dial turned. She screams and jerks. And we hear her beautiful, resonant voice:

JANET

For the next eight years I received more than two hundred applications of electroshock treatment, each one equivalent in fear to an execution.

Eight years! Two hundred shocks! And after all this, her doctor decides on a *new operation* for her, and we all know what that means. Janet's bewildered, clueless mother has agreed. She has signed the papers. Those damn papers. But there's sudden news that Janet has won some huge book award; another doctor takes another look at her and sends her home. She's perfectly normal! All is well! *Go back to your happy life, you're fine!* I hear in my mind.

Janet tries to go back to her life; she tries to *create* a life. She publishes another book, she travels to Europe, she finally gets laid. But when she naïvely offers up her psychiatric history at a job interview, she realizes she's still dragging this thing around, the confused conviction there must be something wrong with her. And she doesn't know how to kick it loose:

JANET

In fear and despair at my life, I needed answers to the questions I still asked myself about my history. I knew that talk of suicide must always be taken seriously. Such talk came readily to me as a shortcut to ensure action.

And she walks *back into* a psychiatric hospital. *Voluntarily*. This I find shocking. I can't understand how she can offer herself up for the rotisserie like that. Is this woman stupid or brave? Or—*is she really* crazy?

JANET

Finally, it was concluded that I had never suffered from schizophrenia. At first, the truth
seemed more terrifying than the lie—how could
I now ask for help when there was nothing wrong
with me?

A doctor tells her any problems she's having *now* are *due to* her prior hospitalization. She really is fine. She can be shy if she wants, feel as awkward as she likes. And she does go on to write more books, win more awards, live a happy life. Crazy or normal, I realize, this woman is amazing; she so strong, so constant.

But I am not. A year later, I am back in a sink on my couch, mired in sobbing and hiding from family and friends, and this time I can't blame it on the dope-you-up antiseizure pills. One morning I realize I've lost four or five months of time. It's gone astray. I think maybe I should call someone. I remember Therapist Steve and his unthreatening macramé plants, but who knows where he is. I borrow a friend's therapist, make an appointment; Therapist Cathy is pretty and young and very tiny, wholly un-Ratched-like, wearing a floral-print dress. She seems harmless, uninvested in me, agenda-free, so I sit on her couch for fifty minutes and choke and bawl about how *there is nothing wrong*. She sends me immediately to a psychiatrist, a clinical, expressionless woman who lectures me for twenty minutes about serotonin levels, runs through a checklist of factors indicating clinical depression, and gives me a prescription for antidepressants. I can smell the thin wet-paper smell of Dixie cups, and I fear this is only the beginning. I hear an iron door clang, I could swear I see a gleam in her eye, and I run back to Therapist Cathy: Can we just try this, first, the two of us, in your safe office with the plush carpeting and the pictures of pretty gardens on the walls? Before the drugs, before the brain chemistry issue and doctors and nurses and the word *clinical*, please? She agrees, reluctantly, but lets the word *hospital* hang in the room: Seventy-two hours, she tells me; if she decides at any time that I'm a real danger to myself, she can have me put in a hospital for seventy-two hours, they can have me for seventy-two hours.

She's telling me this, and I'm thinking about *Planet of the Apes*.[6] I remember lost-in-space traveler Taylor (Charlton Heston), now captured and strapped to a veterinarian's table, rendered speechless from a throat injury, at the mercy of hostile talking gorillas. I remember kind chimpanzee Zira asking orangutan-in-charge Dr. Zaius if she might continue working with her favorite human, Taylor, and Dr. Zaius replies, "Experimental brain surgery on these creatures is one thing, and I'm all in favor of it," while glaring at Taylor, who is trapped in a cage, a leather choke restraint around his neck. Later Taylor, trying to prove his advanced cerebral functioning is no freak accident, finds one of his fellow astronauts, Landon, in a crowd—Landon turns to show us his slack jaw and lifeless gaze, and we see a tidily shaven patch on the side of his head, and a horseshoe of a scar, McMurphy-style, and Taylor screams:

```
                    TAYLOR
    They cut him . . . you cut up his brain, you
    bloody baboon! . . . you cut out his memory, you
    took his identity!
```

And Taylor isn't even suspected of being crazy, but he's a problem, and the same thing is in store for him, Dr. Zaius warns, the "experimental surgery on the speech centers, on the brain. Eventually a kind of living death."

Meanwhile Therapist Cathy is telling me, Yes, we can try this, but she doesn't let me leave until we make a pact: No dangerous behaviors without calling her, first. Agreed, and we plan for me to see her three times a week. I do not mention that I have already been researching suicide—A+, homework-doing student that I am—that I already own a copy of *Final Exit*, already have purchased a pack of old-fashioned razor blades.

But I don't consider buying the razor blades a dangerous behavior. I just need them to make those tiny little practice slices in my thighs

---

6 *Planet of the Apes* (20th Century Fox, 1968): screenplay by Michael Wilson and Rod Serling, based on the novel by Pierre Boulle; directed by Franklin J. Schaffner; with Charlton Heston, Kim Hunter, and Maurice Evans

and forearms, just a warm-up, just to see if I can feel anything, and to see if I'll be able to do it when the time comes. I rehearse and rehearse: Mere kitten scratches. The real time comes, I decide, a month or so later during an inexplicably sobbing-at-two-in-the-morning fit of hysteria; I pick up a fresh blade, try, can't do it. Can't do it for real. So I now have to confront my inability to make a deep and assertive-enough slice to offer escape, and *that* inadequacy makes me paroxysmic. I can't do anything right. What a fake I am. What a wimp, a fucking fraud. Maybe a gun. Maybe poison, jumping off a building, something honest and true, something that once committed to, I can't back out of. Okay, I figure, I should call Therapist Cathy, that's the rule we agreed on, and I don't break rules or agreements because I am such a fucking Good Girl.

But I hear Janet's beautiful, resonant, cautioning voice:

JANET
Talk of suicide must always be taken seriously. Such talk came readily to me as a shortcut to ensure action.

I don't *want* to ensure action, I realize. That's why I can't cut. Action means *hospital*. I think *hospital* and I see pills and needles and too many shuffling people in bathrobes. I see leather restraints on cotlike beds and stained ceiling tiles and drooling and basement rooms. I feel the conductive gel on my temples. I see Ratched and well-meaning Montgomery Clift and a sign that reads PSYCHIATRIC WARD, where Randle, Frances, Catherine, Olivia, and Janet are waiting their turn for the machine. I hear: *Tap.* I think *hospital* and I hear Charlton Heston screaming, "You took his identity!"

And that's my image of *hospital*: It's the place where they steal away what makes you human. Where they silence not only your voice so you cannot tell your story; they silence your brain so you cannot even know what your story is.

I put the blade away and get back into bed. I'm not going that crazy tonight.

At the beginning of *Girl, Interrupted*, pretty, smart, twenty-something Susanna Kaysen is getting her stomach pumped after an overdose of aspirin, while she keeps swearing to everyone that she wasn't really trying to kill herself.[7] Her parents and doctors convince her she needs "a really good rest"; she signs herself into a mental institution, which, again, just shocks me—doesn't anyone ever realize what signing those papers *means*? I was nervous to see this movie; I'm not a convict guy or a 1930s movie star or a housewife or a New Zealander, but I am Susanna-like, a middle-class young woman with a nice life and no apparent problems and a history of minueting with suicide. And Susanna's also a writer—like me, like Janet, like housewife Olivia in *The Snake Pit*. Writers are starting to seem overrepresented as crazy people, I think, although it ultimately was Janet's salvation; I suppose, like arsenic, it can be both poison and cure.

On her way to the institution, Claymoore, the cabbie tells Susanna:

CABBIE

You look normal.

SUSANNA

I'm sad.

CABBIE

(shrugging)

Well, everyone's sad.

And he's right, I think. But when does one person's sadness become another person's lunacy?

One significant difference between Susanna and me, of course, is that Susanna actually swallowed those pills, which puts her in a whole different league—she's the real, impressive thing. But if she's crazier than I am, fellow patient Crazy Lisa (early, unhinged Angelina Jolie) is way crazier than either of us, and puts us both to shame; Lisa is the

---

7   *Girl, Interrupted* (Columbia Pictures, 1999): screenplay by James Mangold, Lisa Loomer, and Anna Hamilton Phelan, based on the autobiography by Susanna Kaysen; directed by James Mangold; with Winona Ryder, Angelina Jolie, Whoopi Goldberg, and Vanessa Redgrave

Randle P. McMurphy of the place, the charismatic, glamorous wacko who brings with her the edge, the danger, the restraints and injections. Lisa takes Susanna under her wing, showing her how to fake-swallow those meekness-inducing pills. She even steals her psych file for her, where Susanna reads that she's been diagnosed with Borderline Personality Disorder, defined by:

SUSANNA

(reading)

" . . . an instability of self-image, relationships and mood, uncertainty about goals, impulsive activities that are self-damaging, such as casual sex. Social contrariness, and a generally pessimistic attitude are observed."

(to Lisa)

Well, that's me.

LISA

That's *everybody*.

The Crazy Girl is the voice of reason—if that's the definition, who *doesn't* have Borderline Personality Disorder? At least sometimes. We should all be in Claymoore. We should all keep Camarillo on speed dial. The arbitrary and generic nature of this labeling reminds me of *Janet Frame, Schizophrenic*; it confirms every fear I've ever had about behaving yourself, and being very, very careful not to sully your permanent record.

The movie offers lots of evidence how normal Susanna actually is, in comparison with all the other women there, and she finally decides she wants to leave. But, as the Chief Doctor points out, "You signed yourself into our care. We decide when you leave."

However, the Doctor also indicates the decision, ultimately, is Susanna's; she needs to decide between two courses of action, namely: Am I sane? Or, Am I crazy? Susanna says those aren't courses of action, but the Doctor insists:

CHIEF DOCTOR
They can be, for some. Will you stay or go?
It's the choice of your life. How much will you
indulge in your flaws?

This takes me aback, confuses me—it's paradoxically empowering and chastising. I like the confirmation that there's an element of choice here, that Susanna can reseize control of herself, *choose* just how far along on the crazy continuum she will go. But I'm embarrassed by the categorizing of depression or emotional fragility as an exaggerated form of self-pity or weakness. A flaw. It echoes Olivia's vengeful, sadistic Nurse: "All you have is an exalted view of your own importance!" Meanwhile, Lisa, the legitimately Crazy One, has run off on a destructive rampage, been dragged back, given electroshock (offscreen, it isn't her movie), and is roaming around shell-shocked with the twitches and the drool.

Susanna's real showdown/reality check comes during a confrontation with her head nurse, Valerie, a no-bullshit Whoopi Goldberg:

VALERIE
You are not crazy!

SUSANNA
Then what's wrong with me? What the fuck is going
on inside my head?

VALERIE
You are a lazy, self-indulgent little girl who is
driving herself crazy! And you're just throwing
it away . . .

Of course, that's me, too. All that sitting around and crying on a brown velour couch . . . just pure self-indulgence, pure laziness, as I've always suspected. Again, it is empowerment combined with admonishment. I'm annoyed; I'm reassured. And added to this a scene from

The Wizard of Oz, on television in the hospital lounge the day Susanna leaves the institution—Dorothy, at the end of the movie, begging Glinda:[8]

DOROTHY

```
Oh, will you help me? Can you help me?
```

GLINDA

```
You don't need help any longer. You always had
the power to go back to Kansas!
```

Fine. The categories are a bit clearer. The lesson: There's *real* mental illness, the Crazy Lisas who are genuine in their craziness. And then there's the rest of us. Who sometimes feel sad (angry, lazy, awkward, trapped) and don't seem to realize that all we've ever needed to do is simply click our heels.

I'll try to remember that, next time.

SUSANNA

```
When you don't want to feel, death can seem like
a dream. But seeing death, really seeing it,
makes dreaming about it fucking ridiculous. . . .
Was I ever crazy? Or maybe life is. Crazy isn't
being broken or swallowing a dark secret. It's
just me, amplified.
```

- - - - - - - - - -

I'm thinking about the images of crazy people in films, and how those images have imprinted on my mind, and my own flirtatious history with bouts of a minor craziness I've been able to stave off, and

8 *The Wizard of Oz* (MGM, 1939): screenplay by Noel Langley, Florence Ryerson, and Edgar Allan Woolf, based on the novel by L. Frank Baum; directed by Victor Fleming; with Judy Garland and Billie Burke

I realize I have forgotten all about *A Beautiful Mind*.[9] I saw the movie when it came out in 2001, and at first I loved it, and then I hated it, and now I go around and around, because it makes me crazy.

Math genius John Nash, while a student at Princeton, is desperate to "distinguish himself" by coming up with a truly original idea—he does, eventually, something about governing dynamics that's referred to (but never explained) as his "equilibrium," the idea that forty years later he'll win the Nobel Prize for. His hope to distinguish himself this way proves to be only half accurate—how many Nobel Prize–winning mathematicians can *you* name? Who aren't *also* famously schizophrenic? It is, alas, his craziness that distinguishes him enough to have the big Oscar-bait movie made about him; sitting in the theatre, I can almost hear the acceptance speech.

But while still a young, Nobel-less mathematician, Nash begins working undercover for black fedora–wearing William Parcher, trying to break Russian codes for the U.S. government. He also meets and marries a beautiful and brilliant graduate student in mathematics, Alicia, who from the day of the wedding never again mentions another word about math. Nash becomes increasingly obsessive about his undercover work until, finally, he has a paranoid meltdown onstage at a math conference; he is tackled, and Christopher Plummer appears, murmuring in that Plummery way of his that's so uniquely soothing and menacing and seductive, all at the same time.

Christopher Plummer is Dr. Rosen, a psychiatrist, and we cut to his office, where Nash is shackled and drooling (Thorazine) and it's revealed that both Parcher and John's college roommate Charles (and Charles's sweet little niece, Marcee, whom we've seen earlier) are, in truth, delusions. Nash is a full-blown paranoid schizophrenic, and who knew? I love this part of the movie; I knew from the first sight of Parcher the character was a delusion, that Nash is going nuts, but the movie faked me out on Charles and Marcee, and I am right there, on the floor of the doctor's office with John, confused, suspicious, roiled. There's nothing unnerving about this to me, however—I don't

9 *A Beautiful Mind* (Imagine Entertainment, 2001): screenplay by Akiva Goldsman, based on the book by Sylvia Nasar; directed by Ron Howard; with Russell Crowe, Jennifer Connelly, and Christopher Plummer

identify with John's craziness (he's one of those *real* wackos), it's just a good directorial trick of shifting perspective.

And then Nash is led into that windowless white room, berobed and frightened; he's quite thoroughly strapped down on a cot with leather and buckles, a rubber guard is gently placed in his mouth, and I know what is coming. "Bathroom," I whisper to my friend, and I slink wimpily out to go wash my hands. I return a few moments later; Nash is back home with the loyal Alicia and their new baby; he's swallowing two bright pink pills every day, he's thick-tongued, fog-brained, and impotent, and getting fed up. He is normal, but dulled. Unbeknownst to Alicia, he stops taking his meds. But we know it, this time, and so we're increasingly on edge, waiting for it, waiting for it . . . A few scenes later Alicia comes upon John about to drown their baby in the bathtub; she races to call Dr. Rosen, as Parcher and Charles urge John to stop Alicia, kill her, she's looking to destroy him! John poises to attack. Alicia is about to escape with the baby when John has an abrupt slam of rationality; it hits him that in all these past years, little Marcee has never grown older. He surrenders. Dr. Rosen wants him back in the hospital immediately, but John refuses; he argues he can reason his way to a steady sanity without the torture of treatment, without the brain-deadening meds. Alicia has to make the choice: She refuses to sign the commitment forms, she puts her hand on John's face and his hand on her heart and tells him "*This* is real." Big . . . *Awww*s from the audience.

At that moment, I want to leave the theatre again. Not to avoid yet one more scene of electroshock—but because I am now appalled by the lesson of this movie. The woman has a child and the mentally ill man she lives with hears a fake man in a black hat telling him to kill. But no, stay with your schizophrenic and dangerous-by-any-objective-standard husband who refuses his pink pills, stay at any risk to your own life or the life of your child. That's beautiful. That's what a woman, a wife, a loving spouse, should do—it's what's noble, admirable, what will move us to tears, make us *Aww* and applaud. Ah, the power of love.

But this is a terrifying, horrendous idea. John *himself* tells her she should leave, that it isn't safe for her or the baby to be around him—suddenly the paranoid schizophrenic is the only person in the movie making sense. How can you *not* leap to aggressive action, how can you not take charge, control, when a person you love ceases to be the same person, is possessed by a soul-sucking demon, has transformed into a peril or a shell? I desperately want her to sign those papers and lock him away, before tragedy strikes.

But it all works out okay for the Nashes. An extended montage skips us ahead thirty-plus years, and no one is drowned, no one is attacked or killed. John learns to snub his delusions and does mention, briefly, that he's now taking some of the "new medications," then accepts his Nobel with a tribute to his loving, loyal, patient wife.

And this brings me right back to loving this movie; I want to believe John is *right*—reject the needles, the pills, the hospitalization, don't give away that part of yourself that distinguishes you. Embrace the devil in the soul, be the mad genius, at any cost; be Woolf and van Gogh. Fight the power. Fight the bland-faced, smooth-voiced people who tell you they can help and then strap you down. Don't listen to the person too clinical or too caring. You can do it yourself. Pull yourself up, choose your course of action, get yourself back to Kansas. Learn and rehearse your lines, give the performance of a lifetime that will give you a lifetime. The movie's message is dangerous; the movie's message is inspiring.

I understand why John doesn't want to take those pills, why Frances refuses to be "dull, average, normal," why McMurphy can't keep from igniting the oil fire of his personality before Ratched's frigid gaze. Because what if it's that tiny, tiny fragment of your beautiful mind that does hold your equilibrium or the true core of your identity? What if it's the exact nerve cells of your uniquely mad genius that wind up with their circuitry scrambled to hell? What if Crazy Lisa is right? What if it's the "disturbed" imaginations wherein lie the sonnets or sonatas, the equations, the chiaroscuros, the distinguishing spark? What are "ideas" without any "emotional energy" as juice? *Memento ergo sum*, and what if it's precisely that off-kilter level of serotonin that allows you access to those memories that make you, you?

I watched the movie again the other day, and I realize I no longer identify at all with John, the crazy one; I identify with Alicia, with her dilemma. Her decision not to commit him is loving, humane, not passive denial—she's the anti-Ratched, for she wants to empower, not control. And I realize I have no idea how my grandfather actually felt about my Aunt Edith, and those decisions that he had to make, time after time after time, to have her locked away. I know he resented the responsibility, yes, but—did he also do it out of genuine concern? Love? A hope that she would be cured? My Aunt Edith probably wasn't going to kill anyone, but she might have wound up in a ditch, beaten or stabbed to death, or self-deadened with suicidal despair. Is it unloving, inhumane, to take away someone's power to self-destruct? Isn't *that* what we really should trust our loved ones to do? And hope they make the right choice? I have to wonder about this now from the other side: Faced with a crashing-and-burning loved one on my hands, would *I* be able to sign those forms?

At the end of *The Snake Pit*, after a tidy Freudian unraveling of her neuroses, Olivia asks her doctor how she can be sure she won't wind up in the pit again; he snaps off the light, lets her stand a moment in the dark, then points out she now knows where the light switch is. *Click.* So although she might find herself in the darkness once again, at least now she'll always have the power to find her way to the light. But what happens, say, to someone like my Aunt Edith—someone for whom even the light switch has no power, no meaning? What about someone who *can't* just click her heels?

It doesn't matter, in a way, that ECT is now, by all accounts "largely voluntary, a last-resort option" and a lifesaver for many people (see: Carrie Fisher); it doesn't matter which way the debate or the proof on it swings; it doesn't matter that I am not clinically bipolar or border-line or that I most likely will not become a paranoid schizophrenic or (I hope) the muttering bag lady on the corner, off her rocker, off her meds, the one I turn my eyes from, or a space traveler flung two thou-sand years forward into an evolutionary quagmire. It doesn't matter whether any of us really does have control over our own mental and emotional well-being—the psychobiologists and the psychosociolo-gists can battle that one out—or agree on a definition of the word "*crazy*," that we often simply fall back on the slippery and subjective cousin-definition of *porn*: "We know it when we see it."

And it doesn't matter, in a way, that my own family members, my friends, the people I trust with the spare key to my life, would never,

I think, I think, sign any papers (I wonder), would never allow the straps or machines or (I hope) the stripping away of me.

Because there is still that thin, shaky line between being crazy and being inconvenient, and who hasn't worried about losing their grip? About losing that weak clutch on sanity, reality, self, or about those things being pried away? "There is a wisdom that is woe; but there is a woe that is madness," says Melville. The threat of that will always loom for me, and perhaps it's the cautionary and inspiring images in my mind of McMurphy and Frances and Janet and John, along with women cast into gloomy pits, or women snapping back on their own lights, and version A and version B of a crazy aunt, that help me keep it all in check, the wisdom and the madness, teeter and threat, the images that show me how to go just crazy enough to empower myself and not the devil in my soul, how not to wind up unself'd and groping in the dark.

HOW
TO BE
LOLITA

THE SCHOOLGIRL, THE NYMPHET, THE MUSE, AND THE INEXORABLE TICKING CLOCK

The Prime of Miss Jean Brodie

Taxi Driver

Bugsy Malone

Pretty Baby

Lolita

Manhattan

MISS JEAN BRODIE

`Little girls!`

she announces imperiously at the front of the classroom, here at the Marcia Blaine School for Girls, calling us to order, demanding our immediate attention.[10] And I pay attention, of course, for I am a little girl, she is speaking to me—although, at six years old, I am younger than Miss Brodie's thirteen-year-old pupils. Perhaps I am even too young to be attending this PG-rated movie, but I am accompanied by my parents, after all, and it's about a schoolteacher and her devoted students in 1930s Scotland, they probably reasoned—if they ever reasoned about such things—so how inappropriate could it be? And how could this impassioned, in-her-prime Miss Jean Brodie (Oscar-winning Maggie Smith at her fine-boned loveliest) offer anything to a little girl but the wisest counsel, the sagest of lessons on life? Especially in that enchanting Scottish burr?

MISS JEAN BRODIE

`Little girls! I am in the business of putting`
`old heads on young shoulders. And all my girls`
`are the crème de la crème! Give me a girl at an`
`impressionable age, and she is mine for life!`

And those unformed little girls, pudgy or scrawny, spotty or velvet-cheeked, with their unfortunate juvenile haircuts and baggy school uniforms, gaze at her adoringly, fully under her spell. I adore her, too—whatever the *crème de la crème* is, it is obviously the best thing to be. Miss Brodie offers a secret knowledge beyond spelling and geography and math; she seeks to illuminate "all the possibilities of life,"

---

10 *The Prime of Miss Jean Brodie* (20th Century Fox, 1969): screenplay by Jay Presson Allen, adapted from her play, based on the novel by Muriel Spark; directed by Ronald Neame; with Maggie Smith, Robert Stephens, and Pamela Franklin

of art and poetry and love, to her girls, "to provide you with *interests!*" she promises, to nurture their natural proclivities for romantic passion, above all else, and I am eager to be privy to these teachings— even if I don't understand everything that is happening in this movie, Miss Brodie's destructive emotional manipulations, or the intricacies of academic politics. I am almost jealous of the special attention Miss Brodie pays to her four favorites—Jenny, Sandy, Monica, and Mary— especially Jenny, whom Miss Brodie deems prettiest, the one who "could be magnificently elevated above the ordinary realm of lovers," the girl most destined to be famous, one day, she says dreamily, "for sex." I do not understand what being famous *for sex* could possibly mean, only that it is, like being the best *crème*, clearly the thing to aspire to, and so I am determined to pay extra good attention that I might learn.

Miss Brodie has recently ended a love affair with Teddy Lloyd, the art teacher with a wife and a flock of children; their once-glorious time together has turned prosaic, lost its idealized sheen, and while he is in despair at losing her, he doesn't hesitate to call her out: "The truth is, Jean, you bounced into bed with an artist, but you were horrified when you woke up with a man!" Miss Brodie is not done with him, however; she sees an opportunity, in pretty-but-bland young Jenny, to create a romantic scenario, a Dante-and-Beatrice-esque love affair between the fortyish Teddy and the budding teen, a relationship that will rejuvenate and reinspire an older man to greatness and awaken the young girl to the glory of sexual maturity. And so, over the next few years, she grooms the clueless Jenny to replace her in Teddy's bed.

But it is Sandy (Pamela Franklin), now seventeen, bespectacled and plain, the one who has developed a resentful edge and caustic wit, the one Miss Brodie has desexualized by deeming her "dependable" and well-suited for an emotion-free career as a spy, who ultimately plays that role. Viewing Teddy's portrait of Jenny, Sandy sees, in its resemblance to Miss Brodie, Teddy's still-infatuated homage; left alone with him, she taunts with her insight, and he, taken aback by her provocative, challenging glare, grabs and kisses her. I am alarmed at this assault, but relieved when she flees safely from the studio, both of us frightened little girls. But very soon we jump back to a scene that jolts and stuns me: Teddy, decked out with paintbrush and spattered smock in rejuvenated, inspired artist mode, is absorbed in a new painting of, it is revealed, Sandy—who is now reclined, womanly and self-assuredly nude on a divan, the artist's muse, the precocious little Beatrice to his middle-aged Dante, the expanse of her bare flesh glowing startlingly bright white against the blood-red drapery of the faux-Neoclassical tableau.

Pamela Franklin was eighteen when this film was made (and extraordinary—to hold your own against Maggie Smith!), as were the other girls of the "Brodie set," some even older, but in the early scenes they are entirely believable as thirteen-year-olds, thanks to subtle tricks of hairstyling and makeup, the oversized desks and shapeless uniforms, their girlish postures and child-timbre'd voices. I have invested in and related to these schoolgirl characters as fellow children, even if they are a few critical years older than I am, and it is a shock to now see Sandy on naked self-display to the lustful gaze of this grown man. She is posed as a knowing, sensual woman, yes, but her breasts are tiny childish almonds, and her face, without her glasses, looks even more pubescently fresh-scrubbed here than in her earlier scenes; is she woman or girl? I can no longer define her, the boundaries and implications of her femaleness have blurred, and I am confused. Her exposed tender skin feels all wrong; it is not the clinical nakedness of the pediatrician's office, or the summertime scampering without bathing suits around the pool under the careless watch of indifferent parents. This intimate scene of adult and child, of man and girl, frightens me, implicates and unbalances me. Sandy's soft naked vulnerability is now somehow mine, and sitting there in the theatre, next to my mother and father, I feel unsafe. I feel danger, and fear, and shame.

And yet. Sandy tires of posing, stands, stretches—like Teddy we are invited to appraise her bare back, dimpled rear end, slender limbs—pulls on a crotch-length sweater. Teddy tosses away the paintbrush and pushes her back onto the divan, mock-bemoaning and self-chastising that he has "a schoolgirl for a mistress," and she pulls the sweater away so he might kiss her throat, her breasts, caress those young shoulders that now definitely have an old head upon them:

```
                        SANDY
    My age does bother you, doesn't it? How
    much longer are you going to be tempted
    by this firm young flesh?


                        TEDDY
    Until you're eighteen and over the hill.


                        SANDY
    I really shouldn't feed your depraved
    appetites . . .
```

she teases, reveling in his passion, and I find myself dizzied again by this next new tilt to the world: *She* is the one in control, here, I realize, with her deliberate unveiling and offering of her firm young flesh. She is in charge, and this adult man is rendered powerless by his hunger for this alluring child-woman. I am not entirely sure what he is hungry *for*, what lies at the core of this appetite, or the mysterious delicious force she possesses, but I am allured, as well; I like the satisfied smile on her face and his mumbling delirium. I have never witnessed this before, the little girl as tantalizer, as temptress; it suddenly seems such a *desirable* thing to be.

This is the perhaps-unwise counsel and secret knowledge that I take away from this film, the new *interest* Miss Brodie may or may not have wished to provide me; that my little-girlness does not only or necessarily make me vulnerable—it is also a source of sexual power.

Taxi Driver and **Bugsy Malone** both opened in theatres in 1976, and both featured a preternaturally mature, whiskey-voiced child actress named Jodie Foster, who seems familiar to me as a tomboyish Becky Thatcher from Disney's *Tom Sawyer*, from suntan lotion commercials and wholesome episodes of *The Courtship of Eddie's Father* and *My Three Sons*.[11] But that innocent little girl is gone. In *Taxi Driver*, Foster plays Iris, a twelve-year-old prostitute, whom an increasingly

---

11 *Taxi Driver* (Columbia Pictures, 1976): written by Paul Schrader; directed by Martin Scorsese; with Jodie Foster, Robert De Niro, and Harvey Keitel

unhinged Travis Bickle (Robert De Niro) spends the second half of the movie seeking to save; I am also twelve years old, and, watching this movie, I grimace and hide my face from Scorsese's blood-spatter violence, I am a little bored by Travis's pursuit of an older uptight blond lady, but I cannot take my eyes off of Iris and her doll-like ringlets, hustling tricks in her midriff-baring blouse, her hot pants and clunky platform shoes. The overt sexualization of this child is even more disconcerting for me than Sandy's abrupt nudity, and I try to block out the sinister voice of Iris's pimp (Harvey Keitel), bartering with Travis for her services:

PIMP

Man, she's twelve and a half years old, you ain't never had pussy like that. You can do anything you want with her. You can come on her, fuck her in the mouth, fuck her in the ass, come on her face, man, she'll get your cock so hard she'll make it explode. But no rough stuff, all right . . . ?

I know just enough about sex, and the words of sex, to be shocked by this speech—made all the more harsh by its *sotto voce* delivery—but not enough to fully comprehend it. All I can really think is *But she's standing right there, she can hear you, and she's only twelve, like me!* But I don't know if I am thinking of Iris, the character, or Jodie Foster, the actress—either way, this is all too assaultively explicit for me to process or make sense of. (And what did my parents think, if anything, watching this movie with their Iris-aged daughter?) I want my Becky Thatcher back; I want this little girl romping safely at the seashore, her mother lovingly, protectively slathering on the Coppertone.

However: at the same time, I can wholly relate to Iris as an object of a certain kind of . . . *interest*, as Miss Brodie might say. My own mother, muddy-brunette and Rubenesque, who still cannot believe she has produced a thin, pretty, blond little girl, likes to dress me in miniskirts and snug or strappy tops, she likes me to curl and pouf my straight, stringy hair and put a little makeup on, has bought me three-inch-high cork wedges and likes to "show me off" this way.

She values the male gaze, has encouraged my flirtatious precocity, and takes an especial delight in the attention my prettiness receives from adult men: The guy painting our house, who offers to "keep an eye on" me while my mother goes shopping, then asks me to keep him company so he won't be lonely while he works ("So, do you like school, do you have a boyfriend . . . ?"); my parents' avuncular, Scotch-drinking attorney, who at parties playfully catches me by the waist and pulls me, giggling, onto his lap and holds me close. By now I have learned there are adult men who are friendly to a cute little girl, and that is all . . . and there are adult men who gaze at me in a certain way, whose smile has a nervous yet appreciative edge, and I understand there is a difference; there is something some adult men want, or need, from me that I instinctively *get*. That I enjoy and encourage. That makes me feel important and adult and wise, gives me a heady thrill. That makes me feel powerful—which I otherwise, in my set-the-table, do-your-homework, little-girl life, do not. I might not think to describe their interest as "depraved appetite," but I recognize the hunger—just as I on some subconscious level understand that Iris's prostitute outfit is designed to enhance the childishness of her undeveloped body rather than hide it, because her value lies in the specific, illicit alchemy of her youth and her sex. In later scenes, when Iris is dressed like a "regular" adolescent—androgynous T-shirt, no makeup, hair as stringy and straight as my own, an ordinary girl I might be in seventh grade with—I find her far less interesting. And I am entirely creeped out, even more than I am by the film's violence or sexually explicit language, to see the scene of this regular-kid Iris slow-dancing with her pimp; "I don't like what I'm doing, Sport," she hesitantly murmurs, now an uncertain little girl, and he reassures her she is his woman, he wishes every man could know what it's like to be loved by a woman like her, how lucky he is to hold close a woman who wants and needs him as she does, the coaxing mantra of *woman woman woman* purred in the ear of this sad child. I recognize and am revolted by the obscenity this so clearly is—but I still relate more comfortably to the Iris dressed in her child-prostitute work clothes, with the assured throaty voice and knowing streetwalker dialogue that makes her seem so adult, so wise and in control. She is a grown woman in the body and skimpy dress of a sweet baby doll, and Travis's chivalric, gory, climactic shootout with her pimp confirms that this is something worth killing for.

Foster embodies that intriguing juxtaposition just as charismatically in *Bugsy Malone*, yet there is a reverse dynamic at play; in Alan Parker's bizarro-world parody of 1920s gangster films, all roles are played by child actors (their tommy guns shoot cream-pie "bullets"), running around in 1920s adult costumes and talking like Jimmy Cagney and Jean Harlow.[12] Foster plays Tallulah, the shimmery, smoky-eyed, speakeasy chanteuse; she is a little girl meant to "pass" as an adult woman, her youth is meant to be entirely obscured rather than exploited, and yet that is still the wink-wink conceit of the film: Look at this child in the dress of a grown-up gangster moll! I am as fascinated by Tallulah as I was by Iris, and there is no creepy Keitel-threat to discomfit me here, no too-graphic sexualizing of Foster's youthful beauty—but she is still suggestively erotic in a way that enthralls me. In her big number, Tallulah slinks around the club in her satin gown, singing oh-so-knowingly and world-wise:

TALLULAH

Lonely . . . you don't have to be lonely . . .

Come and see Tallulah

We can chase your troubles away. . . .

When they talk about Tallulah,

you know what they say:

No one south of heaven's

gonna treat you finer.

Tallulah had her training

in North Carolina. . . .[13]

She drains a cocktail, she perches on a table and strokes her fingers down male patrons' faces and slides hankies from their breast pockets, and all the "men" present (who seem all the more boyish in contrast to Foster's innate maturity) are clearly in thrall to her, too.

---

12 *Bugsy Malone* (Paramount Pictures, 1976): written and directed by Alan Parker; with Jodie Foster

13 "My Name Is Tallulah," music and lyrics by Paul Williams

She is the *crème de la crème* of the speakeasy, the leading lady and star of the show, of this whole movie, for me. I am just as beguiled by Sandy and Iris and Tallulah as all those men are, but I want to *be* these child-women. I want what they have; I want to capture and channel and emulate their satiny female mastery of the world. I am beginning to understand, I think, being famous *for sex*—and, thanks to these cinematic Lolitas, I have determined that power lies in being an innocent little girl with the empowered sexual assurance of a grown woman.

— — — — — — — — —

Thank Heaven . . . for little girls!
Those little eyes, so helpless and appealing . . . !

—Maurice Chevalier in *Gigi*[14]

It is later in that same Iris-and-Tallulah year, I am still twelve years old, and I am sitting on the toilet, peeing, my white cotton panties at my feet. There's a party downstairs—family, friends, very festive—here in my grandparents' house, and I've chosen the upstairs master bathroom to considerately leave the downstairs one for guests. And because it is secluded, I haven't bothered to lock the door. There is a knock, but not much of one—enough that I stop peeing, startled—and the door immediately opens, and my cousin Morris is standing there. He is a cousin by marriage, some lineage through my grandmother's many siblings I can never keep straight; he is fiftyish, a leisure suit, a graying pompadour. He puts on a show of startled—"Oh, sorry, didn't know you were up here, *honey* . . ."—but then lounges in the doorway, studying me, an appreciative smile on his face, while I mumble something like "Oh, that's all right." I even apologize, perhaps, for being there. I am frozen, I am sitting on the toilet, staring at my white cotton panties at my feet. I have never liked this cousin Morris—too huggy, too kissy, too much *honey*—and I am unsure what to do; he is not the candy-offering, trench-coated stranger in the dark alley

---

14 "Thank Heaven for Little Girls," written by Alan Jay Lerner and Frederick Loewe

I have been warned about, he is doing nothing wrong, really, not advancing on me, nothing like Teddy's initial grab-and-kiss assault on Sandy, nothing more wrong than the rudeness at walking in on someone in the bathroom and not immediately retreating. As one should. I can't call for "help"—help for what? What can happen? He is just standing there in the doorway, smiling and studying me. He is a cousin, he is male, he is the adult, the adult male. He finally leaves after a frozen forever, and I pull up my panties, I flush, I wash my hands and count to ten and hurry downstairs, where I hug the wall at the opposite side of the room for the rest of the evening, and tell no one, because: tell *what*? It is a minor incident, a nothing happened; it is a ridiculously trivial thing to remember, after all these years.

But I do remember: My thin naked thighs and the humiliating white glow of my panties and my urine turning green the blue water of the toilet bowl and the ice-clinking party sounds of far-away downstairs, and wanting it to be a nothing thing that isn't happening, here. He is very large, standing in the doorway, and I want to think there is nothing to fear, because, after all, I am in control; I have lured a grown adult man into pursuit of me, away from a party, up a flight of stairs, into standing in a bathroom doorway gazing upon a young girl in an intimate moment. I have driven behavior—see how alluring I am, how powerful?

But I don't feel powerful; there is no glory in this. The assurance of the moment is not mine, I have no mastery, I am no Beatrice, no precious muse to inspire poetry, or great art, or love. I am a toilet *honey*, a dirty underwear girl, a crushable cockroach child. This adult man's . . . interest? temptation? *depraved appetite?* is no comment on me, of course—I am in no way responsible, I'm only a little girl.

But in that moment I can't know that. I'm only a little girl.

"The finest delicacy New Orleans has to offer!" is Violet, the virgin girl-child being auctioned off in a 1917 whorehouse in Louis Malle's *Pretty Baby*.[15] And good lord, is she delicious, beyond merely

---

15 *Pretty Baby* (Paramount Pictures, 1978): written by Polly Platt; directed by Louis Malle; with Brooke Shields, Susan Sarandon, and Keith Carradine

pretty, beyond jaw-droppingly beautiful; twelve-year-old Brooke Shields is simply the most exquisite human being I have ever seen. The film begins and ends with a lingering shot of Violet's face, meant to bookend and illustrate the character's emotional arc, and while the young actress can't quite pull off the shifting nuances of Violet's inner life, that face is mesmerizing. It is a woman's face, with its thick eyebrows and cleft chin and photogenic bone structure (young Elizabeth Taylor rocked her child face the same way), but it is the combination of that seemingly mature façade with the vacuous inscrutability of Shields's expression that both disturbs and delights: This child (Violet or Brooke?) is still a blank slate, we can project and imprint anything onto her we might like, and that is exactly what the men attending this whorehouse auction—and we, the audience, as witnesses to it—are being invited to do. The inner-life of this child (Violet or Brooke?) is irrelevant; it is the experience she can create for us that raises her price, commands our *interest*.

And Violet has been well trained to do this, by the brothel girls who coach her on how to play her role (whimper and cry, then act as if it feels good) and especially by her mother, Hattie (Susan Sarandon), who uses her still-virgin daughter as a lure to arouse her own customers, "inviting" her into the bedroom to stand and watch. Keith Carradine enters the story as Bellocq, a photographer hoping to capture on film the madonna/whore quality Sarandon so gorgeously exemplifies—and he is so fascinated by—and his gentle attentions to her mother inspire a jealous Violet to try out her skills of seduction; initially, her childish flirtations come off as mere brattiness. But by her big Auction Night—where she is brought in to customers, displayed on a platter like a roast pig—she has become a pro; handed over to the stone-faced man who has paid a small fortune for her, she knows exactly how to deliver her lines:

<pre>
                    VIOLET
      I'm glad it's you . . . you look nice. I can feel
      the steam inside me, right through my dress. . . .
</pre>

We cut away from the actual scene, to the other prostitutes waiting for it to be over; we hear Violet scream, but when we all rush in together to check on her, she laughs off the obvious trauma of the experience, affects a matter-of-fact detachment. This is her destiny, after all, the role she was born to play; no reason to make any fuss.

But Bellocq, whose fascination has shifted from Hattie to her little girl, doesn't want whoredom to be Violet's destiny—at least, not as a commodity available to other men. Hattie scores a marriage proposal from a customer and abandons her daughter; Violet runs away to Bellocq, pleading to live with him:

> VIOLET
> And will you sleep with me, and take care of me?

> BELLOCQ
> No. . . .

> VIOLET
> Why not?

> BELLOCQ
> 'Cause . . . 'cause I'm not sure why, actually. . . .

> VIOLET
> You're afraid of me!

> BELLOCQ
> Perhaps. . . .

Give him some credit for being conflicted, I suppose. She pushes him down on the bed, climbs on top of him—again, the illusion of control, this little girl overpowering this adult man:

> VIOLET
> I want you to be my lover! And buy me stockings and clothes.

> BELLOCQ
> You don't know what you're saying, Violet.

```
                    VIOLET
I won't even charge you anything at all. . . .
I know those things better than you. You always
know those things about men when you're a woman.


                    BELLOCQ
Some men are different. I'm different. Well,
maybe not after all. . . . I'm all yours, Violet.
```

And so, he gives in to this temptress. She kisses and caresses him, recites her dialogue:

```
                    VIOLET
I'm going to make you so happy! You're just my
kind of man. You really are. I'm really good you
know, cheri—


                    BELLOCQ
Don't talk to me like that! Please! Don't talk
like a whore!
```

He will refashion her as the innocent maiden he wishes her to be— or whatever he wishes her to be. He gets her a maid, so she can play the lady of leisure; he buys her a doll, "Because every child should have a doll"; he slaps her when he is "tired of having to deal with a child!"; he photographs her alluringly naked and posed Sandy-like on a divan; he ultimately marries her, making her at last all *his*. Are they daddy and daughter, husband and wife, artist and muse? She will be anything he wants—he has "safely solipsized" her, as Nabokov's Humbert boasts of his Lolita—and that's the point. When Hattie returns with her now-husband, who wants Violet to come live with them, go to school, lead the life of a normal little girl, Bellocq is devastated—"You cannot take her! I cannot live without her!"—but even more so when Violet so cavalierly shrugs him off (that emotional mutability and detachment have become her nature), chooses to leave with her mother; that final shot is this new nuclear family at the train station, Violet's new "daddy" posing his wife and new "daughter" for a photo, Violet's exquisite, inscrutable face—is she wondering who or what she is supposed to be now?

I see *Pretty Baby* when I am fourteen. I have a better understanding, I think, of what that male hunger for a little girl is all about: The chance to shape the malleable child to serve the adult desire; the infusion of youth, the transference of a restorative life force that fulfills the vampire's existential need to stave off age, decay, death. But now I feel uncomfortably complicit in the exploitation of this child—if I love this movie so much (and I do), if I am so captivated by that face, the mysterious alchemy of that beautiful old head on those naked young shoulders, am I all that different from those leering men looking to possess her, their dollars at the ready?

And which child is captivating me: Violet or Brooke? As with Iris/ Jodie, I am confused: Is my discomfort due to the demands being made on the character or the actress? This is not the case of an eighteen-year-old playing thirteen (or a nude seventeen); this is not an adolescent dressed up as a mock adult; there is no reassuring distance between the illusion and the reality here. This is an actual sexualized child playing an actual sexualized child. This is Violet running around stark naked in a whorehouse; this is Brooke Shields running around stark naked on a movie set. I've been a naked little girl around other naked little girls my whole life—why are these images suddenly so disturbing to me? It is the context of the film, of course; her juvenile nakedness is meant to be both sexual and innocent, Louis Malle intends to juxtapose the one against the other in order to heighten our awareness of both and thus provoke that discomfort. And it is also my now-fourteen-year-old self, in the process of shifting from my own oblivious childhood to a self-conscious awareness of the realities, and vulnerabilities, of the sexual body.

But if I identify, in my beguilement, with those gazing, beguiled men, I still also completely identify with this Pretty Baby—I am a still-prepubescent fourteen, I am as flat-chested and thin-limbed as Violet and Brooke are, and, in order to hold on a while longer to a self-protective denial of that vulnerability, I still want to believe in the glory, and buy into the illusion, of erotic girl-child power.

-- -- -- -- -- --

S tanley Kubrick, in his 1962 adaptation of *Lolita*, largely avoided the discomfiting question of illusion versus reality by casting, as his titular nymphet, fifteen-year-old Sue Lyon, in part *because* she looked nothing at all like Nabokov's little twelve-year old-girl.[16] It is 1981, my friends and I are on a Kubrick kick, and we go see *Lolita* at the Nuart Theatre, our favorite revival house in Los Angeles. I have not yet read the novel, but am surprised nevertheless by Lyon's mascara'd eyes and developed breasts, her bouffant hairdo, her kitten heels and bosom-enhancing cocktail dress; I'd expected another pretty baby, an adolescent Iris, a nubile Violet, even an almost-legal Sandy in her schoolgirl uniform, and I find it ironic that this most iconic of "Lolitas," despite a few signifiers of youth—the lollipop-sucking on the poster, the Hula Hoop, the stuffed teddy bear on the bed—actually seems older than any of them. She seems older than I am, at seventeen. She certainly seems too old for nymphet-fixated Humbert (delightfully smarmy James Mason, all sweaty obsessive fumbles); when Lolita's mother, Charlotte (delightfully desperate and pretentious Shelley Winters), or Quilty (delightfully Sellers-esque Peter Sellers) keep referring to her as a "little girl," it only highlights Lyon's smooth sophistication, her lack of Shirley Temple cutesiness. Humbert seems to be garden-variety-cheating on a mother with her younger daughter (still a huge *ick*, of course), but not necessarily trying to feed a *depraved appetite*.

Lolita is also far less explicit than *The Prime of Miss Jean Brodie* or *Taxi Driver* or *Pretty Baby*—Kubrick goes for fully clothed innuendo, clever verbal puns, and visual sight gags, playing Humbert's obsession entirely for delightful comedy, and so the disturbing hebephile eroticism is pruned away. (Adrian Lyne tried to correct this in his own 1997 adaptation by casting a far-more youthful *and* sexualized Dominique Swain, and in doing so got back some of the story's sexuality—but lost all its comedy. The novel is a brilliant balance of both, and neither film version gets that right.)

---

16 *Lolita* (MGM, 1962): screenplay by Vladimir Nabokov, based on his novel; directed by Stanley Kubrick; with Sue Lyon, James Mason, Peter Sellers, and Shelley Winters

So, if Sue Lyon's Lolita seems too old to *be* a Lolita . . . what am I? I am seventeen now, and I have only just, at last, gotten my first period: Hello, womanhood! My friend Marie and I have recently been hit on by two fortyish guys in a restaurant, who bought us a chocolate soufflé and ordered us wine and stroked our gleaming bare shoulders and tender arms in a delightfully, satisfyingly mesmerized way, and, like Violet, I am by now a pro at the girlishly flirtatious coo, the promising butterfly side-glance, the bit of dialogue that flatters and invites and yet still suggests a virginal blush. I have mastered illusion—if not with boys my own age, for whom my age holds no special appeal, then absolutely with older men—and playing this role is still one of my favorite *interests*.

And then these older men invite us to Las Vegas for the weekend: *Right now, come on, girls, let's go!* I look at Marie, hesitant; she is equally unsure. And I *am* still a virgin, it is not all illusion—is a Las Vegas weekend with these men my big Auction Night, am I setting a high enough price on myself? Are these men appreciative Teddys, protective Bellocqs, comedically fumbling Humberts . . . or just creepy Cousin Morris's? Marie and I suggest we should maybe call our mothers for permission; the men seem to have no problem with this— perhaps it even underscores our enchanting youth. Marie and I head to the pay phone, dial, explain, ask; both of our mothers are delighted by this possible adventure before us: *Sure, if you want to, sounds like fun, go have a good time!* they say. We are flummoxed by their equanimity; we have expected, hoped, to be ordered immediately home, perhaps told to brush our teeth and put our pajamas on, it is way past our bedtime, and are disappointed to have been given this terrifying degree of agency. Aren't we still little girls? Just a little while longer, please? We lie to the two men, apologizing, that we have to get home, and we flee, just as a terrified Sandy once fled Teddy's studio/lair.

But I feel like a coward, a failure at my role as tantalizing teen seductress; Sandy walked back into Teddy's studio on her own accord, after all, Violet sought out and seduced Bellocq, Lolita was ultimately the one to suggest the game of sex to Humbert. I also feel regret; have I missed out, perhaps, on an opportunity, a precious experience? One that may soon, I am starting to wonder, be increasingly rare?

```
                        SANDY
   How much longer are you going to be tempted by
   this firm young flesh?


                        TEDDY
   Until you're eighteen and over the hill.
```

I remember, and the calendar pages of my young life are fluttering by: I menstruate, I am planning for college, I am almost of legal age, for heaven's sake. How much longer *do* I have, to offer my firm young flesh, to tempt in this so specific way?

And I think back to the film *Manhattan*, which I saw a few years earlier.[17] When the film starts, forty-two-year-old Isaac (Woody Allen) is dating seventeen-year-old Tracy (Mariel Hemingway, mouse-voiced and luminous), and he feels both pride and some awkward shame at this relationship: "I'm older than her father," he sputters to his friends. "I'm dating a girl wherein I can beat up her father." Isaac eventually dumps Tracy for the urbane, neurotic, challenging Mary (Diane Keaton), but when Mary dumps *him* to return to her married lover, his nostalgic longing for the simple pleasures of a romantic and sexual relationship with a teenage girl consume him; he finds Tracy, just as she is about to leave for school in London for six months, and begs her not to go:

```
                        ISAAC
   Do you still love me, or what?


                        TRACY
   Do you love me?


                        ISAAC
   Yeah, of course, that's what this is all about. . . .
```

---

17   *Manhattan* (United Artists, 1979): written by Woody Allen and Marshall Brickman; directed by Woody Allen; with Woody Allen, Mariel Hemingway, and Diane Keaton

TRACY

Guess what, I turned eighteen the other day. I'm
legal, but I'm still a kid.

ISAAC

You're not such a kid. Eighteen years old, you
know . . . they could draft you, in some coun-
tries. . . .

She's correct that she's still a kid, but she's also, paradoxically, the
adult now; the more Isaac tries to convince her to stay—while we
all know what's best for her is to leave—the more he sounds like a
manipulative child, wheedling to get back a once-promised treat now
denied.

TRACY

We've gone this long. What's six months if we
still love each other?

ISAAC

Hey, don't be so mature, okay? Six months is a
long time. . . . You'll change. In six months
you'll be a completely different person. . . . I
just don't want that thing about you that I like
to change.

Of course he doesn't. When I first saw *Manhattan*, at fifteen, I found
this scene so romantic; see how much he cherishes her, he cannot bear
to lose her again—"A mature man *can* find love in the arms of a young
girl, a very young girl . . . !" as Miss Brodie rejoiced about Dante and
Beatrice. But now that I am seventeen—Sandy's age, Tracy's age, *tick
tick tick*—I see it quite differently. The fire in Isaac's loins is not due to
love, or even to lust; it's about that ticking clock. That thing he loves
about her is elusive, fleeting, is slipping away each day: Her luminous
youth. It is his own fragile tether to a life still on the upswing, full of
vibrant promise and fresh discovery, and without that, or when that
tether snaps, when Tracy is more than a technically legal adult, when

she has, with even just six months' more experience, fully transitioned from girl to woman, he will officially begin coasting downward into the denouement of his own existence. Maurice Chevalier sings *"Thank heaven, for little girls! For little girls get bigger everyday . . ."* but the implied cautionary lesson is to thank heaven for them *now*, appreciate them *now*, get them while you can . . . *because* they do get bigger every day, and then the thing about them that allures, charms, revitalizes, is gone forever. When Tracy is older, Isaac will officially become old; her value will plummet, and he knows he better soak up that rejuvenating life energy while it lasts.

Tracy doesn't understand this yet—but at seventeen, I believe I do. The enchanting illusions of Sandy and Iris and Violet and Tracy and Dolores Haze will remain preserved, resin'd forever on-screen, but these films have made clear there is a shelf life to my own Loliltahood; that fragile construct is perishable, has a "sell by" date. As Teddy says, I will be *over the hill* any second now, my alluring little-girlness expired, and my *crème*, no matter if it's been the freshest best, will soon curdle and go sour. What will I have to offer, then, what new role will I play? How will I ever be famous *for sex*?

I will have to find a new source of desirability, I tell myself. A new way to beguile, to be magnificently, unordinarily elevated. But I have no idea how, or what that might be. I'm still only seventeen.

HOW TO
BE
A JEW

QUESTIONS AND COMMANDMENTS, MATZOH, MEZUZAHS, MENORAHS, AND A CRASH COURSE IN CHRIST

Fiddler on the Roof

The Ten Commandments

Jesus Christ Superstar

The Odessa File

The Chosen

t is 1971, and I am a seven-year-old girl living with my parents and four older sisters in our small sepia-toned village of Anatevka, somewhere in Russia, sometime in the very early twentieth century. Our life here is hard but merry; we are always singing. Papa is the head of the household, of course, *the Papa, the Papa!* we sing, *who day and night must scramble for a living, feed a wife and children, say his daily prayers!* But Mama, aproned and head-scarfed, always pounding bread dough or stirring pots of soup, is the one who is really in charge, we all know, the one *who must raise the family and run the home, so Papa's free to read the holy book,* and our home is redolently female: even from here, munching popcorn and watching us rapturously from my scratchy red velvet seat in the dark, I can smell the warm milk from our cows in the barn, the potato-starched laundry flapping sun-hot dry on lines in our chicken-scratch'd yard, the linen pillows oiled with our long brown hair. Our hovel of a house is flurried and flounced with petticoats, it glistens with brass lamps and bubbles of chicken fat goldening those pots on the stove, and the two precious silver candlesticks Mama brings out for our Sabbath prayer, and which she will give to my oldest sister Tzeitel on her wedding day. (Only my three older sisters Tzeitel, Hodel, and Chava appear to have names; we younger two, it seems, are interchangeable.) Our rickety wooden synagogue gleams with the gold Star of David and the shining Torah, is made warm by our heated devotion and our beloved Rabbi, who is all bicker and josh. Somewhere else in our village are glimpses of an expansive cold gray church where cold gray people worship a dead man hanging on a cross, somewhere there are Russians, all of them are the "Others," but as Papa says, *We do not bother them, and so far, they do not bother us.* We keep to ourselves and our traditions, our *Tradition!* Somewhere out there in the world there is, or there will be, revolution, men and women dancing together and peasants rising up against a tsar and the sound of metal swords and screaming horses and people trying to change the workings of the world . . . .

But here, our village soundtrack is a dulcet minor key, a fragile yet tenacious violin song that bursts into hummable melody, it is mournful and joyous all at the same time and makes me want to dance; we pluck our chickens and pitch our hay to the beat, our choreography is wholly expressive of our lives, our faith, our very souls.

But a reminder, a refrain: Papa is the Head of the Family, yes, *who has the right, as Master of the House, to have the final word at home!* He is our benevolent king, our loving, huggable tsar, the patriarch made persuadable by our female kisses or tears. He dances for us in the barn or along a dirt road, arms raised to his buddy-buddy God in both supplication and gratitude. My Papa, his name is Tevye, and he is cheerfully volatile, he dreams of being a rich man, all day long he'd *biddy biddy bum,* but he loves his cart horse and milk cows as much as he loves us, his wife and five daughters, he is all belly and grizzled eyebrows and scratchy beard. Papa explains to me, to all of us, the importance of our *Tradition!,* that

TEVYE

because of our traditions, everyone knows who he
is and what God expects him to do,

how to sleep, eat, work, wear a fringed prayer shawl, cover our heads to show our constant devotion to this God of ours who is thoughtful enough to provide these *Traditions!,* such comforting, tidy rules on exactly how we must live our lives, how we must always behave. Such security, in that directive, instructional love.

Here in our cinematic Anatevka life, here *in the home I love,* it is always a burnished sunrise or sunset. Our Jewishness is the harvest gold of our kitchen appliances, the color of supermarket challah yellow with egg yolks and glistening fat bubbles of Campbell's chicken soup. Our Jewishness is made luminous with candles and copper kettles and fresh milk. We glow with our Jewishness.

I became a Jew when I was seven.

But I was already Jewish, actually, a default Jew by birth, by blood. My father was raised a Lutheran in the backwoods of Wisconsin, trudged every Sunday by his icy single mother to the town church three miles away until he was eight years old and decided "the whole goddamn thing was bullshit"; he refused to have any more to

do with God or religion or spirituality or faith of any kind. But my
mother was Jewish, if unobservant, and so, according to both Jewish
law and Nazi propaganda, I was born a Jew, too. My maternal grandmother was born in Poland to the village rabbi but shed both accent
and religious observation as part of her teenage immigrant assimila-
tion in America; she became even less observant upon marrying my
secular Jewish grandfather, who, if anything, was an anti-Semitic Jew,
a Reagan Republican Jew, disdainful of any public form or expression of religion, embarrassed by Jewish shtick or Catskills humor he
felt evinced a lack of sophistication, and perpetually annoyed with
Israel for always causing so much trouble. My grandparents had been
members of a temple in the early days of their marriage, mostly, I suspect, for the card games and cocktail parties they loved, especially my
dance-on-the-tabletop, former-flapper grandmother. But when they
fell on hard times and could not afford their temple dues—a finan-
cial shame that would haunt my grandfather forever—they asked the
rabbi for some temporary leniency: *Help us out, please, we are members
of this congregation in good Jewish standing,* and were told No. No, you
must leave. Their temple membership was revoked, they were cast
out from the flock, disowned, dismissed, and whatever Jewishness
was left in my grandfather died at that humiliating moment; he swore
he was done with Judaism, forever.

And yet there remained some Jewish markers in my grandparents'
home: A small metal and enamel thing called a *mezuzah* nailed to their
front doorframe; a blue metal can the size of a brick with Hebrew lettering on it and a slot at the top for spare coins, to raise money for some
undefined Jewish organization; and a dark, to-my-child-eyes huge
oil painting of a solemn-eyed, black-garmented man hunched over a
book, which might have been a portrait of my Polish great-grandfather
rabbi or some artist's rendering of Shylock, or simply a generic Portrait
of a Jew. I spent a great deal of time at my grandparents' home as a
child, and this painting, staring down at me on the comfy couch where
I would sleep overnight, confused me, felt both comforting and foreboding. Maybe it was a portrait of God. What did I know?

My own home was an entirely Godless one; both of my parents
were devout atheists, profoundly unspiritual. My family had no religious *Traditions!*, or none that made any sense: a supermarket challah,

or matzoh brei on Sunday mornings, does not a Jewish ritual make. We always had a Christmas tree, because they smelled nice and my mother thought they were pretty and showed off our house to nice effect, and we always "did presents" on Christmas morning, not a celebration of Jesus's birth, but an orgy of competitive, materialist consumerism. Growing up in the 1970s San Fernando Valley, in the Jewishy enclaves of Encino and Woodland Hills, half my friends were Jewish and half my friends were Gentile (not even "Christian," just *Gentile*, broad-spectrum non-Jewish), and I thought that fifty-fifty split was the demographic norm of the entire world until, embarrassingly, my midteens. (Jews are only 1.7 percent of the U.S. population? *Really*? Oh, hello, Buddhism! Hello, Islam!) All my Jewish friends had bar and bat mitzvahs to celebrate their thirteenth birthdays, their symbolic arrival at adulthood, and my family attended these events the way we would attend any birthday party or potluck, my father good-naturedly perching a yarmulke on his blond head. I envied the extravagant parties (and extravagant gifts) that came with the coming-of-age ritual, but had zero interest in the Sunday School God stuff, the learn-a-Torah-portion-in-Hebrew part of it. We never went to temple otherwise, and sitting through all those bar or bat mitzvah ceremonies was both awkward and dull, because I felt like a fraud; the devotion to God, the displays of spiritual communion, were as foreign and meaningless to me as the indecipherable Hebrew words. Once I found a cheap, forgotten menorah tucked in the back of a kitchen cabinet, and, visions of my friends' Eight Nights of Hannukah gifts in my head, I stuck kiddie birthday candles in it and tried to engage my parents in a half-hearted observation (something about oil miraculously lasting eight days . . . ?), but gave up the effort the third or fourth present-free night in.

The most Jewish we ever got was a negligible Passover Seder at my grandparents' house, where we flipped through a few pages of the "Haggadah," a sort of interactive, Manischewitz-stained *Idiot's Guide to Passover*, something about Jews escaping slavery in ancient Egypt, frogs and locusts, right, let's eat! And then came the *afikomen* (Hide the matzoh!), which I, the youngest child, was tasked with finding, which I always did within minutes and then exchanged for $1 from my Grandpa. My strongest memory is a story of four hypothetical Jewish children asking four different questions about the Passover ritual: The wise child, the wicked child, the simple child, and the child who does not even know how to ask, but I could never quite remember which child asked which question (they all seemed equally irrelevant to anything in my own life), and it instilled in me a fear of ever asking the "wrong kind" of question—I certainly didn't want to be labeled wicked, simple, or too clueless to even put a proper interrogative sentence together. But over time Passover simply blurred with Thanksgiving: A loud family affair lacking any real ceremony or meaningful observance of history, of political or religious significance, of any tradition beyond green bean casserole and potato pancakes. (Although the fried onions on top of the green bean casserole were, in fact, a holy rite.)

One ritual I was not privy to, but was mentioned by my mother, was the existence of Yom Kippur, the Jewish Day of Atonement; my grandmother had an old record of Kol Nidre, the ancient prayer or declaration of repentance, and according to my mother, my grandmother would once a year on Yom Kippur lock herself in her bedroom alone, play this record, and cry and cry. I didn't know then, and never will now, what need for repentance drove her to this, moved her so strongly, and in secret, yet: Was it guilt over leading a not-Jewish-enough life? Her failure to pass a true Jewish legacy along to her daughter, her grandchildren? For marrying a man who rejected Judaism? Was she thinking of relatives left behind in a Polish village? Her own long-dead mother and father, that fading Jewish heritage?

As a child, being Jewish meant virtually nothing to me. No one explained exactly what it *did* mean, or might mean; apparently my exposure to all those wedding horas and bar mitzvah chantings was considered religious education enough: Judaism by social osmosis. I once asked a more-Jewish friend to phonetically write out the Hebrew prayer for candles (or was it bread, or wine?) on a paper napkin, so I could memorize it to impress my grandmother, who didn't speak any Hebrew. Being Jewish basically meant making self-deprecatory Jewish jokes when I got a nose job at seventeen. It meant incorporating my grandmother's occasional Yiddish phrases into my speech (*Oy vey! Chutzpah! Kine-ahora!*) to make her laugh. It meant refusing to take the side of Palestine in a sixth-grade debate between Palestine and Israel over territorial rights because it was "against everything I

believe in!" although I believed in absolutely nothing and had no clue
what any of it was about. Nor did I care. It meant wearing a tiny gold
mezuzah necklace my grandfather bought me at a pawn shop, which
I loved because it was gold, a grown-up-looking piece of jewelry, and
still having no idea what a mezuzah actually was. (And I didn't ask:
I'm no simpleton child.)

And it meant the entire family going to see some movie called *Fiddler on the Roof* the moment it hit theatres.[18]

In 1894 Russian writer Sholem Aleichem published several
stories, in Yiddish, about a pious, warm-hearted Jewish milkman
named Tevye, scratching out a living in late-tsarist Russia, dealing
with his strong-willed wife and household of challenging daughters
while struggling to maintain his unsteady foothold on tradition and
faith. There were multiple Yiddish-language stage adaptations of
Tevye the Milkman, or *Tevye and His Daughters*, plus a 1939 Yiddish film
version called *Tevye*, until its incarnation as a big-budget Broadway
musical in 1964 called *Fiddler on the Roof*. The title was inspired by
early Modernist Jewish-themed paintings by Chagall, and you can see
the Chagallian influence in the faintly Cubist set design, the color palette, even Jerome Robbins's innovative angular choreography. *Fiddler
on the Roof* was a massive hit: Record-setting performances, international acclaim, a slew of Tony awards (including one for Zero Mostel's
colorful, iconic Tevye), and endless touring productions and revivals
ever since. No surprise it would become a big-budget, wildly successful and much-loved Hollywood musical in 1971, produced and
directed by Norman Jewison (no, not a Jew), who created an uproar by
casting the thirty-seven-year-old Israeli actor Topol as Tevye instead
of Zero Mostel: He felt Topol's earthy Tevye would be less clownish,
more realistic.

But it is not reality, to my seven-year-old eyes; it is magic. Moviegoing is still a novelty for me, a wonder, a wholly immersive experience; I am enraptured by the beautiful opening images of sunrise over

---

18 *Fiddler on the Roof* (United Artists, 1971): screenplay by Joseph Stein, adapted
from stories by Sholem Aleichem; music by Jerry Bock, lyrics by Sheldon Harnick;
directed by Norman Jewison; with Topol, Norma Crane, Leonard Frey, and Rosalind Harris

a small village, golden fields and blue sky, and the stunning but perplexing silhouette of a man precariously perched on the roof of house, playing a violin (the haunting violin supplied by Isaac Stern). What is he doing up there, this violinist, this fiddle player, I wonder? Fortunately, it is explained to me—to *me*, directly, intimately, by a smiling, warmth-exuding, worn-faced man:

TEVYE

A fiddler on the roof? It sounds crazy, no? But here in our little village of Anatevka, you might say every one of us is a fiddler on the roof, trying to scratch out a simple tune without breaking his neck. It isn't easy. And how do we keep our balance? That I can tell you in one word! *Tradition!* Without our traditions, our lives would be as shaky as a fiddler on the roof!

My introduction to metaphor, and I am in love with Tevye, his paternal wisdom and humor and diastematic grin; I am unaware of the makeup designed to age Topol to Tevye's weary grizzle, the fake white hairs placed strategically into his dark eyebrows. Tevye introduces me to the characters of our village: Our beloved Rabbi, Yente the Matchmaker, and all the Papas and Mamas, the sons and daughters, everyone going about their chores and their *Traditions!* Tevye's three oldest daughters are excited by a visit from Yente; will she bring the man of their dreams, someone slender and pale, or an old, fat, drunken, abusive man? Whatever, they will be lucky to get a man (any man, it is explicitly stated), and I am oblivious to the gender politics here, the disempowerment of the girls, or the valuing of even the most distasteful of men as a "good catch" for these low-rung, dowryless daughters; I'm too curious about the odd wig Yente wears, the wigs I will see on all married women in this village of ours, when their hair is not fully covered by a scarf. With one exception, later.

Tevye dreams of being a rich man, the pride he would take in his home, the leisure he craves to study and discuss his faith with other men of the village; when Tevye is not talking directly to me, he is talking to God, they are on intimate terms: It is a bromance. His daughters run to him for hugs when he enters the house, and it is time for the Sabbath Prayer; Golde, our Mama, lights candles, her bewigged head covered in lace, she and Tevye sing of their wishes for their five daughters, *May the Lord protect and defend you, may you be deserving of praise . . . may he make you good mothers and wives, may he send you husbands who will care for you*, but it is clear the girls need no other care than this golden home, the love of their Mama, but especially their cuddly, adoring Papa; in this house full of women, the Papa's love is even more precious, the thing to be treasured.

I am charmed by the flavor and simplicity of this rural life, the quaint traditions, all the sepia glow (which Norman Jewison achieved by filming through a woman's nylon stocking stretched across the lens). The colorful characters of this village are somehow, oddly, identifiable to me; how is it I recognize the rhythms of their speech? I don't know any Jewish people like this. I don't know any Ukrainian peasants, any rabbis or matchmakers, and my grandmother shed her accent forty years earlier. Why do the candles and lace, the exuberance and bluster of this life, feel so familiar? How can I possibly identify with these long-ago Eastern European peasants as kin? Why do they tap into my blood, why does their song send my DNA spinning in a homey helix'd dance?

The word *Jew* is first mentioned about fifteen minutes in and brings with it the first whiff of conflict—there is news of Jews being evicted from nearby villages—but this conflict is quickly pushed aside for some interpersonal drama: Tevye decides to give his oldest daughter, Tzeitel, in marriage to the rich butcher Lazar Wolf, although we know she is in love with poor Motel the Tailor. Again, the bargaining of his daughter like a prize milk cow goes over my head; it is obvious how much Tevye adores his daughter, for the deciding factor, he soliloquizes for us, is that as the wife of a butcher, "my daughter will surely never know hunger . . . he likes her, and he will try to make her happy." It's a deal! Lazar and Tevye go out to get drunk with their buddies and stumble into a turf war with a bunch of local Russians who, after an ominous face-to-face pause, during which I know, instinctively, I should be afraid of these non-Jewish (Gentile) Russians and their Slavic tough-guy vodka glare, proceed to initiate a dance-off, like a pre–Russian Revolution *Glee*. The Jewish men dance Jewishly, the Russians dance their folded-arms, squat-and-kick-out-legs way, they all dance together, and everything is dandy. To life, to life, *l'chaim!*

But on his drunken stumble home, Tevye encounters the local Russian Constable, who I can tell is really a Good Guy from his twinkling eyes and slight smile beneath his big Russian moustache, and the sincerity of his congratulations to Tevye on his daughter's forthcoming marriage. The Constable then wants to give Tevye a heads-up, a warning, "as a friend," because:

> CONSTABLE
>
> . . . you're an honest, decent fellow, even if you are a Jew.

There it is again, the film's second use of that word, *Jew*, highlighted by the disdainful qualifying phrase. But I trust this Constable guy—he is teasing, doing Tevye some kind of favor, and therefore showing him respect. He means no harm. He continues:

> CONSTABLE
>
> This district is to have a little unofficial demonstration.

> TEVYE
>
> What? A *pogrom*? Here?

I have no idea what a *pogrom* is, but from Tevye's stricken face, it is clearly not a good thing.

> CONSTABLE
>
> No, no . . . just a little . . . not too serious. So if an inspector comes he can see we did our duty. Personally, I don't see why there should be this trouble between people.

After a pause, Tevye says:

TEVYE

You're a good man. Too bad you're not a Jew.

CONSTABLE

(laughing) That's what I like about you, Tevye,
you're always joking.

Another pause. But the Constable's laughter fades, and the pause
becomes ominous, the twinkling eyes grow stern. No, not just stern . . .
it is the slow realization he is being insulted, disrespected, although
I do not understand why this would be so. Being "a Jew" is neither
a good thing nor a bad thing, in my life; it is an absolute irrelevance.
But the tense moment is over; he leaves Tevye alone in the night, to
ask of God:

TEVYE

God, did you have to send me news like that
today? I know we are the chosen people, but once
in a while, couldn't you choose someone else?

Chosen for what? I wonder.
When Tevye breaks the happy news to Tzeitel, she is distraught:

TZEITEL

Papa, I can't marry him, I can't!

TEVYE

What do you mean, you can't? If I say you will,
you will!

It is the first real moment of distress, for me, far more alarming than
the steel-eyed Constable. Tzeitel drops to her knees, begging her Papa,
and the bluster of this most loving and affectionate and generous man
has on a dime turned angry and chilled. He is shocked by her disobe-
dience, that she would even *think* to cross him, to follow her own will!
The benevolence is gone, replaced by his disapproval. The threat of

rejection. I cannot imagine being rejected by the adult men in my life; my own father bears no resemblance to blustering Tevye, he is usually somewhat quiet and remote in our home, upstaged by my emotionally dramatic, scene-stealing mother, but his love for me is a given, a source of absolute security I have never had reason to question.

But I recognize this adoration for the *Papa*, this craving for his approval and love, for that is my maternal grandfather's role in our family; my Grandpa Al is the true Head of our House, our own indulgent patriarch whom we all defer to and wish to please. He is the classic adoring and adored Grandpa, who buys me gold Jewish jewelry at pawn shops and takes me shopping for school clothes and makes me root beer floats when I sleep over at their house and we sit together to watch *Mannix* and *Barnaby Jones*, just the two of us. Affectionate and generous and loving, yes, a man I cannot imagine ever turning angry or chilled. But this moment forces me to imagine it. To see myself, on my knees, begging my grandfather, my Grandpa, my *Papa* for . . . his love? No, it is a comfortable impossibility.

Impossible yes, for Tevye and Tzeitel as well. "All right," Tevye says to Tzeitel, regretful but tender. "I won't force you," he tells her. Of course not—what father could ever force his beloved daughter to do something she didn't want? I am relieved, reassured.

A brief relapse, though, when Motel announces his and Tzeitel's desire to marry:

TEVYE

This isn't the way it's done! Not here, not now!
Some things I cannot, I will not allow! *Tradition!* Marriages are arranged by the Papa!

But at the sight of Tzeitel's pleading eyes, the realization that she loves this man, he gives in. Of course he does—all he wants is his daughter's happiness, after all.

Cut to: Happy preparations for the happy wedding. During which, a short scene: The Constable, meeting with a Superior Officer, has attempted to call off this thing called a *pogrom*. The Superior Officer is suspicious:

SUPERIOR OFFICER
Do you *like* these troublemakers? These *Christ-killers?*

I'm confused; didn't the *Romans* kill Jesus Christ? I'm sure I've heard that somewhere, although I am unclear who or what "the Romans" were. Or even who or what *Jesus* actually was in the scheme of things, other than the guy who started Christianity. Wasn't that what the crucifixion was all about, the Roman President or someone not liking this guy Jesus (who was actually, confusedly, *Jewish*, it is coming back to me, probably from some Christmas special on TV, so why would the Jews kill him . . . ?), but the Constable hastily assures him, No, no, he will take care of it, and it's on to the wedding, a lovely but odd ritual of braided candles and men in funny hats, and veiled Tzeitel walking in circles around Motel, and lots of wine being sipped. Tevye and Golde sing about how grown up their daughter is, *is this the little girl I carried? Is this the little boy at play? What words of wisdom can I give them?* Then it's party time, where for some reason, the men are dancing on one side, the women on the other, separated by a rope. But Perchik, a young Communist student Tevye has taken a liking to, who is sweet on Tevye's next daughter-in-line, Hodel, scoffs at all these old-fashioned traditions, even challenges the Rabbi to come up with some religious rationale for why men and women dancing together is a sin. The Rabbi draws a blank (what possible reason could there be?) and Perchik leads Hodel out to dance. And then Motel dances with Tzeitel! Tevye, now feeling left out, dances with Golde! Everyone dances! This is a great wedding, now familiar as some cousins, or family friend's. I can practically taste the chicken breast and rice pilaf that will be served to us soon, can almost hear Karen Carpenter crooning *We've only just begun . . . .*

Until. Enter the (Gentile) Russians on horseback, carrying torches and clubs. The gaiety stops, the wedding guests freeze. I do not know what is about to happen, but I sense I should be frightened. The horses charge, swords are drawn. The celebrating Jews (*Christ-killers, trouble-makers*) scatter in terror.

But it isn't such a big deal. It's a few seconds of melee, some ripped-open feather pillows, some broken glass, a few spilled cups of wine. A table is overturned. A drunken wedding-guest uncle would do more damage. I won't realize until many years later that this depicts The Most Benign Pogrom Ever; there is no blood, no crushed skulls, no degradation. Just as the Constable had said, in his friendly warning; nothing too serious. He even apologizes to Tevye, in a way:

CONSTABLE

Orders are orders, understand?

Tevye's face is stricken, he is silent, unmanned, powerless to do or say anything, but we would not be able to hear him anyway over the suddenly overwrought music that tells us this is traumatic, a Tragedy. I'm not buying it. No real damage has been done, after all. I suppose a pogrom really isn't such a big deal. More like a rudeness, an inconvenience.

No, the big deal comes toward the end of the movie. Tevye has given his blessing to Hodel marrying Perchik; they have asked for his blessing, not his permission, once again breaking *Tradition!*, and once again Tevye is swayed by his desire for his daughter's happiness. But when the third daughter, Chava, wants to marry Fyedka, a strapping and sensitive Russian youth, Tevye has had enough. He's done. "I am the Man in the House! I am the Head of the Family!" he asserts, outraged. Told by Golde that Chava has run off and married her Gentile Russian boyfriend anyway, he declares:

TEVYE

Chava is dead to us! We'll forget her!

Chava shows up (no wig, her hair visible beneath her shawl) to plead:

CHAVA

Papa, stop! At least listen to me! Papa, I beg you to accept us!

And he pauses, one final time, to ask of God:

TEVYE

```
How can I accept them? Can I deny everything I
believe in? On the other hand, can I deny my own
daughter? On the other hand, how can I turn my
back on my faith, my people? No! If I try to bend
that far, I will break!
```

And he roars away from her, plodding off with his milk cart while she stands, abandoned at the side of the road, still begging him to look at her, listen to her. But he is deaf to her pleas. "Our daughter is dead," he will repeat to Golde, and the rest of the family now cowers before him and his cold, deadening rage. And so Chava is disappeared, erased, snipped out of the family album, and I feel the chill of this in my bones. His cuddly warmth has turned terrifying, turned to threat. No, it has now gone well beyond threat: It is an actual retraction of his love, the cancellation of a relationship, the abandonment of a human being. It is an act of deliberate cruelty. Like Chava, I am crying, disconsolate. This is frightening.

But the ostensible tragedy of the story arrives with the Constable, and the edict that everyone, that is, all the Jews, must leave Anatevka. They are cast out from their home, their beloved village. Final shots of everyone packing up, the Rabbi praying, holding the Torah like a baby, the golden color palette now bleached of color, reduced to grays, black mud and white snow, desolate and cold to match the bleakness of loss and defeat. All warmth is drained from this movie—except when Tevye says a loving, gentle good-bye to his animals. Leaving them behind has him in tears, turns him tender with grief. Softhearted, sentimental Tevye.

And then Chava arrives, with her Gentile now-husband Fyedka.

CHAVA

```
Papa? We came to say good-bye.
```

Tevye, packing up the wagon, ignores her.

CHAVA

```
We are also leaving this place. We are going to
Cracow.
```

FYEDKA

We cannot stay among people who can do such
things to others.

CHAVA

We wanted you to know that.

Tevye ignores them louder.

FYEDKA

Some are driven away by edicts. Some by silence.

CHAVA

Good-bye, Papa!

Stony silence from Tevye. I guess he is still too sad and upset about
having to leave his animals to acknowledge his daughter's existence.
Chava says good-bye to Golde, to Tzeitel. Good-bye! Goodbye! Then,
a quiet:

TEVYE

And God be with you.

It's a mumble, barely audible. No embrace, no real farewell. He
doesn't even look her in the eye. What good will God "being with
her" do her? I wonder. Without her beloved Papa?

Because isn't her Papa, in a way, her religion? Isn't that, shouldn't
that be the real faith, the sanctified, sustaining love between them?

But she is grateful, promises to write to them in America. Will they
ever be truly reconciled? Ever embrace, or touch? Ever see each other
again?

And these unanswered questions are the most disturbing thing to
me, as the village empties out, everyone trudging through the snow,
burdened with their meager belongings, their bundles and wheel-
barrows, the old men stopping one last time to stand in a circle and
pray together (just the men, only the men), and the Fiddler following
after them to play his final violin song, a sweetly mournful refrain of

Tradition! The true tragedy of the story is not the eviction from Anat-evka; they're off to America, aren't they, the Promised Land? They'll find a place to live; Tevye can find a job. (And as I grow older and watch and rewatch this movie on network television, I will think they are actually lucky to be evicted, for surely it's better to settle into a Lower East Side tenement existence than to live—or not live—as Ukrainian Jews in Revolutionary Russia, or World War II. Doesn't the eviction ultimately *save* their lives?)

No, the true Tragedy, the saddest and most chilling thing, is a father choosing *faith* over his daughter. Choosing a belief in a set of arbitrary rules, some fantasy *Tradition!* What about your actual daughter? I think. Isn't *she* your "people," your own family, your own daughter, that you are turning your back on? Flesh and blood and breath, standing right there in front of you, begging for your love, your acknowledgement? She is not a concept, a philosophical abstraction. She is not a thing to be believed in or not. She is real, she exists.

But it isn't just, or really, about his faith, I finally realize. I finally understand. Chava's breaking of *Tradition!* is a rejection of him. Of the Papa. Of his role, his supremacy—and that is the *Tradition!* that gives him his only purpose in life. He is a poor, persecuted Jew in the world, and this is his only semblance of power, of authority, the thing that gives him any purchase or foothold at all up on that shaky roof of his. He loves his daughter, yes, but love is conditional: Your love is expressed through obedience to me, and in exchange I will love and protect and honor you. Your vulnerability is my strength, the thing upon which I can balance and lean. And if you cease to be vulnerable, if you push me too far, disobey my directive, instructional love, challenge my absolute tsarist rule, you will be disowned, cast aside, so that I can hold on to my *Tradition!* and thus not lose my own precarious footing. Do not question my authority; if you do, you will cease to exist, and I am willing to pay that price.

This is the lingering, subconscious moral, for me, of *Fiddler on the Roof*; it is not about the precariousness of early twentieth-century Ukrai-nian Jewish life, it is about the precariousness of love. A father's love. But I won't truly realize or understand this for another fourteen years.

For now, at seven, I will suppress this disquieting family dynamic. I will ignore and compartmentalize this moral and instead accept the narrative archetypes as presented: The threatening, bad-guy Gentile Russians, the blustering, adoring Papa and his loving family. I will hold on to the comforting and bloodless fairy-tale Judaism, the song-and-joyous-dance Jewishness, the big happy familyness, the candles and lace and melodious *biddy biddy bum*, I will bask in the golden warmth and stocking'd sepia glow of it all.

My German/Lithuanian maternal grandfather, Albert, my adored and adoring Grandpa Al, was proudly American-born, no fresh-off-the-boat immigrant, he. He grew up in Chicago during the Roaring Twenties, the era of speakeasies and bathtub bootleg gin, Dillinger and Capone, and my grandfather's father, Benjamin, ran a service station that, as the family story goes, catered to the Mob. Benjamin was called "Benny the Jew" by Mobsters, perhaps even nicknamed by Capone himself, it was implied. Benny the Jew did not bother the Mob, and they did not bother him; as the story goes, they regularly arrived in a fleet of sleek black roadsters (after viewing Public Enemy gangster movies, I project tommy guns, fedoras, and cauliflower ears onto the scene) to have their tanks filled, their windows washed, their oil checked, perhaps a bullet hole patched up by Benny the Jew; they wordlessly tossed their bills (perhaps even joshed with Benny a bit, for Benny the Jew was an affable guy, knew his place, accepted their money and business with the mercenary pragmatism of his race) and zoomed benignly off on their Mobster way.

My grandfather apprenticed with his father Benny the Jew, learned to patch tires and check radiator hoses and keep his eyes down, his bulbous Jewish nose minding his own business. As the story goes, one day when my grandfather was eighteen and preparing to marry my (Polish Jew, freshly immigrated) grandmother, one of those sleek black cars pulls up. A Capone Mobster leans out the window, queries all tough-guy Cagney-like:

"You. Yeah, you. You Benny the Jew's kid?"

My grandfather, I imagine, pauses briefly (bullet hole in the passenger door), then nods. It has to be claimed; his heritage, ancestry, race are as obvious as the nose on his face.

The back passenger door of the car opens, a shadowy leather seat, maybe a whiff of cigar.

"Get in."

There is no decision to be made. He sets down his rag or oil can, wipes his hands on his coveralls, crawls in with as much shaky Semitic dignity as he can muster. The Mobsters and the story take my grandfather to a tailor in the city, who measured and chalked, sheared through a high-quality black wool, tailor-fit him with his wedding suit, spanking black and new. Courtesy of Capone, a thank-you to Benny the Jew for all those years of faithful service.

You Benny the Jew's kid?

I wonder about that brief beat between query and claim, what my grandfather thought or felt. Did he look around for his father—in that moment not his Papa, not a venerable, patriarchal Benjamin, but a mere "Benny," infantilized by the diminutive—for protection or guidance? Did he know instinctively or by experience how powerless, how useless his father would be?

But *is* it a moment of powerlessness, of shame? Of Jewish emasculation? Or a summons to adventure, perhaps, a lingering penny-comic fantasy about to come true, an invitation to the ultimate club of invulnerable mobster machismo? (Alcatraz and syphilis are still years away in Capone's own emasculated future.) Is my grandfather Al, Benny the Jew's kid, afraid or elated? Is it an initiation into adulthood, a symbolic leaving of the gas station/home? Is the fitting of a wedding suit the making of an adult man?

I have no idea—I first hear this story when I am very, very young and it has been handed down, told and retold with the intention to amuse and delight, the assertion of a tiny glamour. There is no violence, no degradation, here. It's a story told with pride, meant to prompt images of Cagney and De Niro. Al Capone bought my grandfather his wedding suit: A charming family anecdote. Is it even true?

And what does Jewishness have to do with it? What if it were a story of Benny the Episcopalian, or Benjamin the Gas Station Guy?

But: *Benny the Jew* has such a ring to it. It reduces my great-grandfather Benjamin to that diminishing diminutive, plus a racial label. It is definingly pithy, to the point. The first time I ever hear this story as a child, the word *Jew* makes me instantly uncomfortable. The harshness of that

J, the deep-voweled, yet abruptly cut-off *ew* triggers unease. The word *Jew* feels fraught; for years I wiggle my syntactical way around it, I restructure sentences to use the swooshier *Jewish* instead. "The Jews" isn't as bad—the plural *s* again softens it somehow, dilutes its razor edge. One time I asked my cousin Sandra, who is a self-described Professional Jew, a high-level executive at a Jewish organization (once recruited as a spy for Israel: Another bit of family mythology) if *Jew* was a negative word, a slur. She thought a moment, then said: "Only when it's preceded by *dirty* or followed by *boy*."

But I am still disquieted by it. *Jew*. I don't hear it that frequently in real life, but in the endless movies of my adolescence and young adulthood, I will hear it increasingly often, and it is rarely said with careless affection or clinical disinterest. The word *Jew* has sneer inside of it. It will become a word spat from the mouth of the brown-shirted Nazi, the Aryan street thug, the Mengele-esque concentration camp officer. It is a hastily stitched yellow star scar of a word: *Juden, Juif. Jew*.

- - - - - - - - - - -

There are no "Jews" in *The Ten Commandments*.[19] At least, not in Cecil B. de Mille's Technicolor, bombastic, bare-barrel-chested and heaving-bosomed 1956 version of *The Ten Commandments*. There are "Hebrew slaves," there are "The Israelites" and "The Levites," but to my nine-year-old self, watching this three-hour-and-forty-minute depiction of Moses delivering an Enslaved People from bondage in ancient Egypt, it takes me several scenes to piece together whatever history I have gleaned from all those nonsensical Passover Seders to realize: *Oh, this is all about the Jews!*

The Ten Commandments—a huge hit upon its theatrical release, and one of the highest-grossing films ever made—was first shown on network television in 1973, becoming a national, annual Easter/Passover event (the one year it didn't show, the network received millions of complaints—angry Jews, angry Christians, or both?). I think that first

---

19 *The Ten Commandments* (Paramount Pictures, 1956): screenplay by Æneas MacKenzie, Jesse Lasky Jr., Jack Gariss; directed by Cecil B. DeMille; with Charlton Heston, Yul Brynner, Anne Baxter, and Yvonne De Carlo

year I sat down to watch it on television with my parents and brother. Or maybe I'm remembering the following year, watching with my grandparents, on one of those many sleepover nights. Maybe I'm simply remembering all the multiple viewings to come, Oh hey, *The Ten Commandments* is on, let's watch!, the annual wallpapering onto our lives of de Mille's final epic, year after year after year—as with so many rituals, the singular moments blur, meld, and in doing so create a solid, if unspecific, foundation of experience.

Wherever I am, the opening, very Biblical-sounding Voiceover informs me how authentic this experience will be: "Those who see this motion picture—produced and directed by Cecil B. DeMille—will make a pilgrimage over the very ground that Moses trod more than three thousand years ago" (wow!), and that the movie has been written "in accordance with the ancient texts of Philo, Josephus, Eusebius, the Midrash, and . . ." (here comes a new screen and a fancy font) *The Holy Scriptures*! (God gets a screenplay credit.) The Voiceover continues: God saying there should be light, and then creating life on earth, including Man, who was given dominion over everything. But Man wanted dominion over Other Men, too, and the Conquered were made to serve the Conquerors, and so did the Egyptians cause the Children of Israel (that's the Jews, by the way) to serve with rigor, and their lives were bitter with bondage (images of slaves pulling big Sphinxes with ropes) and their cry came up to God, so God decided to send them a Deliverer, upon whose mind and heart would be written God's laws and God's Commandments. One man, to stand alone against an Empire! (If God was just going to send a Deliverer at some point, I wonder, maybe He could have *not* created the Men who wanted dominion over Other Men in the first place? A whole people had to be conquered and suffer for centuries just to create that one job? *Oy vey*.)

And that one man, of course, is Charlton Heston (whom I recognize from a traumatic drive-in viewing of *The Planet of the Apes* when I was four or five. Oh, my parents . . .) who begins as a Hebrew baby boy floated away for safety down the Nile, is adopted and reared by a childless Egyptian princess, and thus becomes a beloved Prince of Egypt, in love with Nefretiri (Anne Baxter in a Cleopatra wig, who includes a pneumatic *Moses, MOses!* in every line reading) and inspiring the jealous rival hatred of Pharaoh's son, Rameses (Yul Brynner, bald with a side ponytail, and so hunky). Ramses wants the Hebrew Slaves to work harder to build their cities and not be distracted by rumors of a mythical Deliverer, so Moses is sent by Pharaoh to go deal with it, and we are shown our first images of these problematic Children of Israel, of which there seem to be only two types: Buff and gorgeous, like Joshua the stonecutter and Lilia the Water Girl, or old, decrepit, and stringy, but all of them in distractingly dark body makeup (is this Jew-face?), the naturally blue-eyed tricked out in dark brown contact lenses. Moses is clearly a Good Guy (he thinks the slaves should be given some food, and an old woman should not be crushed to death by a big rock), and even debates religion with Joshua:

MOSES

You do not speak like a slave.

JOSHUA

God made men. Men make slaves.

MOSES

If God is almighty, why does He leave you in bondage?

JOSHUA

He will choose the hour of our freedom and the man who will deliver us!

Again, if God can pick and choose this kind of thing, then why would He choose to allow the bondage in the first place? But perhaps this is a childish question. Or the too-simple inquiry of the simple child.

Moses is eventually outed as a one-time Hebrew baby and decides to own it; he cuts off his own side ponytail, dumps Nefretiri, and will now live with his true brethren

                          MOSES
    in order to find the meaning of what I am! Why a
    Hebrew or any man must be a slave!

and we cut to the mud pits, where, the Voiceover informs us, the
Hebrew Slaves have served in "bondage without rest, toil without
reward. These are the children of misery, the afflicted, the oppressed,
century after century . . ." and again, I'm wondering: century after
century? What in the world is God *waiting* for?

   Moses's true mud-pit and brick-making brethren all think he must
be the Deliverer they've waited four hundred years for—he is both
doubtful and modest ("It would take more than a man to lead them
out of bondage, it would take a god!"), but Pharaoh decides to banish
him to the desert anyway. Moses wanders through sandstorms and
over rocks, sucking moisture from his robe and feeling tortured by
doubt, and eventually finds a family of sheepherding Bedouins; he
chooses from among the bevy of simpering, giggling, man-obsessed
daughters (echoes of Tzeitel, Hodel, and Chava here, with nothing
else on their girlish minds) to marry the wise and spotlessly-white-
clad Sephora (Yvonne de Carlo, but she is, really, Lily Munster).
Sephora tells him God actually lives just over there, on Mount Sinai
(the image of a mountain glowing with orange smoke, looking a little
like a school science fair exhibit), but Moses isn't so quick to buy it:

                          MOSES
    If this god is God, He would live on every moun-
    tain, in every valley. He would not only be the
    god of Israel, but of all men. It is said He cre-
    ated all men in His image; then He would dwell in
    every heart, every mind, in every soul.

                         SEPHORA
    Why do you want to see Him, Moses?

                          MOSES
    To know that He is, if He is. To know why He has
    not heard the cries of slaves in bondage . . .

how many of my people have died because He has
turned away His face?

Yup. This is still my question and will remain my question forever regarding the existence—the theory?—of God, or a god, or gods.
Sephora offers the "Oh, but us lowly humans can't really understand
God's plan, just trust, believe, have faith, and it'll all be okay" perspective, but Moses insists:

> MOSES
>
> For me, there will be no peace of spirit until I
> hear the word of God! From God Himself!

Which is either pretty darn cocky or maybe the start of a common
sense, empirically based, scientific-method attitude. He climbs the
mountain, finds a burning bush, all orange-glowing and chatty:

> MOSES
>
> God, I am here! Lord, why do you not hear the
> cries of the children in the bondage of Egypt?

> GOD
> (I guess, or THE BUSH)
>
> I have surely seen the affliction of my people
> which are in Egypt, and I have heard their cries
> . . . for I know their sorrows. Therefore, I will
> send thee, Moses, unto them that thou mayest
> bring thy people out of Egypt!

It's about time. Moses finally accepts the existence of this God and
that he must really be the Deliverer; all doubts resolved, he descends
from the mountain now with a wild Wolfman Jack pompadour and
a dazed gleam in his eye—the gleam of the true believer, I suppose,
although to me he just looks a little demonic, possessed. He returns to
Egypt and confronts Rameses (now Pharaoh):

MOSES

Thus sayest the God of Israel: let my people go!

Rameses refuses, of course, so Moses warns him God isn't going to like it—in fact, He is going to smite the Egyptians and visit all sorts of plagues upon the land: The Nile turns to blood (but looks very much like Willy Wonka's chocolate river), and flies, frogs, boils, and so on, none of which we get to see, which is disappointing.

Moses threatens that God will kill all the first-born sons of Egypt, because "It's the Lord who executes judgment" (so this wonderful true God of Israel has no problem serving as a war-mongering executioner of how many people . . . ? This kind of hypersensitive, quick-trigger deity will turn on you in a heartbeat), so Rameses decides to kill all the first-born sons of the Hebrews. This eye-for-an-eye pissing contest could go on forever: Well, now God will kill the *second*-born! So now Rameses will kill the third-born! Now God'll kill first cousins! (And what about the first-born *daughters*, I wonder? Apparently, they are not a threat.)

When the Hebrew slaves go around swiping lambs' blood on their front doors, so God, or the Angel of Death sent on God's behalf, will "pass over" their houses and instead wreak vengeance on the Egyptians, I finally get it: A-ha, this is all a set-up for the story of *Passover*! This is what the last three hours, and all those endless Seders, have been about, the lamb shank and bitter herbs and talk of plagues! Meanwhile, God/Death Angel, represented by dirty-looking gray-green smoke, is crawling around Egypt smite-killing first-born Egyptian males. We see them drop like flies, we hear the screams.

MOSES'S SISTER MIRIAM

Death is all around us!

MOSES'S BROTHER AARON

But it passes those who believe in the Lord!

Which is illogical and confusing: Why would God/Death Angel *need* that gross-out signal of the lambs' blood smeared on front doors?

Wouldn't He know who believes in Him or not, isn't that the whole point to this one true God? And wouldn't He, like an omniscient real estate agent, know who lived where, be able to tell the good Children of Israel homes from the bad unbelieving Egyptian ones?

Pharaoh's own son dies, and he cracks, announces the Hebrews are bondage-free; they all take off to the Land of Milk and Honey with their unleavened bread (matzoh!), in a crazed exodus sequence of packing and camels and caravans and flocks of geese, babies being born on the road and thousands of extras in dark body makeup. But then Pharaoh changes his mind, and his troops race after the fleeing Unbondaged Israelites, backing them up against the coast of the Red Sea. Moses assures everyone the Lord will save them: Roiling black clouds, churning sea, a glowing orange pillar of fire swoops in and opens up the water so everyone can run across the ocean floor (including a really panicked goose, who seems to have a good grip on his motivation), and even pre-CGI, it's a nifty effect. Pharaoh's troops are all drowned. Moses leads everyone safely to the foot of Mount Sinai, then climbs up for another klatch with the Burning Bush, where he receives a tidy To Do and Not To Do list scribbled by bolts of gold fire on mountain stone: Thou shalt not steal or commit adultery or bear false witness or take my name in vain or covet your neighbor's stuff, Thou shalt keep the Sabbath holy, Thou shalt honor your mother and father, and so on, all ten of them boomed in God's booming voice (actually Charlton Heston's voice, though uncredited).

Moses carries these stone tablets down the mountain to share these obvious and common sense "do unto others" lessons with his people, but while his back was turned, the Hebrew Unenslaved had decided to hold a desert rave. Music, dancing, the liquor cabinet raided. Moses, like any dad who comes home too early/unexpectedly, is roy-ally pissed off:

MOSES

Woe unto thee, O, Israel! You have sinned . . . you are not worthy to receive the Ten Commandments!

But we're *free* now! the Partying Kids of Israel protest.

MOSES

There is no freedom without the law! Who is on
the Lord's side, let him come to me! Those who
will not live by the law shall die by the law!

So, those who believe in the Talking Burning Bush and Gold
Sharpies of Fire are fine; everyone else is screwed. Apparently this
passive-aggressive God is still pissed off with the believers, too, and
makes them wander in the desert for forty years, until Moses, now
all Santa Claus'd with his white beard and hair, sends everyone off to
cross the River Jordan while he does some final wandering by himself, for some reason. He waves good-bye, as crystalline beams of light
beam down from heaven, a beaming, approving God, now, and it's
the end, The End, THE END.

Thus concludes the history of how the Hebrews (Jews) were delivered from bondage, yes, I get that, but the emotional core of the story
is Moses accepting his role as Deliverer, and all his doubts magically
resolved, his religious faith and destiny made cinematically manifest. His doubts are resolved, but mine are created, raised, *clarified*, by
this movie: My nine-year-old Godlessness is made equally manifest,
confirmed. And while I have a clearer understanding of the story of
Passover, and how dramatic narrative can be more stickily instructive
than a dry, sermony Haggadah, I do not identify with these Children
of Israel or their spiteful, manipulative God at all. This story has no
resonance for me as a history of "my people."

But *is* it "history" or just a good story? There is a paradox, here; if
I accept this tale as history, if I credit that word with factual, empirically based knowledge, supported by documentary evidence, then I
am still being asked to take a leap of faith re: the miraculousness of
it all, the Burning Bush and parting Red Sea and the very existence
of those "Ten Commandments" tablets. A made-up story is actually
easier to "accept" at face value. Entertain me, illuminate me, even,
slip in a tidy moral or two; I won't question provenance. I won't ask
for footnotes. This story of Pharaoh and Deliverer works just fine for
me as another fairy tale, as impersonal epic, a spectacle of bombast
and unrelatable, laughably histrionic victims and villains. Tell me that
story. It's good fun. I will happily watch that story, year after year after

year on network television. Just don't ask me to *believe* it or accept it as fact.

And it is also a story that, in hindsight, feels ironically and paradoxically de-Jewed. The notable absence of that one word, *Jew*, intrigues me. Why the avoidance of that label? Is it merely an attempt to stay true to the Old Testament's rare use of the word, or a writerly effort to be consistent amid all the tortured faux-Biblical dialogue? Is it an example of the anti-Semitic fashion of 1950s Hollywood? We have our hero, Moses, the venerable Jewish patriarch/prophet, but best we not make him, or anyone else in this story of Jewish liberation, *too Jewish*, too explicitly *a Jew*. Perhaps this was more palatable to a largely (98.3 percent) non-Jewish audience? Perhaps this fits better with the "history of the Jews" as the necessary and mere Old Testament prologue to the arrival of the *true* hero in the *real* story of our shared humanity: the New Testament Jesus Christ?

But of course, at nine, I am as ignorant of Christian theology as I am of Judaism. And I ask no questions of my parents, for they are even less interested in theological debate or semantics than I am.

Fortunately, 1973 also brings an instructional companion piece to *The Ten Commandments*: The arrival/transformation to the screen, like *Fiddler on the Roof*, of another wildly successful Broadway musical, this one about the final days of Jesus Christ. And also, like the film version of *Fiddler*, directed by Norman Jewison. (Still not a Jew.)

----

*J*esus Christ Superstar was not my first "rock opera"—my parents had taken me to the Los Angeles premiere of *Hair* at the Aquarius Theatre when I was six years old, so I was already a connoisseur of the form.[20] But it is my introduction to a living, breathing (and singing) cinematic Jesus, one more vibrantly alive (and hot) than the museum icons shown in textbook color plates. *Jesus Christ Superstar* is my crash course in Christ.

20 *Jesus Christ Superstar* (Universal Pictures, 1973): screenplay by Melvyn Bragg, Norman Jewison, and Tim Rice; music by Andrew Lloyd Webber; directed by Norman Jewison; with Ted Neeley, Carl Anderson, Yvonne Elliman, Barry Dennen, and Josh Mostel

EXT. JUDEAN DESERT—DAY. A beat-up VW bus arrives, a huge cross strapped on top like vacationers' snow skis, a hippie-styled troupe of "actors" exit and, to a visceral electric guitar (I am already bouncing in my seat, feeling the fevered pulse of this desert rock), proceed to costume themselves in cheerful "Hey, let's put on a play!" style. An exquisite-faced guy (blue eyes, cheekbones, scraggly blond goatee) garbs himself in a gleaming white robe that puts Sephora's to shame and instantly becomes the object of everyone's rapt and loving attention.

Standing apart and scowling is a black guy in a red dashiki; this is Judas, I will soon learn (and be very confused by, given that at age nine, I didn't know any African American Jews, and for another ten or fifteen years I will believe that Judas was in fact black, just as I will believe for quite a long time that Jesus, a Mediterranean Jew, was a blue-eyed blond, reinforced by the tradition of other Aryan cinematic Jesuses like Max von Sydow, Robert Powell, and Willem Dafoe). Judas is distressed by how all the Jesus-love has gotten out of hand, everyone running around crazy with *too much heaven on their minds*, that Jesus is going to get all of them (that is, the Jews) in big trouble:

JUDAS

Listen Jesus, do you care for your race?
Don't you see we must keep in our place?
We are occupied!
Have you forgotten how put-down we are?
I am frightened by the crowd
For we are getting much too loud
And they'll crush us if we go too far . . . .

Other guys in massive onion-shaped black hats sing in frighteningly ominous baritones about the problems this Jesus guy is causing, he's on a *rabble-rousing mission*, he is dangerous and must be stopped, this *miracle wonderman, hero of fools*:

CAIAPHAS

(Head Black-Hatted Guy)

I see bad things arising!
The crowd crowned him king,
which the Romans would ban
I see blood and destruction
Our elimination because of one man!

Oh, these guys are also Jews, I realize, some kind of High Council; I thought they were the bad-guy Romans. Meanwhile, Jesus's followers are distressed by the lack of information Jesus is giving them about *the Buzz*, what they're all supposed to be doing, what is their end-game, here? Maybe they should march on Jerusalem or something? Mary Magdalene, the local heart-of-gold prostitute, insanely in love, is worried that Jesus isn't getting enough sleep. But Jesus is pissy that his (male) followers aren't just following him blindly. Why are they pestering him with silly questions? He is upset they just aren't into him enough, not loving him enough, that none of them—*not one!* of them—really cares if he comes or goes:

JESUS

You'll be lost, you'll be sorry,
When I'm gone!

he whine-sings, sounding like a petulant bad boyfriend, or a five-year-old throwing a tantrum. His followers (groupies?) try desperately to persuade him of their devotion; *Christ, you know I love you! Christ, what more do you need to convince you? There must be over fifty thousand, screaming love and more for you! And everyone one of fifty thousand would do whatever you ask him to!*, that last bit sounding disturbingly cultish to me. (It is 1973, after all, and I live in Los Angeles, and Charles Manson and his do-whatever-he-asked-them-to followers are still fresh in the news, still fresh in my nine-year-old mind.)

But it's still not enough blind devotion; Jesus pout-sings some more about how no one, not the fifty thousand, not the Romans or the Jews (the Jews are more explicitly *the Jews* here, now that we're in the New

Testament) understand power or glory or anything. They just don't get it. Nobody understands him, poor guy.

I certainly don't—we don't see him *do* anything to earn all that love. One of the High Council Jews bemoans how *A trick or two with lepers, and the whole town's on its feet!*, but we don't even get to see that. (I would have liked to see that leper-trick of his; I have no idea what a leper is.) Nevertheless: He is hot, this Jesus. Ted Neeley's performance was both panned and praised, but you can't argue with the guy's charisma or the throbbing intensity of his rock opera vibrato. It makes sense, in a way, for him to be Big Man of Judea. As Caiaphas sings: *One thing I'll say for him, Jesus is cool!*

But still, what to do about this *Jesus-mania?* Only one option:

CAIAPHAS
We must crush him completely!
For the sake of the nation
This Jesus must die!

Meanwhile, Jesus actually does throw a tantrum, in the temple: Tables overturned, stuff smashed, a little like the pogrom in *Fiddler*. (But wasn't Jesus against violence? I understand he's upset they're selling stuff in the temple, but this just feels like a wanton destruction of property.) He storms off and is accosted by ragged sick people, blind people, people missing limbs (I imagine there are lepers in the crowd, but it's hard to tell), who swarm him creepily, begging for healing and help, until, overwhelmed, he finally loses his shit, scream-singing, *Don't push me, don't crowd me, there's too many of you! Leave me alone!* Perhaps this is meant to humanize him, show his undivine vulnerability, but what did he expect? It doesn't seem very, well, *Christian* to yell at them that way, or to heal some lepers and not others. And how does Jesus and/or God select whom to heal, and whom to ignore; is mercy, grace, blessing, whatever you call it, so arbitrary, so inconsistent?

How many people have died, because He turned away His face?

By now Judas is really worried, because *Jesus can't control it like he did before!* He goes to Caiaphas, and in exchange for thirty pieces of silver tells him where The Last Supper (which I think was a regular

old Passover Seder for these Biblical Jews, right?) is being held th
night. Cut to a picnic in the Garden of Gethsemane, where Jesus (terrible host) berates his followers (all men, no women, not even to serve
the food, not even the faithful, besotted Mary M.) for all the bad things
they are going to do: Betray him, deny him, and, once again, just not
love him enough:

JESUS

For all you care, this wine could be my blood!
For all you care, this bread could be my body . . .
I must be mad
Thinking I'll be remembered
I must be out of my head
Look at your blank faces!
My name will mean nothing
Ten minutes after I'm dead!

Jesus sings his doubts straight to God now, Tevye- and Moses-like,
gazing up at the heavenly clouds (the usual "visual" stand-in for
God—if God is everywhere, why can't He ever be represented by a
cricket or a rock?), about how fed up he is with everything. He wants
to know why he has to die for this to all work out—will that really
make any difference?

JESUS

If I die, what will be my reward?
Can you show me now that I would not be killed
in vain?

Show me just a little of Your omnipresent brain
Show me there's a reason for Your wanting me to
die

You're far too keen on where and how
And not so hot on why . . . .

And yet decides in the next beat to stop browbeating God, and just
go along with His plan:

JESUS

All right, I'll die!

Just watch me die!

See how I'll die!

Take me now

Before I change my mind . . . .

Jesus is arrested, passed from Caiaphas to Pontius Pilate (finally, a Roman), who tries getting Jesus to admit he's planning a big coup as King of the Jews, which Jesus entirely denies. Bored by this petty Jewish criminal, Pilate passes him along to King Herod, who is in charge of the Jews, and we troop off to a porcine, granny-glasses-wearing, half-naked, poolside-lounging Herod (played in hilarious Richard-Simmons-meets-Bob-Fosse fashion by Josh Mostel, son of Zero—a *Forgive me, please,* to the Mostel family by Norman Jewison?), who, in the show-stopping number, part ragtime, part burlesque, entirely high camp, taunts him:

KING HEROD

So you are the Christ

You're the great Jesus Christ!

Prove to me that you're divine

Turn my water into wine!

That's all you need do

Then I'll know it's all true!

Come on, King of the Jews!

Oh, what a pity, if it's all a lie!

Still I'm sure that you can rock

The cynics if you try!

I'd only ask what I'd ask any superstar . . . .

I agree: Show me the miracles! But this is all beneath Jesus, whose silence throws Herod into a snit: *You're a joke, you're not the Lord! You are nothing but a fraud!* So it's back to Pilate. By now a mob—a Jewish mob—has inexplicably gathered, ranting and raving that Pilate must crucify him! *Crucify him, crucify him!*

A-ha: The "Christ-killers" I have heard about! So the Romans were, in fact, the good guys, it's the *Jews*, yes, such troublemakers, who are suddenly, misguidedly out for Christ's blood. So, what is with these vengeful, angry Jews? There has been no actual threat made against them, no "Get your Jesus in line or you're all in trouble!" edict; all the doom and gloom has come from other Jews like Judas and Caiaphas projecting their anxieties. The Romans haven't seemed all that concerned about some lowly carpenter wandering around. Are the Jews so paranoid, so hungry for a prophylactic scapegoat? And where did this sudden clamoring mob of Jesus-denying Jews come from? Just minutes ago they were all over their rock star Jesus, hoping to touch the hem of his spotless white robe.

Poor Pilate actually pleads with the mob:

PILATE

What do you mean, you'd crucify your king?
He's done no wrong
No, not the slightest thing!
I see no reason, I find no evil
This man is harmless
So why does he upset you?
I need a crime!

But the crazed Jews are relentless, so to appease these "vultures," Pilate agrees to have Jesus (bloodlessly) flogged, begging the tight-lipped Jesus all the while to help him: Please say something, Jesus, save yourself, help me to help you! The bloodthirsty Jews are unsatisfied, so Pilate at last has no choice: You want your guy dead? Okay, fine, whatever.

Cut to a 1970s lounge act: Judas appears (reanimated, as he hanged himself after tipping off the Romans—the image of which taps into the visual rhetoric of lynching and is far more disturbing than the sanitized images of Jesus being flogged or crucified) in a V-necked white jumpsuit, back-up singers in fringed white disco-wear, and a groovy gospel choir behind them:

JUDAS AND SINGERS

Jesus Christ, Jesus Christ!

Who are you, what have you sacrificed?

Jesus Christ Superstar

Do you think you're what they say you are?

intercut with more "realistic" images of Jesus dragging his cross (which seems to weigh about ten pounds) through the streets, still being taunted by the screaming crowd of murderous Jewish vultures. Suddenly the music stops: the sound of hammering (what is being hammered is out of frame), and the image, mostly in shadowy silhouette, of Jesus being raised on the cross. Mary M. is there, crying, faithful to the end. There is the sound of mocking laughter—*Jewish* mocking laughter, of course—that a few years later will sound exactly like nasty schoolmates laughing at pig-bloodied Carrie at the Prom.

JESUS

Father, forgive them. They know not what they do . . . .

"They" meaning, of course, the Jews. Who, in addition to being fickle and bloodthirsty Christ-killing vultures, are so, so ignorant.

The troupe, back in street clothes, reboards the bus, with the noticeable exception of Jesus, or the actor playing Jesus, whom they are leaving behind; the Mary M. actress and the Judas actor gaze reverently back to the final shot: A silhouette of the cross, the setting sun.

After the movie, I will ask my parents to purchase the hypnotic, addictive soundtrack on cassette, and for months I will walk around the house with my tape recorder, blithely singing *Christ, you know I love you! I believe in you and God so tell me that I'm saved! Jesus, I am with you! Touch me touch me, Jesus! Jesus, I am on your side, kiss me kiss me, Jesus!*, just as I did with the Broadway soundtrack for *Hair*, when I walked around at age seven singing about fellatio and cunnilingus.

At least I have a better understanding, I think, about the Christ-killing rap, why some Christians get so upset with us Jews; the Romans technically killed Jesus, yes, but only because we forced them to. We gave them no other choice, us Jewish rabble-rousers.

But, wait . . . didn't Jesus *have* to die in order to save everyone, or something? In order for Christianity to even exist? Wasn't that the whole bizarre *plan*? Doesn't this mean Judas—and by extension, the bloodthirsty Jewish mob—actually did do the right thing? Exactly what God wanted? Everything still seems like our fault, though, somehow.

So, how responsible am I for killing Jesus Christ, little half-Jewish Valley Girl that I am? Should I feel guilty? Should I feel guilty that I don't feel guilty? I'm still so confused.

Sometime during the year of Heston-Moses and Blond Rocker Christ, my father provides some new context, another jigsaw piece to this puzzle of Jewish identity. We are sitting in a movie theatre (of course), probably on a Saturday afternoon while my mother is off shopping, waiting for Coming Attractions, although I have no memory of what movie we are actually there to see. My father—my devout atheist, once-Lutheran father—begins talking about a thing called "The Holocaust" (a word I don't think I have ever heard, perhaps only overheard in a low-voiced adult conversation or two . . .), which happened a long time ago over in Europe when millions (a word, like *Holocaust*, too abstract to carry any real meaning) of Jews were rounded up and put in camps and then killed by the German Nazis for no other reason than that they *were* Jewish. And while we don't practice or believe any religion in our house, not Judaism or Christianity, my mother is Jewish, my grandparents are Jewish, and so I am, too, and it is important that I know that. It is important I understand what a special thing that is. It is something I must *never forget*. It is an inescapable part of me, in my very blood. Judaism is not just about "faith" or some bullshit religion: It is a racial and cultural and historical heritage.

Surely I must have had questions about this (the wise child? the wicked child, simple child? No, at this moment I am indeed the child who doesn't even know how to pose an actual question, not about this), but the lights dimmed, the curtain went up, the Coming

Attractions began, and there in the dark cinema I am once again made Jewish, have once again become *a Jew*—but defined now by something both too abstract and too horrifying, too staggeringly relevant and weighted with responsibility: Judaism as death warrant.

My first Holocaust film—what an obscene way to phrase that, the genre-fying of genocide—was not, technically about the Holocaust: *The Odessa File*, in 1974, is a peppy Cold War thriller, set in 1963 Berlin.[21] Jon Voight is Peter Miller, an apple-cheeked (and so Aryan) journalist with an ebb-and-flow German accent, who comes into possession of a diary written by an old Jewish man who has just committed suicide by gassing himself. Twelve minutes into the film, Peter sits down to read this hand-scribbled account of the old man's experience in WWII; he is immediately engrossed, and the groovy espionage music fades to a quavery voiceover:

> SALOMON V.O.
>
> I am Salomon Tauber, and I have stayed alive this long only because there is one more thing I wish to do. The friends I have known, the sufferers and victims of the camp are long dead, and only the persecutors are still around me. I see their faces on the streets . . . and in the night I see the face of my wife, Esther, and I remember how she clung to me on the train as we pulled into the station at Riga . . . .

The bright saturated colors of early '70s film transform to grainy black-and-white images: Dazed, dull-eyed men, women, and children huddled together in an enclosed cattle car, rocking listlessly to the movement of the train. Jewish Stars of David glow achromatically white on coat lapels. Salomon and Esther cling to each other, yes.

---

21 *The Odessa File* (Columbia Pictures, 1974): screenplay by Kenneth Ross and George Markstein, adapted from the novel by Fredrick Forsyth; directed by Ronald Neame; with Jon Voight and Maximilian Schell

SALOMON V.O.

We had been three days and three nights in that cattle car, without food or water. The dead, and there were many of them, were crowded in among us.

The Jews stumble from the train, stagger around the platform. SS Officers herd them, carrying truncheons, guns, whips. They converse in German without subtitles, *Ich Ich Ich,* sounding disconcertingly like bar mitzvah Hebrew. There are barking German shepherds. There is barbed wire. The bodies of dead Jews are dragged off. There is a hint of smoke in the air, as if a sheer black stocking has been pulled over the camera lens.

SALOMON V.O.

It was there I first saw him: Captain Eduard Roschmann, the SS Commandant of the camp. The Butcher.

And there is SS Roschmann, the Commandant, an unnervingly handsome Maximilian Schell in a well-tailored coat, collar turned dashingly up, a skull decorating his black cap.

SALOMON V.O.

Roschmann had a hobby. He liked to destroy human beings. First their soul, then their body.

Jews standing on footstools have ropes around their necks; Roschmann, *Ich*-ing, kicks the stool out from beneath an adolescent boy. His feet dangle in space. Jews kneel at the edge of trenches, are shot in the back of the head by Nazi officers, fall conveniently forward. Roschmann plays a game; behind the next-in-line kneeling Jew, a young boy, he smiles at another officer, puts his finger to his lips, and shoots into the air. The boy, unharmed, falls forward. The boy then gazes up at the Nazis, his face blank. Roschmann chuckles, nods to the officer, who aims into the trench, shoots the boy. The Nazis laugh, joke around. Their unsubtitled German is an appropriately incomprehensible language for incomprehensible actions.

                    SALOMON V.O.
Sometimes, Roschmann amused himself by kicking
those about to die as they huddled together naked,
stripped of dignity and all hope. He enjoyed
watching the dogs feed on them while they were
still living.

We are not shown any of this. More trainloads of Jews arrive.

                    SALOMON V.O.
Roschmann had many of the women, children, and
elderly exterminated on arrival—they were more
valuable dead: Their clothes, their hair, their
teeth, were a cash asset.

We do not see these images. We see only Salomon and Esther, being
marched down a street. A hollow-eyed Esther is loaded onto a van,
while musicians play; Salomon, stumbling, is held back by Roschmann's truncheon. Esther, realizing they are separated, screams and
screams. When Salomon struggles, pleads, Roschmann beats his face
until black blood drips. He can only watch, helpless.

                    SALOMON V.O.
The expression in Esther's eyes has stayed with
me always.

The van is sealed, driven off, the Jews packed inside suffocated by
carbon monoxide.

                    SALOMON V.O.
After her death, my soul died inside me. But my
body and mind remained alive. I was determined
to survive and tell what Eduard Roschmann did to
our people here.

Salomon informs us that after the war, Roschmann disappeared,
but:

SALOMON V.O.

```
I bear no hatred, no bitterness toward the German
people. Peoples are not evil, only individuals
are evil. If, after my death, this diary should
be found and read, will some kind friend say Kad-
dish for me?
```

Back to Peter in his apartment, pensive, closing the manuscript; the final few moments of the movie focus on his obsession with finding Roschmann and bringing him to justice—in doing so, he discovers Roschmann has come under the protection of the Odessa, a cabal of postwar Nazis who have reassimilated themselves as ordinary upstanding German citizens, dedicated to (1) helping other Nazis on the run, and (2) sabotaging the State of Israel. Peter's boss is opposed to this investigation ("Dead Jews don't sell papers!"), his mother is opposed to this ("Don't do this, people want to forget the horrors of the war!"), but Peter persists, eventually going undercover as an Odessa operative and confronting the now-aging Roschmann, who has been hiding in plain sight as a successful German businessman. There is a big spy-thriller twist/revelation at the end, and we conclude with a repeat of Salomon's voiceover insistence that he bears no bitterness, that peoples are not evil, his wish that someone say Kaddish, the Jewish prayer for the dead, for him—which the Ayran Peter does.

But, no, these are not the final moments of the movie: This is the movie itself, a well-crafted Cold War espionage entertainment. The black-and-white, voiced-over sequence of Salomon's experience at Riga, of Roschmann's sadism and butchery, is less than six minutes long. It is the excuse for the movie, the inciting incident, the trigger for Peter's actions; it is the Holocaust as MacGuffin.

It is unclear if Salomon's depiction of the camp is news to Peter, in 1963 Berlin, but it is news to me: I am ten years old, these are my first images of the Holocaust, and they *are* the movie, for me—they become the movie, they expand to fill the entire two hours and ten minutes of screen time, they enter my consciousness and nightmares. These images are all I will remember about *The Odessa File*. I have little memory of "my experience" watching this film. I didn't exist during the movie; I disappeared into those images. Those faces, those eyes, the white stars, black blood.

From this film dates my determination to own my Jewishness—as a cultural and historical identity, if not a religious one. My blondish hair and my Anglo last name do not announce me as a Jew, I can "pass" so easily, and for years afterward I will find a self-righteous satisfaction in asserting my Jewish self to the world—the usual surprise on someone's face confirms my understanding that to 98.3 percent of the people around me I may well be *different*, be the *Other*: Former Hebrew Slave, Child of Israel, member of the Levite tribe. Christ-killer, troublemaker.

This film also instilled in me a visceral discomfort with anything German (despite my own German ancestry), the *Ich, Ich, Ich* now the onomatopoeic equivalent of barbed wire, the dread of the Teutonic replacing any abstract fear of pogroming Russian Cossacks. The accent alone makes my stomach clench, makes me frightened, suspicious, angry; this is absolute bigotry on my part, a reverse discrimination, I know; I am not responsible for killing Jesus, and contemporary Germans are not responsible for the Holocaust. But I can't help it; I am no Salomon.

For years after *The Odessa File*, for all of my young adulthood, I will seek out other "Holocaust movies," ostensibly to comprehend the incomprehensible, but also in search of those images to feed and fuel my outrage and fear. Now that I have found a source to my own relevance in the world, I do not want to let it go. I will carry Salomon's bitterness for him, keep it beating and warm, keep it alive.

Fictional films about the Holocaust are a disparate lot, dramatically and aesthetically. We can watch the corruption of the human soul (*Inside the Third Reich; Holocaust*); the creation of a human soul (*Schindler's List*); moments of triumph (*Defiance; Escape from Sobibor*); false sentimentalizing (*Life Is Beautiful*); the ultimate irony (*Europa Europa*); the corrosive power of memory and guilt (*Sophie's Choice; The Pawnbroker*); the eroticization and fetishizing of evil (*The Night Porter*); the crushing of the human spirit (*The Grey Zone*); the resilience of the human spirit (*Holocaust; Playing for Time; The Pianist*); to list a very, very few.

But those films that choose—attempt?—to accurately dramatize the extermination of the Jews ultimately draw from and contribute to a shared iconography. They are the images that have become tropes: Haystacks of naked skeletal bodies. Hair being shorn. Piles of emptied suitcases, of eyeglasses, of shoes. A sampling of teeth gleaming with gold fillings. The smashed windows of Kristallnacht; a bloody, skull-crushing, degrading pogrom. A cattle car packed with human beings. A "selection" of human beings, sent to the left or the right. Smoke rising from chimneys. The barking German shepherd. The barbed wire. A can of Zyklon B. A gate sign reading ARBEIT MACHT FREI. Naked bodies crammed into a "shower" room. Tattooed arms. Lamp shades. A swastika armband. All those yellow or black-and-white Jewish stars on lapels. The visual semiotics of the Holocaust.

The threatening, sneering, scarring sound of *Juden*.

Lord, why do you not hear the cries of the children?

For years I watch this kind of movie, movie after movie, in theatres, on television, at revival houses, wherever I can find them, until the images begin to blur; the repetition and sheer accumulation of them eventually dilutes their power. I numb out; and then, ashamed of my numbness, ashamed to be so safely insulated, I keep watching, trying to keep my anger aflame. *Never forget*—that is what I try to do. I keep watching, seeking a bolstering horror fix, another horror rush. And then I am ashamed at my need for what feels like cheap, righteous thrill, the sense that I have made a pornography of it all, and I stop watching this kind of movie. I'm happy to forget, for just a little while, for now.

The Chosen, in 1981, is more oblique.[22] I go to see this movie precisely because it is not, to my understanding, about the Holocaust; based on the award-winning 1967 novel by Chaim Potok, it is about the challenging yet profound friendship of two very different kinds of Jewish boys: Reuven Malter (Barry Miller), the

---

22 *The Chosen* (Chosen Film Company, 1981): screenplay by Edwin Gordon, based on the novel by Chaim Potok; directed by Jeremy Paul Kagan; with Robby Benson, Barry Miller, Maximilian Schell, and Rod Steiger.

ball-playing, jazz-loving, kid-next-door son of a widowed Jewish
intellectual (Maximilian Schell, all the more handsome now), and
Danny Saunders (Robby Benson! Robby Benson! his dark side-
curls framing those crystal-blue eyes), the prodigy son of a revered
Hasidic rabbi (Rod Steiger, hammy, white-bearded, and stern) in
early- to late-1940s Brooklyn. Both families are haunted by the war
and the emerging revelations of the concentration camps, of Hitler's
atrocities, yet they inhabit two wildly different worlds: Reuven's
father is a fierce advocate for the creation of the secular state of
Israel—"Only a Jewish state, a Jewish homeland, can give meaning
to these savage acts! Only a Jewish state can guarantee it will never
happen again!"—and is also a loving, tender father; Danny's father,
Reb Saunders—who rejects Zionism, for "The Messiah and the
Messiah *only* will bring the Jewish people to their homeland!"—
has raised his son in the strictest, most sheltered and sequestered
religious observation, including a chilly absolute silence. Reuven is
stunned when Danny tells him that, outside of studying Torah, his
father never speaks to him:

REUVEN

I'd hate that. To not have my father talk to me . . . .

Reuven is destined for his own academic career, Danny is destined
to follow in his father's footsteps as a leader in the Hasidic community,
and the weight of these opposing destinies draws the boys together,
while the opposing philosophies of their fathers threaten to tear them
apart. Danny tries to illuminate Reuven to the power of orthodox
faith, explains how the founder of Hasidism in the 1700s believed that

DANNY

To be a good Jew didn't depend on how much you
knew, but on how much you *felt* . . . .

but we eventually learn that Danny secretly dreams of attending a
secular university in order to study psychology and psychoanalysis.

Meanwhile, Reuven finds himself drawn to the deeper mystery of faith—his own dream will be to attend rabbinical school—and yet he is saddened to see Danny's struggle with the pain of his silent relationship with his distant father, the brewing tension between them over Danny's yearning for a life beyond their figurative Hasidic walls. By the end of the movie, Reb Saunders gives in: He summons Reuven for a talk (Reuven is surprised by this until his own father tells him Reb Saunders actually wants to talk to Danny, through Reuven) and tries to explain, with Danny present, that he and his son were close when Danny was a child, yes, but as Danny got older, Reb Saunders felt his son's intellect was developing to the detriment of his compassion and so decided he must raise him

> REB SAUNDERS
>
> through the wisdom and the pain of silence. To teach him other people are alone, are suffering, other people are carrying pain. And he learned through the wisdom and the pain of silence that a mind without a heart is nothing.

Reuven, clearly disapproving, does not respond, so Reb Saunders asks—still of Reuven, not Danny:

> REB SAUNDERS
>
> So, you think I've been cruel? Maybe. But I don't think so, because my beloved Daniel has learned. So, let him go. . . .

And he finally turns to Danny:

> REB SAUNDERS
>
> Daniel? You heard?

> DANIEL
>
> Yes, Papa.

REB SAUNDERS

And when you go forth into the world, you will be
proud, and go forth as a Jew? And you will keep
the commandments of a Jew?

Daniel begins to cry.

REB SAUNDERS

Maybe you should forgive me. For not being a
wiser father. . . .

They embrace; now both of them are crying, and I am crying, too, for it is so moving to watch this stern patriarch soften, express weakness and doubt, accept Danny for who he really is, to share in this loving reconciliation between parent and child.

I am also moved during the scene when the United Nations votes *Yes* on a resolution to support the state of Israel, the first step in the actual creation of a Jewish homeland; Reuven and his father, listening to the news on the radio, are overwhelmed with joy, and although I consider myself shamefully apolitical, when the newscaster announces, "We have a State! After two thousand years of exile, we can go home again!" I cry, too; I have never felt "exiled," and yet, in some odd way it feels good to have a "home," to know a home exists. I remember that sixth-grade debate, and I am embarrassed not just by my eleven-year-old's lack of understanding, but also by my lack of interest in even *trying* to understand, my lack of curiosity about the world, and I am surprised and grateful I feel so deeply about this, now.

But watching this film, I am finally—it's about time, I am almost eighteen years old—awakened to the gender politics at play in these Jewish lives, a theme almost invisibly woven throughout the films I have seen. In the end, Golde was not really in charge of anything beyond what kind of soup to make; she had no say in the tearing apart of her family, could only cower and weep before Tevye's decisive rage. Her household of strong-willed daughters, like Moses's giggling sisters-in-law, or his own wife, Sephora, were kept far too busy cooking and cleaning—*And who does Mama teach, to mend and tend and fix? Preparing me to marry whomever Papa picks? The daughters, the*

daughters!—to play any role in life beyond nurturing mother or supportive wife. The women of Christ's Judea are backup singers, backup
dancers, but other than Mary Magdalene (who was most likely not a
prostitute, but a woman who left her husband and children to follow
a different path in life), they are virtually absent from any significant
event; all these women peer through curtains at the goings-on during
temple services, are hidden away in the kitchen while the men celebrate the Sabbath with food and drink and intellectual debate, they
wait, freezing, by the side of a road for the men to finish their prayers.
At a wedding in *The Chosen*, the women are not merely separated by a
rope, as in *Fiddler*, but by an actual wall, lest there be, what? Contami-
nation? Temptation? Separate is not equal. Danny's mother (no wig,
but her head always so snugly wrapped in a white scarf it looks as
though she's undergoing chemo) is only ever seen cooking or cleaning
or serving tea. At some point, Reuven begins crushing on Danny's
younger sister Shaindel, teasing her about reading a book:

REUVEN

Aren't you supposed to be helping your mother in
the kitchen?

SHAINDEL

Is that all you think a girl does? Cook and clean?

and of course he thinks that; we haven't seen a woman in this entire
movie do anything else. Danny, feeling he must dash Reuven's hopes
of a relationship with Shaindel, explains her marriage has been
arranged since she was just a child, to the son of another rabbi:

REUVEN

Does she like him?

DANNY

I don't know. I've never asked her.

Because it is not, of course, of any consequence how she—or Tzeitel,
or Mary M.—might *feel* (despite the Hasidic honoring of *feeling*) or
might wish to live her own life, not in the face of a Jewish *Tradition!*

of patriarchal hierarchy, one that relies on those man-written religious texts as supporting evidence of the will of God.

This film is not intended to be a story of women, or of mothers and daughters. But as in other cinematic depictions of the lives of Jewish women, in their very invisibility, or in the visibility of their home-and-hearth roles, their story is still being shown. And it is a story of oppression-within-oppression, of limitation and squandered potential, one that leaves me with a sour undertaste, but also a relief, a gratitude that in my own irreligious, very un-Jewish upbringing, I was spared all that. I am glad to be separate from these "true brethren" of mine.

And yet. Early in the movie, Reuven is surprised Danny has no idea who Errol Flynn is, and Danny must explain: "I've never been to a movie. We don't go to the movies." Looking to broaden Danny's perspective, Reuven takes him to a museum for the first time, where they pause for a long while before a marble female nude.

                          REUVEN
        What do you think?

                          DANNY
        It's a deception. Have you noticed how we have no
        pictures or paintings on the walls of our house?
        It's because the images detract from what's real.
        And what's true.

                          REUVEN
        I see you haven't stopped looking.

                          DANNY
        That's because it's beautiful.

Next up for the boys, a movie house, for some Van Johnson musical confection; Danny is unimpressed, bored. But then the newsreel begins: The "Nazi Murder Mills," with documentary footage of American troops liberating the concentration camps. Here we go, I think, begin the parade of those brutal, brutal images I have seen so many times by now. *Again*, really? I do not want to watch them again, I do not want another fix—or want to trigger the need for another fix—but I find myself shaking, my heart quickening. And I realize what is moving me, here, is *Danny's* reaction to them. It is his first time seeing these images, and his horror is newborn and unfiltered, uncynical, raw. There are tears in his eyes, his jaw is both tightened and slack, his face seems to lose its shape; he is disappearing into these images, the way I once did, and watching his pain both shames me and reawakens my own. This image of Danny, a fictional character in a fictional movie, does not detract from what's real, or from what's true; it brings me back to what is real and true, an essential part of who I am, as a human being and a Jew, and for that I am also grateful.

I will never forget.

The expression in Esther's eyes, on Daniel's face, will stay with me, always.

- - - - - - - - - -

YENTL

Papa, please forgive me
Try to understand me
Papa, don't you know I had no choice?
Can you hear me praying?
Anything I'm saying?

Papa, how I love you
Papa, how I need you
Papa, how I miss you
Kissing me good night[23]

M y grandfather Al didn't get a first-born son, his own ben-Albert. His first child was my mother, Beverlee, born in 1933. A chubby, frizzy-brown-haired, big-personality little girl, one who decided, very

---

23 "Papa, Can You Hear Me?" from *Yentl* (MGM/UA, 1983): music by Michel Legrand, lyrics by Alan Bergman and Marilyn Bergman

early on, that she was not going to be ignored—a defining moment of my mother in childhood is a cinematic one, captured on old Super 8 film: My grandfather loved taking home movies, and we have a flickery scene of a dozen assembled kids where we see my mother determinedly pushing (shoving?) herself to the front of the crowd to wave and beam and mug for the camera. All her life she would envy the slim blond Gentile girls around her. But if she wasn't ever going to be blond or thin or pretty, she was always going to be noticed, damn it, be the star of the show.

But her father adored her—this according to my mother, who loved telling me the stories of his adoration, spoiling her with riding lessons and fancy clothes and taking her off to Chicago jazz clubs when she was only fifteen and sixteen and (then voluptuous) could pass for twenty-five. Whatever made her happy. Through her two marriages and two divorces he still always did for her, took care of her; he would always be the dependable male presence in her chaotic life, always be the Papa, the benevolent Daddy-King who enabled and indulged her, paid her bills, bought her jewelry and furniture and cars, babysat her own daughter (me) so she could both remain a child and keep the wild party going, stay at the center of every shot, every scene. She filled the screen, indeed, was larger than life, charming and charismatic, needy and narcissistic, and entirely exhausting.

She and my father divorced when I was twelve, and in the following years her unthinking dependency on my grandfather increased. (Her dependency on me, too—it became my responsibility to take her contact lenses in/out every morning/evening, because her porcelain fingernails were too long. For an example picked at random.) She clung harder to my grandfather, relied on his willingness to manage the majority of life's basic logistics for her, while simultaneously plunging into a crazed second adolescence: She and a flock of other fortysomething, recently divorced and disoriented, once-voluptuous, now-overweight women established a favorite booth at a local supper club, where the befriended waitresses and bartenders would comp their drinks or slip an extra baked potato onto a shared steak dinner, and they could drink martinis and dance disco and distract themselves from their upheavaled lives three or four nights a week.

There began a stream of men in and out of our house—my mother and I shared a bathroom, and I never knew what strange guy might be exiting the shower in the morning, a flowered beach towel around his waist. These were generally unsavory characters, guys who were typically unemployed or unsavorily employed: Drug users and dealers, mostly, guys with records and rap sheets, guys in between their "own place" (hence, their presence in our house), guys with nagging ex-wives and girlfriends and assorted children, guys who would disappear from my mother's giddy frame of reference (and our house) after a few appearances and soon be replaced by another.

My grandfather was increasingly annoyed, frustrated, appalled. I was busy at school, with friends, with my first after-school and weekend job at a bakery; I didn't question any of it. I was usually asleep when my mother came home in the middle of the night, wafting cigarette smoke and martinis and the latest guy's syrupy aftershave. I didn't mind that I began eating dinner and sleeping over at my grandparents' house even more often, spending several nights a week watching TV and slurping those root boor floats with my Grandpa, or happily going clothes shopping together. I thought it was edgy and sophisticated when my mother threw parties where strangers got black-out drunk on generic vodka or snorted coke off the modular glass coffee table it was my responsibility to Windex twice a week. I was unaware when my mother planned to mortgage our house to cover some guy's bail, a plan that finally galvanized my grandfather to anger; fearing *I* would wind up homeless, he flat-out refused to "help her" with the mortgage process. I heard about that one only several years later. Maybe that particular guy is still in prison. But my grandfather's anger and resentment took hold, began to boil. This is not how a woman should live her life. This is not how a woman must behave. Not a mother. Not his daughter.

Some things I cannot, I will not, allow!

The final blow came while I was far away; I was twenty-one, on a scholarship year in France, lonely and disoriented and drinking way too much myself, when I heard there had been a blowout between my grandfather and my mother. I have heard multiple versions of the story over the years from various family members: No two versions match. But the essential moment seems to be a disrespectful comment made by my mother to my grandfather; in some versions it is an ill-timed teasing, a foolishly blurted joke; in others it is an all-out nasty "Fuck you, Dad, I don't need you or your help! You don't own me!" Either way, my grandfather swore he was done with her, forever. She was disowned, dismissed, cast out from the flock. Declared dead.

My mother was hysterical. She left him desperate phone messages, wrote desperate letters, pushed and shoved herself as best she could to the center of the frame. She pleaded and implored, and not just with my grandfather, but with my grandmother, too, begging her to mend the rift—which my grandmother, very ill and very soon to die, was unable to do; my grandfather was unpersuadable—*Chava is dead to us! We will forget her!*—and I imagine my grandmother lying help-lessly in her bed, crying, dying, consumed by this new failure, this new guilt.

And so my mother begged me to intercede, to persuade him. After all, my grandfather adored me, was so proud of me, never denied me anything. Surely he would listen to me.

But there was, in fact, a *Tradition!* in our family: My grandfather's habit or ability to "be done" with people, to assign blame and villainy and all the evils of the world to someone he decided had done him wrong—an old business partner, a family friend, a brother-in-law, his own sister. This affectionate, generous, loving man had a reserve of impressive angers that would coalesce and be visited upon the latest person to betray or insult him, to question his dominance, and that would be that: An emotional pogrom. He had no religious faith, but he held a strong, unquestioning belief in his own authority as Head of the Family, *to have the final word at home!*

I was the adored granddaughter, yes, one who had never done a single thing to displease him, and yet . . . . My grandfather's love was precious to me. It was the thing to be treasured. It meant the golden warmth of home, far more than the house I shared with my mother, the place I could always go and curl up to sleep on a comfy couch, even as an adult, *here in the home I love,* secure under the portrait gaze of a solemn-eyed, black-garmented man—a watchful ancestor or a protec-tive god. My grandfather's love provided balance. A steadying glow. It was not something I was going to risk. Not even for my mother. Because if my Grandpa could deny his own once-beloved daughter this way—if a father's love was indeed so precarious—could his anger not also fall upon and obliterate me?

So I never pleaded for my mother, I never stood up to him on her behalf. I made pitiful excuses to her: *Oh, I'm waiting for the right moment; Oh, you know how stubborn Grandpa is, I might just end up making it worse* . . . and after a while she ceased asking. Her exile from our family was a price I was willing to pay. I remained her daughter, of course, I split holidays in threes ("celebrations" now with grandfather, mother, father and stepmother), I took care of her as best I could, took on many of the responsibilities my grandfather once managed. But when I was with my Grandpa, I stayed quiet on the subject. I told myself it would make no difference, anyway, that I had no power to persuade him with my kisses or tears: The belief system I created for myself. And he, oddly, almost never mentioned her to me again. Perhaps he sensed that to explicitly recruit me as an ally would put me in a painfully untenable place. Or perhaps he felt no need to recruit me, secure in the knowledge he was doing the right thing, teaching his daughter and all of us a valuable lesson this way. Or maybe, on some level, he felt shame. Maybe he feared losing my love as well. I was grateful for the silence, happy to carry this particular pain inside of it, next to my own shame; I never mentioned her to him again, either. I never asked a single question.

I am the wicked child, yes.

My mother finally gave up trying—*Some are driven away by edicts. Some by silence*—and it destroyed her, physically and emotionally. He died a few years later, without ever seeing or speaking to my mother again; no embrace, no real farewell. At his funeral, while some rabbi my grandfather had never met said Kaddish, I held her hand while she bawled. She died a few years ago, still enslaved by the bondage of pain.

Is it too late for me to repent? Lock myself in a room and cry to a recording of Kol Nidre? Pray, to someone, or to something, for forgiveness? Speak directly, intimately to God, send up my apologies and cries for deliverance?

Just before my grandfather died, he took me furniture shopping. I had just moved into my own place for the first time and needed a dresser; of course my Grandpa took me to get one. As we roamed around living room arrangements and bedroom sets and dinettes, he spotted a kitchen table and four chairs, vaguely Danish modern. He stopped, pointed it out to me approvingly. I didn't need a kitchen table, I reminded him.

No, for your mother, he said, nodding, thoughtful. That would be a good table for her. I think she'd really like that. Don't you think?

And God be with you.

I stayed very quiet, not wanting to startle him, the way you deal with a sleepwalking person. He has forgotten, I thought. Just for the moment, he has forgotten to deny his own daughter. He has forgotten to hate her, forgotten his own belief system, the arbitrary rules wherein he is justified in being so angry and resentful that he can strike someone figuratively dead. The faith that has sustained him, allowed him to feel powerful and strong, given him a foothold on the shaky roof of his own life.

Or maybe, like Reb Saunders, he is trying to talk to his child through me.

Yes, I murmured. I think she'd like that. I'll let her know.

Thou shalt honor thy mother and thy father.

- - - - - - - - - - -

Before she died my mother often said how she wished she could believe in God, in the thought of heaven or some kind of fabulous afterlife one could draw comfort from when the real-life present was an experience of pain and despair. She envied people of faith their faith, some sustaining, comforting thing they could escape to.

But, she would say, laughing, it's such bullshit!

Would I have any religious faith if I had been taught to? Would I believe in God if I had been taught to? Would I be a better person? A better daughter? A better Jew? All I can do now is ask the questions.

Because I'm a terrible Jew. I mock the stories and traditions, I believe none of the theology, I reject the idea any of us have been divinely chosen for anything. I am offended by the misogyny, the intolerance, the self-righteousness. There is no rocking the cynic in me; I remain a profoundly unspiritual, irreligious person. I have no heaven on my mind, my feet are solidly on this earth, and when I die, when my footprints fade, I believe I will be, simply, gone. God does not dwell in my heart, mind, or soul; I believe there is no Divine Plan for me, or anyone else, no approving beams of heavenly light or roiling dark clouds to signify displeasure, no tidy instructions on how to live, no holy book or stone tablets or Higher Power to guide us, or watch over us, Glinda-like, on the yellow brick road of life. I have faith in human acts of kindness, in compassion and empathy—I do my best, and often fail—and I do not believe we need Commandments from on high or a magical Man in the Sky to tell us that this is how we should behave.

But there is history, and there is the legacy of culture and life experience, and the inheritance of DNA, and I am a believer in all of that. And I believe in the seductive power of ritual, the self-created structures or beliefs we imbue with resonance—we all need the comforting illusions of stability and security in this shaky rooftop thing of a life. Tevye is right; we are all fiddlers, trying to scratch out a simple tune without breaking our necks.

So I will still watch a Papa struggle to love his daughters, and feel mournful and joyous all at the same time, whenever they are on television; once a year I'll still watch Moses lead his people to safety and be just a little swept up in his determined heroism, despite myself; I will still rock out to that superstar Jesus Christ and keep my eyes open for miracles; I will still feel Daniel's and Salomon's pain, and keep it alive as best I can. I'll still listen out for whatever wisdom and guidance I might find in that resonant, booming voice in the dark . . . be it Heston's or God's. This is my own way of ritual, of keeping the faith, of asking questions in order to find the meaning of what I am.

HOW TO
LOSE
YOUR
VIRGINITY

LEARNING THE MECHANICS AND METAPHYSICS OF SEX

Romeo and Juliet

Little Darlings

Fast Times at Ridgemont High

The Other Side of Midnight

Coming Home

Don't Look Now

Looking for Mr. Goodbar

All That Jazz

Body Heat

Last Tango in Paris

W e needed signed permission slips from our parents for the field-trip screening of Franco Zeffirelli's *Romeo and Juliet* in 1976—all that potentially traumatizing passion, after all.[24] My friends and I were dying to go; we'd read the play in our seventh-grade drama class, our teacher emoting the text for us, offering an exegesis of Queen Mab's dream and the more arcane metaphors, but really, it was all about the poster: Two naked teenagers gazing affectionately at each other in rumpled sheets, unencumbered by any literary or historical context. And rumor had it there was (more) *nudity* and *sex* in the movie, this was Shakespeare made really *hot*, and that guy playing Romeo looked really *cute*. And he was, that tousle-haired Leonard Whiting, in his Renaissance Faire tights and blousy shirt. Olivia Hussey was a total babe as Juliet, too, all rosebud mouth and wide-set olive eyes, a river of silken black hair; at seventeen and fifteen, they were an improvement—and a controversial one—on the thirty- or fortysomething Romeos and Juliets of film versions past, the appropriately seasoned Norma Shearers and Leslie Howards, who, to our eyes, made passion look so boringly, uninterestingly *adult*: An old-movie, ancient-history, irrelevant kind of love.

But now, on a Saturday afternoon with my classmates at the Nuart Theatre for this educational screening of the most recent incarnation of Shakespeare's star-crossed lovers, Leonard and Olivia, in their wide-screen, English-accented glory, are far, far beyond *cute*; their beauty is unearthly, gasp-inducing, almost painful to look at. And their physical desire for each other is revelatory; we were expecting a love story, sure, but are surprised to feel the awakening of our own nascent, adolescent lust.

I have a rudimentary understanding of the biological basics of sex and reproduction, of course; when I was six or seven my mother read

---

24 *Romeo and Juliet* (Paramount Pictures, 1968): screenplay by Franco Brusati, Masolino D'Amico, and Franco Zeffirelli, based on the play by William Shakespeare; directed by Franco Zeffirelli; with Leonard Whiting and Olivia Hussey

through the unprurient *How Babies Are Made* book with me, chapters
sequencing in greater sophistication from flowers to chickens to dogs
to humans, all illustrated with cartoony paper cutouts; I understand,
in theory, about the egg-and-seed workings of fertilization, that Penis
A inserts into Vagina B. By now I have been taken to the occasional
movie *rated R for sexual content*, watched late-night TV soap operas,
and cringed my eyes away from the gross sex scenes—who wants to
see grown-ups behaving like that? And I am, at twelve, a veteran of
playtime doctor's appointments with pantsless and hairless neighborhood boys, of bottle-spinning kissy games and those awkward and
giggly few minutes "in heaven" at lights-out rumpus room parties,
everyone's nervous breath both sweetened and soured by candy and
punch, many of us secretly hoping indignant parents would snap on
the lights and put a stop to all that fun. I have discovered the hand-
held shower massager and the perfectly-placed Jacuzzi jet in our pool,
and my own clever, dexterous fingers, although these early explora-
tions, while successful, were blank-minded and unimaginative—I
didn't yet have a bank of visual imagery to draw on, could only rely
on the instinctive, if uninspired, physiological mechanics.

But I have never really experienced, or even *seen*, true adolescent
arousal before—and now, watching this Romeo and Juliet's unhinged
passion, I am aroused, too, to see these dewy-skinned children feeling
a mutual lust, seeking out sex. They fling themselves at each other,
they pant and heave and moan with longing, and my popcorn breath
is quickening, too. Watching these turned-on sixteenth-century teens,
I am made dizzy by a sudden flushing heat. I am both stimulated and
a little embarrassed; I glance at my friend Marie—is she feeling this,
too? This curious, enflaming, quivering thing?

But there is no actual sex. Spotting each other at the Capulets'
masked ball, Romeo and Juliet flirt "palm to palm," followed by a
brief touch of virginal lips: "Then have my lips the sin that they have
took?" she asks. "O, trespass sweetly urged," he says, "Give me my
sin again!" If this is sin, they, and we, couldn't care less—and how
could anything these rhapsodically beautiful creatures do together be
a sin? Passion ignited, they continue making out until interruption
by that busybody Nurse. In the balcony scene, piqued by the danger
they risk, they kiss full-mouthed and ravenously, as if to swallow each

other whole. Their shared desire is consuming, and so is mine; by now I am past the initial shock of their exquisiteness and am impatiently, breathlessly awaiting something more. Oh, wouldst thou leave me so unsatisfied? For perhaps the first time I realize the story of sexual love does not end with a kiss, as all those G-rated fairy tale romances with their chaste, happy-ending pecks wanted me to believe; it only begins with one.

And finally, finally, what we have been waiting the whole movie to see, what our parents signed those permission slips for: A sleeping Romeo, lying facedown but breathtakingly peach-skin naked, draped across a sleeping Juliet, whose long hair is arranged artfully across her uncovered, surprisingly full breasts—is that a nipple? I am hoping so; I am as hungry to see Juliet's naked flesh as I am to see Romeo's; give me my sin again. Yesterday they secretly married, last night was the wedding night, but Zeffirelli has passed over depicting an off-text deflowering consummation in favor of this quiet morning-after scene, which is simultaneously less frightening, thanks to the absence of any penetrative explicitness, and more astonishing, more disconcertingly alluring in its intimacy; they have shared a vow, have shared a bed, are sharing breath, bodies, and hearts, are fully naked together in the full creamy light of a Verona dawn, and that experience has until now been unimaginable to me. Romeo stands, strolls to the window, and I am overwhelmed by the perfection of his unselfconscious, rear-view nudity. Juliet pulls the sheet over her breasts—audible groans of disappointment from the boys in the theatre, and I stifle mine. But there is more; while they lovingly, iambically debate whether it is the night-ingale or the lark they hear outside the window—is it still benevolent night or cruel, discordant day?—Romeo returns to the bed, throws back the sheet, and throws his graceful naked body full-length upon Juliet's, and I imagine the impact of this embrace, the pressing of my naked back into the mattress with someone's weight, my someday breasts in someone's mouth.

But it is so far away from me, up there on-screen; I want this, for absolute real, and I am not even sure what *this* means. I want to be crushed this way, by a beautiful boy and his gleaming limbs and insistent physical love, I want to be a naked-flesh body pressed against the length of another person's love-damp heat, a lyrical fusion of both skin and soul. The scene's innocent eroticism is safe for me to enter into, and also tantalizingly adult; it strikes a match, triggers a longing, begins a craving for an experience I do not know how, at twelve years old, to find or have or make happen. Wherefore art thou, Romeo?

I'm not alone in this; "I envy Juliet," fifteen-year-old Ferris (Tatum O'Neal) breathes in romantic longing to her camp counselor Gary (Armand Assante, in his Euro-gorgeous, heavy-lidded heyday). In *Little Darlings*, Ferris is the spoiled, sheltered rich girl stuck at summer camp with scrappy, street-wise Angel (Kristy McNichol) and a cabin of bored sister-campers led by Mean Girl Dana, who takes pleasure in taunting Ferris and Angel about their sexual inexperience: Are they "women, or little girls"?[25] They're both, of course, with their coltish womanly bodies; they are in the precise, blurry moment of transition, trying to balance their confusion and fear with their needful craving, their cool self-defensive posturing with their emotional vulnerability. I am the exact same age as these girls; I am equally virginal, equally yearning and afraid. I have recently had my first grown-up date, with a cologne-drenched eighteen-year-old guy, who took me to a comedy club, encouraged me to slurp at his rum and Coke (fake ID—he was posturing, too), and, after an agonizingly stilted drive home in his Camaro, walked me to my front door and thrust his tongue in my mouth until I mumbled a dismissive *Thanks, good night!* and escaped into the house. For every second of that kiss I was equal parts repulsed and thrilled—I felt violated and objectified (not that I knew that word or concept), grossed-out by the sloppy invading tongue; but I also felt let down he did not press me for something more, something else, that he did not overpower me all night with his naked, insistent desire and poetic pentameter until the arrival of the lark, the herald of the morn. I was so relieved he never called me again; I was bitterly wounded to be so rejected.

Dana proposes a Ferris v. Angel contest: Which of them will "become a woman by the end of the summer"? Whoever loses their virginity first wins, and everyone takes sides. Ferris selects counselor

---

25 *Little Darlings* (Paramount Pictures, 1980): written by Kimi Peck and Dalene Young; directed by Ronald F. Maxwell; with Kristy McNichol, Tatum O'Neal, Armand Assante, and Matt Dillon

Gary, seeks to seduce him with mature overtures—a late-night visit to his cabin in her nightgown, suggesting she needs an understanding ear for her problems, *How about a glass of wine*, she proposes, *How about that Shakespeare?*—until he bemusedly, but kindly, shuts her down. There is no question, for him, that she is still a child—although, he reassures, if she were twenty-one, he'd probably fall madly in love with her. And she prances away across the lawn in her embroidered nightgown, validated and relieved, happy to linger a while longer in the sexless safety of her star-crossed-lovers dreams.

But this is really Angel's story; she sets her sights on Randy (Matt Dillon), a kid from the boys' camp across the lake—and "sets her sights on" is the right phrase, for *Little Darlings* is the rare film to delight in the female gaze; when Angel meets Randy, the camera lingers, from her point of view, on his alabaster skin and pomegranate lips, the slope of his sculpted muscles, the snug fit of his jeans. He is much prettier than she is, and she is perfectly happy to gaze upon him with us, to share the visual feast of this lovely boy. But their first "date," an illicit hookup in some kind of barn, shakes her composure. She wants to desire, and to be desired, and she is terrified at the unfamiliar reality of both. She cannot bring herself to undress; she picks a fight until he—confused himself, he is also only fifteen—tells her off, snaps she is not even his type, "a kid your age!" She feels wounded, in spite of her anxiety. "I'm not sexy to you, am I?" she asks, again seeking the paradox of a safe rejection and a validation of sexual allure, all at once.

Their second date begins with more promise; Randy feels terrible for having been unkind, he is all sincere boyish patience, is authentically tender and sweet. Even the barn seems romantic now, a hidden love nest in the darkling rain. When Angel, trembling, confesses she is scared, he tells her he is, too.

ANGEL

    Don't laugh . . . right now, do you care about
    me, a little?

And in answer he kisses her, tenderly and sweetly, and *Yes*, we think, this is perfect, the perfect moment, perfect boy—did you see those lips?—this is it, go for it! We are all Team Angel; win that contest!

But we skip ahead, to the aftermath. And it is a painful aftermath to see. For all the tender sweetness, this was not a good thing. Angel and Randy are not curled up like Veronese lovers in a shared, newfound physical intimacy, to a melodic Nino Rota score; they are on opposite sides of the barn, pulling their clothes back on in stunned silence, and Angel's face—Kristy McNichol is heartbreaking in this scene—is profoundly sad.

> ANGEL
>
> It wasn't what I thought it would be. . . . God, it was so *personal*. Like you could see right through me. . . . Making love is . . . it's different from what I thought it was going to be like. . . .

He finally guesses it was her first time. "Christ, why didn't you tell me?" he asks.

> ANGEL
>
> I thought it would turn you off. Virgins are weird, right?

He tells her she's beautiful, that he thinks he loves her. But she is the wise one: "You don't have to," she tells him. Love won't change what just happened between them—or what didn't happen.

> ANGEL
>
> God, I feel so lonesome . . . .

she says, although he is standing right next to her, fully present, trying to understand her feelings, to fuse and connect and share. A beautiful, sensitive boy, a romantic summer night in a barn, an experience she *wanted* to find, have, make happen—and still. She has misjudged the power of sex, not just to pleasure, fulfill, create intimacy, but its equally powerful opposite: Sex as pathway to a lonely emotional emptiness. Back with her cabinmates, Angel lies, tells them nothing happened, willingly loses that contest; it *is* so personal, it isn't something to trade in for a victor's sash and tiara, a false-god title, a cheap trophy to display on the mantel. "Oh, it was nothing, still is nothing," her mother had told her earlier, in response to Angel's tentative inquiry about sex, what it's like and what it all means. But now, at the end of the film, wise Angel confronts her: "What's this crap about sex being *nothing*?" she lectures; it *is* something, or at least has the possibility to be something, and she knows that now. She has lost the contest but won that insight.

Little Darlings is also unusual in its focus on the female experience of sexual awakening. Most loss-of-innocence movies are all about the boys, the ill-timed and indiscriminate hard-ons, the premature ejaculations and locker room ribbing played for snickery comedy. But the experience of allowing another human being to enter your body is an especially vulnerable one, and *Little Darlings* is the only movie I had seen, to date—or perhaps have ever seen—that is willing to treat that with the respect it deserves. (While still being hilariously funny—food fight! Stealing a condom dispenser from a gas station bathroom! Cynthia Nixon as a flower child!) The movie is not antisex—it simply asks that we appreciate the power and potential of sex.

And it is hugely impactful on me. A summer later, at sixteen, I find myself with my first real boyfriend, my own beautiful and sensitive boy I feel I could gaze upon forever. He is more man than boy, actually, he has hit six feet and shaves every day, has a torso that widens to a glorious peach-skin capital *V*; he is the one in our group we all—boys and girls, gay and straight alike—turn to for erotic leadership in our pack-wolf craving for a whiff of actual grown-up Sex. My friends and I have begun obsessing over who will lose her virginity first, replicating discussions from a few years earlier about who would be the first to get her period, and, in doing so, have created a de facto contest of our own, an unofficial Virginity Sweepstakes. And here this sexy, delicious boy has turned his gaze upon *me*. I cannot believe my good fortune. Surely he is the one, right? The guy I will *lose it* to? (A phrase I dislike—I don't want to lose anything; I want to *find* something, a transcendently new thing to value, about boys, about bodies, about life, about myself.)

The first time he kisses me—sitting alone on the floor together at one of those rumpus-room parties, but with higher stakes, now, with beer replacing fruit punch and no one's parents even bothering to be home to watch over us anymore, and Bread singing *"I want to make it with you"* on the stereo—I feel my first jolt of desire at another person's touch, my first startling crotch-throb, the first time I ever feel myself go swollen and heated and wet. And that begins a long summer, at the beach, in our cars, in our own homes undisturbed by absent or distracted parents (or any busybody Nurse), in ongoing battle over jean zippers and shirt buttons and hormonal irreconcilability. I spend the summer panting and moaning with lust, but also squirming away at the last second from his curious hands and mouth, his eager hips. I am terrified, and I do not know why, or of what. What am I waiting for, I wonder, someone sweeter, cuter, *sexier*, more popular? I have grabbed the brass-ring boyfriend, and this is a good guy who will, I'm pretty sure, tell me afterward I am beautiful, that he thinks he might love me, even if only out of good manners. But . . . does he *care about me, a little* . . . ? Do I even care about *him*? I can't really know, and he probably doesn't know, either. We are sixteen, and our emotions are obscured by that swollen wet heat.

But I can't do it. Some instinct—or the memory of Angel's stricken face, her bewildered loneliness in the aftermath of sex—says, *Wait*: This is an important something, and you do not have to make this important something happen *right now*. There is no contest, no race to a finish line. And as sweet and tender as this man-boy of mine is, he only tussles and pleads so respectfully so far—*a kid your age!*—and by September he gives up, and it is over.

I am torn between relief and devastation (*Virgins are weird, right?*); I dramatically take to my bed for several days, an abandoned, rejected Juliet, pretending I have the flu. I feel so very alone, and yet—thank you, Angel!—I know it is better to feel lonesome without him than feel lonesome with him. I am ready for the longing, yes, but not the con-summation; I am not ready to be possessed—or to possess—because I am not yet in possession of myself. I am not ready to be *seen-through*; I need my invulnerable opacity, the embroidered nightgown, just a little while longer.

LINDA

Stacy, what are you waiting for? You're fifteen
years old! I did it when I was thirteen. It's no
huge thing, it's just sex,

counsels so-*mature* Linda (Phoebe Cates), The Worst Best Friend in
the World, to baby-faced Stacy (Jennifer Jason Leigh) in *Fast Times
at Ridgemont High.*[26] Stacy has just started high school (filmed in the
unnamed San Fernando Valley, where I live), she and her friends
work at the Mall (the unnamed Sherman Oaks Galleria, where I have
spent my teenage years eating corn dogs and buying tank tops while
waiting for life to flicker on), and everyone is singularly obsessed with
sex: Getting it, talking about it, puzzling through the shifting boundaries of physical and emotional intimacy while trying to pretend it is,
of course, *no huge thing*: It's *just sex.*

Stacy worries whether or not she will be any good in bed, and
Linda assures her there is no such silly question of "good" or "bad":
"You either do it, or you don't." The actual experience is meaningless—it's all about getting to list it on your résumé. She is appalled
Stacy has never given a blow job, and, with patient-teacher voice ("It's
so easy, there's nothing to it, relax your throat muscles . . ."), gives
her an impromptu lesson using a carrot in the school cafeteria—it's
free advertising for the boys leering nearby. There is so much pressure to *do it* already, get it over with, what are you waiting for, what's
the big deal, what's *wrong* with you? It is a culture of disdain for and
diminishing of any aspect of sexuality beyond the genital, a celebration of cool-chick emotional indifference. It is, in a way, sex reduced
once again to a cartoony, two-dimensional paper cutout. Insert Penis
A in Vagina B; it's so easy, a child could do it, and you're *already fifteen*!

And then the loss-of-virginity moment: Stacy has found her
Romeo/Gary/Randy, a twenty-six-year-old Guy she served pizza
to at the Mall and told she is nineteen. After being tucked into her

26 *Fast Times at Ridgemont High* (Universal Studios, 1982): screenplay by Cameron
Crowe, based on his book; directed by Amy Heckerling; with Jennifer Jason Leigh
and Phoebe Cates

stuffed-animal-festooned twin bed by her mom ("Good night, Stacy!" mom chirps), she sneaks out the window and waits at the corner for his chariot to arrive, while Jackson Browne croons on the diegetic soundtrack how that girl's *just got to be somebody's baby, she's so fine . . . .* The Guy tells her she looks beautiful—smooth, this guy, I can almost smell the Aramis—and suggests they go to The Point, the local baseball dugout/sex lair. And here, as in *Little Darlings*, director Heckerling focuses on the female experience rather than the male; the Guy kisses her, teases whether or not he'll get to first base—an oblique request for permission to proceed, the Guy's not an asshole—unbuttons her shirt and crawls on top of her. But we barely even see his face; it is Stacy we focus on, her wincing in pain and unease, her dissociative stare at the graffiti over his shoulder. The scene's final visual is a long shot; we are suddenly watching them from a distance in the dark, reflecting the emotional detachment of the moment, watching the Guy's white naked body pumping away.

JACKSON BROWNE

She's probably somebody's only light
Gonna shine tonight
Make her mine tonight
Yeah, she's probably somebody's baby, all right . . . .[27]

The next day, Stacy tells Linda "it hurt *so bad!*" (referencing the physical pain), and Linda's sage, so-*mature* counsel is: "Don't worry, just keep doing it, it gets better," meaning that with Stacy now liberated from that annoying virginity-albatross—cherry popped, hymen broken, maidenhood breached, the terminology just gets worse—the act can become even *more* meaningless, now, hooray. And for most of the movie Stacy follows Linda's advice, hoping to figure out or find that something of value, about sex, about boys, about herself. She tries, and fails, to sexualize an adorable restaurant date with an equally virginal nerd who's been crushing on her, then seduces the nerd's cooler best buddy, which results in another dreadful scene of clumsy genital

---

27 "Somebody's Baby," by Jackson Browne and Danny Kortchmar

mechanics that leaves her lying there, naked and vulnerable and hurt as he scurries away. She winds up pregnant, has to ask the guy to chip in for an abortion, has to get a ride to the clinic from her brother . . . the sadness, loneliness, and confusion just keep snowballing along.

But for me this isn't a "wages of sin" lesson. Heckerling isn't judging Stacy; this is not a "Don't Lose Your Virginity" story: It's a "How *Not* to Lose Your Virginity" tale. This film, so familiar to me in its geographical landmarks and teenage angst-ridden sexual strategizing, is an instructive, confirming deterrent. I am now eighteen, I am still a virgin—Linda would be so horrified—and watching this movie, I am so relieved that I withdrew from the contest, took myself out of the running, that I resisted the Danas and Lindas and older Guys in their slick cars. Stacy finally works up the nerve to tell Linda: "I figured it out. I don't want sex. Anyone can have sex"—she wants a *relationship*, and romance; a screen scroll at the movie's end tells us Stacy and the sweet nerdy boy are still dating, but they "still haven't gone all the way," and that is the coming-of-age charm that elevates *Fast Times at Ridgemont High* above the usual teen-sex-comedy fare. Like Stacy, I've learned I want to be somebody's baby, too. I want to be somebody's only light. I want the loving gaze as well as the lustful one, the meeting-of-souls balcony tryst with someone willing to risk death for me, a someone who will so overwhelm me with his beauty I am in haste to shed modesty and clothes and girlhood and throw my full-length womanly nakedness upon him. And I'm glad I could learn that without having to publicly fellate a carrot (thanks for the tips, though) or lie wincing on a baseball dugout bench.

However . . . by the time I am twenty years old, I find myself identifying with Stacy's concern that the whole world is having sex but her, that she is being left behind, left out of all the fun. I am once again hearing: *Do it* already, get it over with, what are you waiting for, what's the big deal? But the difference is, this time the voice is mine. I have aged out of the contest, the sweepstakes is over (although I am at last almost old enough to do it with camp counselor Gary . . .), and I have, by now, eagerly watched enough sex in mainstream movies (and the rare pre-Internet porn video), ranging from soft-filter lovemaking to relatively graphic fucking, to have accumulated a stockpile of instructive and stimulating images.

At thirteen, lurid, guilty pleasure *The Other Side of Midnight*[28] revealed to me the amazing fact that, unlike the static illustrations in *How Babies Are Made*, sexual intercourse is more than mere insertion of Penis A into Vagina B; it actually includes *movement*! Thrusting, rubbing, pumping. *Coming Home* introduced me to the intriguing concept of oral sex; the scene of Jon Voight going down on Jane Fonda was educational for both the explicitness of its spatial relations and the expressive intimacy between the two characters.[29] (However, I saw this movie with my mother, when I was fourteen, and I do not recommend that experience.) *Don't Look Now* was also illuminating due to its candid and legendary "Are Julie Christie and Donald Sutherland *really doing it*?" scene of a grieving couple attempting to lose themselves in emotionally and physically naked gymnastics.[30] *Looking for Mr. Goodbar* taught me a woman can both be on top and be taken from behind; *All That Jazz* showed me how to make a guy come in his pants; sweaty William Hurt opening sweaty Kathleen Turner's legs in *Body Heat* didn't really teach me anything I didn't already know, but wow, the look on his face . . . .[31] And, of course, *The Last Tango in Paris*'s famous lesson on butter and anal sex.[32] (i.e., how *not* to have anal sex.)

Yes, I have paid rapt attention to and taken notes on all of it; I have the mechanics down, thank you, my imagination has been both

28 *The Other Side of Midnight* (20th Century Fox, 1977): written by Herman Raucher, based on the novel by Sidney Sheldon; directed by Charles Jarrott; with Marie-France Pisier

29 *Coming Home* (United Artists, 1978): written by Waldo Salt and Robert C. Jones; directed by Hal Ashby; with Jane Fonda and Jon Voight

30 *Don't Look Now* (British Lion Films, 1973): screenplay by Allan Scott and Chris Bryant, based on the story by Daphne Du Maurier; directed by Nicolas Roeg; with Julie Christie and Donald Sutherland

31 *Looking for Mr. Goodbar* (Paramount Pictures, 1977): screenplay by Richard Brooks, based on the novel by Judith Rossner; directed by Richard Brooks; with Diane Keaton; *All That Jazz* (20th Century Fox/Columbia Pictures, 1979): written by Robert Alan Aurthur and Bob Fosse; directed by Bob Fosse; *Body Heat* (Warner Bros., 1981): written and directed by Lawrence Kasdan; with William Hurt and Kathleen Turner

32 *Last Tango in Paris* (United Artists, 1972): written by Bernardo Bertolucci and Franco Arcalli; directed by Bernardo Bertolucci; with Marlon Brando and Maria Schneider

inspired and enflamed. So, can I please just *get laid*, already? I am dying to put theory into practice, to seek out sex for the sheer sake of sex, for absolute real, to find and have and make that experience happen. I am old enough to sign my own permission slip.

There is a guy in my college Shakespeare course whose witty insights and wire-rimmed glasses I have appreciated; we run into each other one Saturday morning at the Nuart's Shakespeare Film Festival, and we formally begin dating. He is funny as hell and smarter than I am (which I have come to appreciate as an aphrodisiac), and after three weeks of dinners and foreign films and *Trivial Pursuit* (I always lose), I inform him one evening over sake and tempura that I have purchased contraceptives that afternoon, and if he's up for it—which he is—I'm ready to *Do It*, which we do.

It is no quivering, enflaming thing, we are not breathless and exquisite teenagers overwhelmed by heat, there is no fusion of souls. It's clumsy and definitely a bit mechanical—not quite the paper cutouts of that children's book, more like a series of IKEA instructional pictographs, now. And despite the extraordinary patience and tenderness of this lovely guy, it is incredibly painful. But I am referencing only the physical pain. In the aftermath, there is no stunned, stricken silence, no sad emotional reckoning; if anything, I am surprised by the sweet comedy of it all, how there is a new laughing and joking between us that is very dear. I am not feeling a transcendental intimacy, but neither am I feeling emptiness or loneliness or regret. I have lost nothing; I have found an extraordinary new thing to value. Sex, for me, will never be *just sex*, nor do I want it to be. I want my Shakespeare *and* my porn, illumination and obliteration, transcendence and raw sweat, connection and escape. With each new lover, I will become a weird virgin all over again, because the experience of sex with a new body and heart and soul will always be different, be re-created anew—it will always, or can always be, the First Time.

HOW TO
BE A
DRUNK

THE LOG BOOK OF A DISTINCTIVE ALCOHOLIC

Sarah T.—Portrait of a Teenage Alcoholic

The Lost Weekend

Arthur

Days of Wine and Roses

When a Man Loves a Woman

Who's Afraid of Virginia Woolf?

Valley of the Dolls

The Morning After

The Lonely Passion of Judith Hearne

Opening Night

Bridget Jones's Diary

Breakfast at Tiffany's

Raiders of the Lost Ark

Leaving Las Vegas

Flight

love alcohol. I love to drink alcohol. I love the grapefruity redolence of Sauvignon Blancs from New Zealand and the juniper berry kiss of gin. I love the flirty burn of tequila liberally citrus'd with fresh lime. I love the velvet tongue of Merlot, the apricot honey of an ice-cold IPA beer. I love the celebratory Kir Royale, Champagne turned ruby with just a touch of crème de cassis, and I love the low-maintenance flexibility of that frosted bottle of vodka in the freezer, just so happy to go along with anything in the pantry or fridge: OJ, a few mashed raspberries, the juice from a can of lychee nuts. Sometimes I honor the vodka by drinking it straight up, all ice-and-diamond clean.

I love the sound FX of drinking, the mimetic hum: The chuckle of a liberated cork, the shaking shaker of crushed ice, the gasp and fizz of a cracked-open mixer, the trickle-and-splash sound of cola hitting the waiting rum.

I love the mise-en-scène of drinking, the aesthetics of all that crystal and glass: The fat breast of a brandy snifter, the hieroglyphic martini glass, the elegant phallic flute. I gaze at these glasses posed just so in my hand and marvel at my sophistication. I see lovely Romy Schneider in *Le Vieux Fusil*, lifting the nose veil on her 1930s cocktail hat to sip her *coupe de Champagne*; youngish Melanie Griffith in *Working Girl*, flirt-shooting tequila with Harrison Ford and delicately swiping lime pulp from her preplumped lips; Barbra Streisand seductively stroking her breast with a glass of sherry in *On a Clear Day You Can See Forever*; Meryl Streep's Sophie in *Sophie's Choice*, being brought back to life and love by a single sip of a red wine so exquisite it is what, if you have lived the life of a saint, the angels will serve you to drink in Paradise.

What I don't love is anything fruity and disingenuous: Margaritas, daiquiris, mai tais, any trendy, girly, garish concoction. I'm turned off by the banality of paper umbrellas, the cloying simple sugar syrups. Give me the honest bite of clear, pure ethanol—let me hold my jeweled glass to the light, revel in its power, its authentic, unambiguous intent.

I also do not love raucous drinking, frat-boy swilling, sports bar rowdiness, the inelegant kegger or red plastic Solo cup, the hint of eruption *tick-ticking* behind a boozed-up lack of control. I like the well-mannered bar, the leather booth, the candle's flicker, one's sensibilities and imagination set gently aflame; I like my drinking atmospheric, soft-filtered, refined.

But most of all, I love the feel and effect of drinking: The absorbing swell of the alcohol in my mouth and throat; the initial belly-warm and faint blush in my cheeks; the expansive, generous alchemy that will make me a wittier, sexier, more interesting and insightful, both more vulnerable and more impervious, more fearless, more charming and delightful me.

I decided to become an alcoholic when I was eleven years old.

Back then, though, it was really because of my friend Sarah. Sarah T. Maybe you met her, back in 1975? She was a few years older than me, she was fifteen, with ripply Mona Lisa hair, a lingering layer of baby fat pouting her cheeks. She was so shy, struggling with a new school, her parents' divorce, never quite at ease in her tender puppy skin. She totally botched her try-out for the glee club out of sheer nerves, a pained insecurity about her place in the world made embarrassingly public, rich fodder for Mean Girls. But boy, get a few drinks in her, and wow. She blossomed, went full swan, got all on-key and giggly and happy happy happy. Other kids flocked to her instead of ignoring her, complimented her cute outfit, remembered her name. Poured her more drinks.

My friend Sarah T. was not a real person, of course, but the titular character of *Sarah T.—Portrait of a Teenage Alcoholic*, one of those "social issue" network television Movies of the Week from the 1970s, meant to be instructive and realistically gritty yet still exploitative ratings-grabbers, part of an often-named "Portrait of . . ." craze (*Dawn: Portrait of a Teenage Runaway*, starring Jan Brady; *Sharon: Portrait of a Mistress*; *Alexander: The Other Side of Dawn*), showcasing distressed women and teens.[33] I loved the edgy tease of these movies, the subliminal "this could be you" threat if my own safe, normal, middle-class suburban

---

33 *Sarah T.—Portrait of a Teenage Alcoholic* (Universal Television, 1975): written by Esther Shapiro and Richard Alan Shapiro; directed by Richard Donner; with Linda Blair, Verna Bloom, Larry Hagman, Mark Hamill, and Michael Lerner

life ever took the slightest wrong turn. One bad decision on my part, they implied, one step outside my own Good Girl persona, and I could wind up in reform school, or vomiting in the gutter, or turning tricks for the first savvy pimp to hustle and pick up frightened naïve runaway me at the bus station. These movies made me feel a longing: I was the most boring adolescent ever, the easiest, most issue-free child, no problem to anyone in a household full of people with voluble, visible problems, and the problem with being no problem is that you go about in that cloak of invisibility: Attention need not be paid. Or, if it is paid, it is a passing pat on the head, an approving dismissal, an overloud laugh track and a cued round of auto-applause. A tribute to the persona, not the person. Being such a Good Girl, I always feared Something Bad would happen to me; I was worried Something Bad never would; I longed for Something Bad to offer me a kind of distinction. These movies of tortured souls trapped in disturbing narratives offered an alluring paradox: Both happy fantasy and a cautionary lesson.

Sarah T. begins with a faux beer commercial, beer-drinking fun people having lots of beer-fueled fun—"*So, go where you want to go! Be what you want to be! Happiness is Corey's Beer!*"—then freeze-frames to give us the stern voiceover:

STERN VOICEOVER

There are approximately half a million preteen and teenage alcoholics in this country today, and the number is growing. Three out of every four teenagers do some drinking. One out of twenty has a serious drinking problem. One in ten will become an alcoholic . . . it may take an adult fifteen years to become an alcoholic. It takes a teenager fifteen months. . . .

These statistics sound impressive, but I ignore them because they are inviting me to do math. I do appreciate the ironic underscoring of fun beer commercial images and PSA-style warning, but I am only mildly interested in what else might be in store; I have never seen a movie about an "alcoholic" before, nor met one in real life—to my knowledge—and the word itself is so clinical, so far off in the abstract realm of adults and adult-size problems given quantifiable, diagnostic labels. I consider changing the channel.

But another freeze-frame, now on a teenage girl's sad, pudgy face:

STERN VOICEOVER

This is Sarah Travis. She is fifteen years old. She's an alcoholic.

And I immediately recognize this Sarah Travis as Linda Blair, possessed child of *The Exorcist* and anguished runaway from last year's television Movie of the Week *Born Innocent*, famous for its never-again-shown-on-television shower room rape scene. Linda's Kewpie-doll face and her bewildered adolescent angst make her so sweetly vulnerable. So relatable, like a friend. I am intrigued. What will befall this sweet girl this time, what perilous devil will be seeking her out?

The cautionary narrative begins at a cocktail party thrown by Sarah's mother and new stepfather, where the stepdad's new boss urges young Sarah to have a drink—"It'll help the medicine go down!"—and this kind of party is also relatable, so, so familiar to me; my parents are famous for their wild bashes, where I am trotted out to pass around mini quiches and stuffed mushrooms to increasingly drunk and raucous adults, sent off to bed at midnight, and awaken in the morning to find people in mod polyester sleeping off their hangovers on the harvest-gold shag carpeting of our living room. Sarah demurs, but when the boss's back is turned, she finishes off the adults' drinks all on her own: She drains glass after glass, and even with the medicinal grimace, it's clear she is actually a seasoned pro at this adaptive technique. This has never occurred to me. I have never tasted alcohol in my life.

The next morning, Sarah listens to her hungover mother and stepfather bemoan how much booze they'd gone through (also a scenario I relate to, and a conversation I could repeat word for word). Her beloved, failed-artist father visits, carrying around a six-pack in a shopping bag (Larry Hagman, perhaps Method-acting from his own alcoholic life), popping beer after beer as he leads Sarah on with a fantasy of their running off to live in the woods, where he will do his painting and they will escape all life's problems, just father and daughter together.

Meanwhile, to deal with life's problems, Sarah has a repertoire of tricks: A liquor store delivery is achieved by pretending her (off somewhere) mother is in the shower and getting the delivery guy to leave a bag of booze; she filches from the liquor cabinet in her picture-perfect older sister's apartment; she waters down the household bottles with a chemist's precision; she sneaks vodka into her soda can from a bottle of cologne she keeps in her locker at school. I applaud all this ingenuity and deception; it is evidence of the deep-running rivers beneath her flat-affect surface. Her secrecy grants her power, significance, a complexity beyond her years. This is no boringly normal teenage girl with standard-issue issues: This is a girl containing multitudes, layers upon layers of pain. If only anyone would pay attention, look beyond the placid façade.

On a blind date with her stepfather's boss's son Ken (a pre–Luke Skywalker Mark Hamill), he offers her a drink at a Popular Kids party, and, after token protest, she sucks one down. She is initially a hit; she loosens up, dances, jokes, sings in that movie-party way, where everyone suddenly gathers round to listen and applaud. But, after sneaking more drinks from the bar, she tips her hand when she becomes a sloppy drunk, shoving a plate of potato salad into a Mean Girl's chest and barely able to stagger home to her horrified mom and stepdad. Mark Hamill/Ken gallantly takes the blame, and her parents, after an ostensible display of disapproval, shrug it off: "So, she had a little to drink. At least she's not into drugs." I agree with her parents; the applauding party kids, the appreciative gleam in Ken's eye, were well worth whatever minor downside was created by a few belts. It isn't as though she's a heroin addict.

But the liquor store delivery guy gets wise and cuts off her supply; the housekeeper, the only adult who seems to offer her any understanding or solace, gets fired for "getting into" the family liquor, triggering a new source of guilt and despair; and Ken, watching Sarah at a beach party guzzle gin through a straw from a spiked watermelon like a starving piglet, is getting worried, realizing he has not, in fact, been the corrupting influence:

KEN

You don't drink like a beginner, Sarah.

SARAH

Oh, come on! You make me sound like some major
alcoholic freak. I don't see any purple cockroaches climbing the walls. Look, I take a drink
every now and then because it makes me feel
better, makes all the hassles with my parents and
the stuff at school go down a little easier. I
don't have to drink. I can quit any time I feel
like it. I just don't feel like it.

Exactly. No biggie. Sarah is called in to a conference with a guidance counselor and her mother for slipping grades, missing class,
etc., but Mom is distracted, eager to accept Sarah's lame Good Girl
excuses, and I'm not worried, either. I'm just not getting the real peril,
here. But Sarah is devastated to discover Ken has been dating other
girls (she by now has fallen madly in love with his kind blue eyes, his
cool truck, and his sweet horse); she polishes off a carafe of wine while
babysitting a toddler and is found passed out on the couch. I have just
begun babysitting, myself (conscientiously, of course—perhaps more
so than the parents who leave their four-week-old baby in the care
of an eleven-year-old girl who has never held a baby before), and I
find this lack of responsibility disturbing. Her parents flip out, but
primarily over how it will *look*, what people will think. And Sarah, out
of tricks and rendered ironically invisible amid all this concern about
"appearances," finally confesses:

SARAH

Mom, listen to me. I've been drinking for nearly
two years now. Almost every day. I've snuck booze
from the house and I've stolen it from liquor
stores. Who knows, I probably would've drunk rubbing alcohol if I couldn't get my hands on anything else.

Still, she's been keeping it together, hasn't she? Her drinking seems more like, well, an edgy hobby. A bad habit, maybe a step or two beyond biting your nails or chewing your hair. But it's off to a Therapist for family counseling. Mom's in denial. Sarah's only fifteen, she's a Good Girl, it isn't like she's hanging out on Skid Row, etc., until the Therapist cuts through the shit:

```
                    THERAPIST
Seems to me that a fifteen-year-old who drinks
every day has a lot to say that nobody is lis-
tening to.
```

```
                      MOM
Believe me, I've listened!
```

```
                    THERAPIST
But have you heard? Kids develop alcohol prob-
lems like anyone else. Because they're lonely or
troubled or frightened. Booze helps them to live.
To face social situations, to get through the
day. And it works. For a while. And then it stops
working. Because alcohol is a mean and sneaky
drug. It giveth, and then it taketh away. And one
day, you know, it's going to kill you.
```

Lonely or troubled or frightened . . . well sure, why *wouldn't* she, why wouldn't *anybody* like this magical elixir, then? I see all those empty sour-smelling glasses I help my mother wash after a wild bash, all those clinking bottles I gather up to put in the trash. The Therapist says "it works for a while," but clearly the reward here is real and enduring; if it didn't keep working, if it didn't taketh away the loneliness or fear, why would adults keep doing it? It doesn't seem to be hurting anyone, let alone killing anyone.

Mom refuses to consider Alcoholics Anonymous. Her child is not *an alcoholic*—gasp!—so why would she send her off to hang with a bunch of old winos?

                    THERAPIST
We're a country of whiskey-heads. Sarah gets permission to drink every time she sees you and your
husband hoist that old five o'clock pick-me-up.

But Sarah is skeptical of the scarlet *A-for-Alcoholic* label, too:

                     SARAH
If I was . . . how could I tell?

                    THERAPIST
Well, you cross a kind of imaginary line. You
begin doing things that are destructive to yourself and the people around you. And you recognize
that, and you know.

Which actually reassures her, and me, given Sarah's basic level of
undestructive functionality (that babysat toddler was perfectly fine,
after all). She goes to an AA meeting anyway, where she is startled to
meet kids her own age, even younger. Yet Sarah still denies she's *an
alcoholic*. If I *were*, she tells another Teenage AA Girl, so what, I'd just
admit it!
    Of course you would, the Teenage AA Girl agrees with her:

                 TEENAGE AA GIRL
Nothing hard about admitting it. Except then you
have to give up the booze. And Lord knows no dedicated, hardworking alcoholic wants to do *that*.

Sarah's beloved, fuckup father reveals his lack of interest in her
coming to live with him in his failed-artist-in-the-forest life; devastated by yet another rejection, Sarah now goes off on a desperate
mission for booze, finally offering herself up to a gang of twentysomething guys if they will buy a bottle for her. This negotiation is the most
painful thing in the movie to watch, so far, my first cringe, my first real
glimpse of that warned-about peril. This is not good. Drunk out of her

mind, Sarah steals Ken's sweet horse, rides into traffic, and gets the horse killed, a scene I can watch only peripherally, feeling frightened and a little sick. Okay, we have entered the "destructive to yourself and those around you" phase. Her Therapist confronts her:

```
                    THERAPIST
    You've crossed that imaginary line, remember?


                     SARAH
    So do something! Help me!


                    THERAPIST
    Look, you have a choice. You can sink into the
    bottom of a bottle of booze and drown. Or you can
    climb out. Now, I can't make that choice for you.
    I can't frighten or coax you into it. You have
    to do it alone. After that, there will be people
    to help you. I'll help you. You know the words,
    Sarah. I can't say them for you. I can't believe
    them for you.
```

Mom insists the answer to all this mess is to simply forget any of this mess ever happened. Clean slate. Fresh start. Problem solved. But Sarah has finally had enough:

```
                     SARAH
    Mom. I'm an alcoholic.


                      MOM
    Don't be foolish!


                 FUCKUP FATHER
    Honey, we all got problems!


                     SARAH
    I'm an alcoholic!
```

It is her epiphanous moment, her first step, it is the last line of dialogue; the final shot of the movie is her heading to join the Teenage
AA Girl, who is waiting for her, and we are clearly meant to be left
with both a lesson learned, and with hope: Sarah has made her choice,
she has said the magic *I'm an alcoholic* words at last, the incantation by
which all that angst will, somehow, be wonderfully rechanneled into
a normal, stable, productive life.

But this is not what I am left with. *Portrait of . . .* movies are not
made about normal, stable teenage girls, after all, only about girls
with problems. With distinction. Parents might *listen to*, but they
do not *hear* unless peril raises its hand and yells *Present!* I should be
appalled by all the deceit, by a fifteen-year-old girl prostituting herself
for alcohol; I should be horrified by the brutal death of a sweet horse.
And I am. This is horrible. But that degree of dysfunction and damage
feels unimaginable to me, both implausible and unnecessary; no one I
know has a horse, and my parents' unlocked liquor cabinet is stocked
for the Apocalypse. Sarah went about this badly, let it get out of control, is all. I want the distinction without the messy fallout, a manage-
able fairy dusting of Something Bad, and I see no reason why I can't
achieve this, why I can't stay on the Good Girl side of the imaginary
line, flirt but not dance with the demon, yet still have *the problem*. I
want the problem. I want to *be* the problem, authentically visible and
voluble, just for once.

So, after I watch this movie—which I watch alone in my bedroom,
on my own little TV in my pretty, pink-canopied bed, my parents off
somewhere—I get a juice glass from the kitchen and fill it to the brim
from an open gallon jug of red wine I find in the liquor cabinet. I sneak
it to my room—I am creating secrecy, subterfuge, although there is no
one around to appreciate it—and force myself to drink it down, with
my own medicinal grimace. I don't like the thick, furry, vinegar taste,
or the magenta toothpaste foam, afterward. I wait to feel something:
A desire to sing or dance, a blossoming, a distinctive deepening of
my soul, even a sighting of purple cockroaches on my pink bedroom
walls, but it giveth me nothing. I merely get sleepy, and I go to bed.
I try again the next night, and the next, for two full weeks. Nothing
happens, nothing at all, and when the bottle is empty I throw it clink-
ingly in the trash without anyone noticing a thing. I contemplate

opening another bottle, but I am unsure how to work a corkscrew. I sample other open liquor: Gin, vodka, tequila, Scotch, and find them worse than the wine. How do adults and disturbed teenage girls drink this stuff, anyway? I can't keep this up for another fourteen and a half months, I realize. I feel like a failure, an unlayered, uncomplex, invisible girl.

And why would anybody bother to listen to me, I think, if I have nothing of perilous distinction to offer? But perhaps, I fear, so quietly I cannot even hear it myself, perhaps it is because I really have nothing of interest to say.

- - - - - - - - - - -

We meet *The Lost Weekend*'s Don B. much like we met Sarah T., *in media* alcoholic *res*: The opening shot is a bottle of booze dangling from a rope outside an apartment house window, and thus begins director Billy Wilder's bitterly noirish depiction of an alcoholic spiraling out of control.[34] Don Birnam (played by cast-against-type Ray Milland, whose suavity meticulously disintegrates over the story's three days, the black-and-white cinematography silvering his forehead sweat) has been ten days sober and is preparing to leave for a wholesome weekend in the country with his enabling brother (*with plenty of buttermilk and fresh well water to drink!* his brother enthuses). But Don evades his brother and well-meaning girlfriend, Helen, to go on a mini-binge. He steals money from his housekeeper, buys two bottles of cheap booze, and stops at a bar for "one straight rye" from his Disapproving Barkeep, Nat. (I have never heard of "rye" as a drink and am initially confused it has something to do with the rye bread my mother buys at the Jewish bakery.) A theremin begins wailing, what will become our Pavlovian audio-marker for Don's craving, his descent into hell. He bolts the rye, the shot glass leaving a glistening wet ring on the bar top, as he plots how to smuggle his bottles out to the wholesome country:

---

34 *The Lost Weekend* (Paramount Pictures, 1945): screenplay by Charles Brackett and Billy Wilder, based on the novel by Charles R. Jackson; directed by Billy Wilder; with Ray Milland and Jane Wyman

                              DON

```
What you don't understand, all of you, is I have
got to have it around. So I know I can have it if
I need it. I cannot be cut off completely. That's
the devil, that's what drives you crazy.
```

A second wet ring on the bar top, a third. Nat the Disapproving Barkeep counsels moderation, but the rye does its thing, inspires poetic loquacity:

                              DON

```
It shrinks my liver, doesn't it? It pickles my
kidneys, yes. But what does it to do my mind? It
tosses the sandbags overboard so the balloon can
soar. Suddenly I'm above the ordinary. . . . I am
one of the great ones. I'm Michelangelo molding
the beard of Moses, I'm van Gogh painting pure
sunlight. I'm Horowitz, playing the Emperor Con-
certo. I'm John Barrymore, before the movies got
him by the throat. . . .
```

Back at home, his brother is finally furious: "I've dragged him out of the gutter too many times . . . why kid ourselves? He's a hopeless alcoholic!" (point: alcoholism as moral failure), and his girlfriend despairs: "He's a sick person! It's as though there's something wrong with his heart! You wouldn't walk out on him if he had an attack! He needs our help!" (counterpoint: alcoholism as physiological addiction). But Don has gone from loquacious to belligerent; he throws them out and blissfully pours himself another drink while an overhead close-up of his glass brings us swimmingly deeper and deeper into the oily glittering booze, right along with him.

Unlike Sarah T., Don knows full well he's an alcoholic. First thing in the morning, he's back at the bar, telling Nat

                              DON

```
I can't cut it short! I'm on that merry-go-
round, and I gotta ride it all the way, around
```

and around, till that blasted music wears itself
out. . . .

He should write a novel, he tells Nat, call it: *The Bottle: Confessions
of a Booze Addict, the Log Book of an Alcoholic.* He flashbacks for us how,
when Helen discovered his drinking, he tried to dissuade her from
hanging around, but she is the archetypal loyal girlfriend, clinging to
both denial and pragmatism—so what if he gets drunk now and then,
she says, a lot of people do!

> DON
>
> Sure, the lucky ones, who can take it or leave
> it. But then there are the ones who can't take
> it, and can't leave it, either. What I'm trying
> to say is, I'm not a drinker. I'm a drunk. They
> had to put me away, once.

> HELEN
>
> After all, you're not an embezzler or a murderer!
> One cure didn't take, is all. There must be a
> reason you drink, Don! The right doctor could
> find it.

> DON
>
> Look, I'm way ahead of the right doctor. The
> reason is me, what I am. Or rather, what I'm not.
> What I wanted to become, and didn't.

> HELEN
>
> What did you want to be so much that you're not?

> DON
>
> A writer. Silly, isn't it?

Ah, this is a Tortured Artist story, then! Echoes of Sarah's father,
popping open another shopping bag beer, dreaming. Don tells us he
reached his peak at nineteen, the college Hemingway, a short story

published in *Atlantic Monthly* and being considered a genius, all that
promise, how he started a failed novel, then another and another, only

DON

by then, somebody began to look over my shoulder
and whisper in a thin, clear voice, like the E
string of a violin: *Don Birnam*, it whispered,
*it's not good enough! Not that way. How about a
couple of drinks, just to set it on its feet?* So,
I had a couple. What a great idea that was! That
made all the difference! Suddenly I could see the
whole thing, the tragic sweep of a great novel,
beautifully proportioned. But before I could
really grab it and throw it down on paper, the
drinks would wear off, and everything would be
gone, like a mirage. And then there was despair,
and a drink to counterbalance the despair, and
one to counterbalance the counterbalance. And
I'd sit in front of that typewriter trying to
squeeze out one page that was halfway decent.
And that guy would pop up again. The other Don
Birnam. There are two of us, you know. Don the
Drunk, and Don the Writer. And the Drunk would
say to the Writer, *Come on, you idiot! Get some
good out of that portable! Let's hock it. Pawn
shop on Third Avenue, it's always good for $10.
Another drink, another binge, another bender,
another spree* . . . I tried to break away from
that guy a lot of times, but no good. Once I even
got myself a gun and some bullets. I was going to
do it on my thirtieth birthday. Here are the bullets. The gun went for three quarts of whiskey.
The flopped suicide of a flopped writer.

While I am enthralled by this speech, indeed hope to one day be
such a tortured artist as this tortured genius Don Birnam, whose delicate sensibility grants a justifying glamour to his story, I do wonder:

What if Don were a bank teller or mechanic? Would we be invited to sympathize with his struggle in the same way? Would a dentist or construction worker be given a dramatic monologue with the same rhetorical flourish? What happens to the alcoholic who isn't a member of the Tortured Artists' club, who isn't "above the ordinary"? Do we devalue his struggle, his tortured soul? Simply dismiss him, label him *a drunk*?

Back in present day, Nat counsels Don, well, maybe he should just go ahead and kill himself if things are so bad. But something about flashbacking, remembering Helen's early faith in him, creates a fresh hope: No, Don tells him, I'm going to do it this time! I'm going to write!

And he rushes home to that portable typewriter, to a fresh page rolled in, to a close up of:

> THE BOTTLE
> a novel by Don Birnam
> To Helen, with all my love

He stops typing. He stands up. He removes his coat, his hat. He wipes his silver-sweat brow. He paces. He lights a cigarette. Cue the theremin's shimmery wail, enter the seductive, dancing devil. Don searches desperately for his hidden bottles, *just to set it on its feet*, until at last he spots the shadowy overhead glow of a bottle tucked in the ceiling light sconce and drinks himself to near oblivion. The next morning he rips his page from the typewriter, goes to hock it, but all the pawn shops are inexplicably closed. (A friendly Jew on the street informs him it's Yom Kippur. Which Don and a general audience might not know is the Jewish Day of Atonement, but is surely a deliberate wink by Billy Wilder, a Jewish refugee from the Nazis.) Back at the bar, he begs for a drink, until Nat, disapproving as ever, pours one, just one, wisely intoning:

> NAT, THE DISAPPROVING BARKEEP
> One's too many, a hundred's not enough.

And the one certainly isn't. Don hustle-flirts a Bar Floozy out of some cash (the lower-stakes male equivalent of Sarah T.'s whoring herself out), falls drunkenly down a flight of stairs, and lands himself in a hospital ward full of shaking, sweating, screaming men. Bars on the window, locked doors, a wiseacre Male Nurse who welcomes him to "Hangover Plaza! The Alcoholic Ward!" and warns of the oncoming DTs, the pink elephants and beetles Don will soon be seeing. . . . But Don manages to escape. He threatens a liquor store guy for a bottle of rye and back at home guzzles, gulps, swallows, belts, as the theremin wails. He spies not pink elephants or purple cockroaches, but a whiskery, beady-eyed mouse chewing its way at him through a hole in a living room wall, and now a *bat*, yes, a Halloween-style bat, all witchy flapping wings, swoops battily around the apartment, attacking the mouse as black blood trickles down the wall. Don screams and screams, in full-on *delirium tremens* frenzy.

He is saved by the loyal Helen, of course, whose leopard coat he steals and hocks, this time not for booze-fund cash, but for a gun. Helen finds the gun; *why*, she asks, *why?*

> DON
>
> It's best all around! Don Birnam is dead already . . . of alcoholism, of moral anemia, fear, shame, the DTs. . . .

Helen pleads he has so much to live for, his talent, his ambition (and her love, it is implied), when Nat the Disapproving Bartender *deus ex machinas* with Don's typewriter, miraculously found by someone on the street. Helen insists this is a sign. Don is *destined* to be a writer, see? It is his purpose in life, see?

> DON
>
> *Write*, with these hands, and a brain all out of focus? I'll be sitting there, staring at that white sheet, scared. . . .

She shows him the title page of his novel, *The Bottle*—see? He must write about that!

DON

```
About a messed-up life, about a man and a woman
and a bottle, about nightmares, horrors, humili-
ations, all the things I want to forget?
```

Yes, Helen insists,

HELEN

```
Put it all down on paper! Get rid of it that way!
```

Of course he can write the story, now that he knows the ending, the happy, happy ending! He can help so many people with his story! All he has to do is write it down (oh, that little part . . .).

And Don envisions the finished book, yes, he will put the whole *Lost Weekend* down on paper, every minute of it! We pan out of the apartment—to notably non-theremin music—and return to our opening shot, of that dangling, suspended bottle, while Don wonders how many others out there are like him?

DON

```
Poor, bedeviled guys, on fire with thirst . . .
such comical figures to others, as they stagger
blindly to another binge, another bender, another
spree. . . .
```

It is nice that an appeal to Don's empathy is what seems to work its magic here (clearly embracing the *alcoholic* label is not in itself sufficient for transformative epiphany), and equally nice it is limited to the last three sentimental minutes of the film, allowing Wilder to spend his and our time in shadows over sunshine. But this happy ending, like Sarah T.'s, seems tidy, tacked on. Is this, in fact, a "happy ending" for Don, or the first of several false starts, just one more cure that probably won't take? Is empathy truly so motivating? Is the creation of art so effective and cathartic an exorcism? And if it is, then why does that not stave off the devil, why do artists become Failed Artist-Drunks in the first place?

I watch *The Lost Weekend* during my "Afternoon Movie" phase when I am twelve or thirteen, my after-school homework-delaying habit. I'm intrigued by the mostly bleak nihilism of Don's story, but, as with Sarah T., there is a comfortingly unrelatable level of dysfunction, here; I have never seen adults scream about bats and mice during my parents' wild bashes, hospital stays are for surgeries and broken bones, and Don's middle-aged, male, 1940s experience is even further away from me than Sarah's contemporary troubled teen-girlhood. I don't really long to emulate, or recognize myself at all in this sad, tortured man. But I am still made uncomfortable and wary and tense watching this old movie over my cookies and milk; it disturbs and stays with me, and it will be a long, long time before I understand it is not because I see myself in Don's messed-up life and despairing bedevilment—it is because I see my father.

My father is a talented artist, a sculptor in wood and clay. He grew up poor, isolated, and fatherless, in the backwoods of Wisconsin, where whittling was a cheap and available form of both entertainment and industriousness—a knife, a stick, and there you are: A toy, a Christmas present, a slingshot—and the concept of being *an artist* simply did not exist. A man finished up some schooling, got a decent job, married and raised a family, and didn't dream of more. His trajectory speed-bumped when at seventeen he got his high school girlfriend pregnant; he dropped out of school, they married, had five children over six years, and my father scrambled to earn that living, often working two or three jobs at a time. At some point his wife "threw him out of the house," and my father, who boasts himself an open book on the vagaries of his life, has always been a little vague on those details. He left Wisconsin without looking back, eventually landed in Los Angeles, and got that decent job working for a toy company, slowly working his way up the corporate ladder and away from the loser backwoods hick he once was, or thought he was. One night he spotted my voluptuous, sophisticated mother (black sheath dress, cigarette holder) in a Hollywood bar and sent over a drink. She sent it right back, but her gesture was meant as flirtation, not dissuasion, and they were married soon afterward.

My father's "first family" was not a secret. There was a framed photo of my father, his first wife, and their five children in his bottom nightstand drawer, and I was mildly curious about it: Who was this first wife, who were these three little girls and two little boys with my father's blond hair and serious Midwestern faces? But growing up, I didn't feel what people seemed to think I should: Intense curiosity about these half brothers and sisters, a familial longing to connect with them, and/or—the most typical assumption—feeling threatened by the existence of these children my father could so casually leave behind. Wasn't I worried, it was implied, that my father might also abandon me, my brother, my mother, his "current family," someday?

No, I wasn't. My father was the one who took me to the ER in the middle of the night when I had the stomach flu and scraped up my vomit from that harvest-gold shag carpeting. He took me to get my ears pierced when I was twelve. He danced with me at weddings and bar mitzvahs. Summer weekend days he and I spent at the beach, with a well-stocked Styrofoam cooler; I'd play in the waves, and he'd look up from his paperback every few sentences to wave and make sure I was okay, to assure me he was there. My mother's love was high volume, dramatic, always on display, ultimately a self-reflective showcase: Look at my pretty little daughter, see what I have created! But my father's love was a quiet, stabilizing theme in my life, as sustaining and taken for granted as air to breathe. The special bond between us was part of our family mythology. We were alike in temperament—"You take after your father *so much*," I often heard—both of us happy in solitude and silence, and we could sit together for sweet, peaceful hours in the evenings, after a clattery family dinner, just father and daughter together, in the corner of the garage set up for his sculpting "hobby"; I would do homework while he sculpted amazing works of art from wood or clay and, every night, steadily put away a bottle of wine. The most comforting smells of my early childhood were linseed oil on fresh-sanded walnut wood, the earthiness of fresh-turned clay, a whiff of Coppertone mixed with Coors beer from that well-stocked Styrofoam beach cooler, and the juniper berry gin kiss from his nightly after-work martini.

All right, it wasn't always so peaceful and sweet. The wine, the beer, the martinis did have a positive effect on him, at first; like Sarah, it made him feel better, made all the hassles of life and the stuff at work and whatever else haunted his soul and pricked his tender skin go down just a little more easily. You could see the tension dissipate, the jokes and participation in the world made more effortless. He became a wittier, more charming, more delightful him. But the nightly predinner martini became two or three, the glass of wine at dinner became two, became that Buddha-shaped gallon jug of Almaden. "Incidents" began, at dinner parties at friends' houses, at my parents' own epic parties; my father would have "a little too much" and get . . . different. Get loud, at first all happy life-of-the-party guy, his joshing notched up a few decibels, but then an anger seeped into every remark, his jokes now edged with something indifferent and mean. He would get so unlike himself, the calm and so-present Daddy-himself I knew, the man who taught me poems and held my hand during scary medical tests. The tension that dissipated after the first drink or two would return but simmer and expand and reform itself into a different shape; later, watching *Raiders of the Lost Ark* for the first time, I would see a visual approximation of this when, the Ark finally being opened, a pearly smoke escaped to become beautiful spectral angels swirling around before retransforming into snarling, horrific demons that made the Nazis scream.

I barely remember what came next, though: The *tick-ticking* rowdi-ness, the raucousness, the inevitable eruption. But I know it did, just slightly off-screen. I can still feel it in my gut, the body-memory of a clenched stomach. Sometimes the monster you don't see is scarier than the one you do. Did it happen when I wasn't present, left at home with a babysitter? Did I, sensing the smoke turn malevolent and dark, learn to strategize myself out of the way, distract myself in my room with TV or a book? What I remember most is the morn-ings after: Feeling frightened and confused because my father had "taken off" in the car—disappearing to no one knew where, and hopefully not killing himself or anyone else—and asking my mother what happened, when was Daddy coming home? But my mother would be hungover herself, and hysterical, and after this happened several times I'd learned to comfort her: Don't worry, Mom, he'll come back, really! And he would, a few days later—after the binge, the bender, the spree at some motel or hotel somewhere, he'd show up back home, quiet and abashed, and everyone would drywall and spackle and paint over the "incident" in exactly the same way as the guy my mother hired to fix the latest fist-holes punched through the walls of our house.

And yet, it just didn't seem like a big deal. It was the late '60s, the early '70s, the era of the sunken living room and Dean Martin getting urbanely sloshed on TV, the ubiquitous wet bar tricked out with the accoutrements of drinking: Every house had a martini shaker, multiple groovy ice buckets, jars of cocktail onions and maraschino cherries and green olives, wooden toothpicks with jewel-colored cellophane-laced tips, the two-foot-tall bottle of chartreuse Galliano and a set of fancy liqueur glasses, cans of tomato juice kept in the mini fridge for weekend hair-of-the-dog Bloody Marys. As Helen points out, *everyone* got drunk now and then! There was no deception, no subterfuge necessary: Sure, let's open another bottle, let's have a nightcap, another round, one for the road! It's always the five o'clock cocktail hour somewhere! And any violence was again, for me at least, off-screen; my father never laid a hand on anybody, preferred to take out whatever alcohol-fueled rage and frustration he felt on the drywall, or in the solitary shelter-escape of an anonymous motel room, or internalize it into self-loathing and despair. His anger was never directed at me; I don't remember ever feeling afraid of him. And I wouldn't be afraid *for* him for many years yet.

But it was impossible not to breathe in something else, along with his aerated love and juniper-berry breath: For the child of a drunk, there *is* always, always, Something Bad about to happen, just waiting to erupt. You can never trust the charming, delightful thing, the love that gets showy and loud; it will disappear in an instant, turn ugly and mean, become that lurking monster capable of who knows what kind of terrifying hurt, and you can only hope the quietly authentic love will return with the real person in a few days, sweetened with apology and guilt. But maybe one day the real person will head out the door and will be gone forever. So don't ever let your guard down. Hold your breath. Keep your stomach clenched. The dancing smoky demons are just waiting to make you scream.

The first time I ever got officially drunk was New Year's Eve, 1978. I was fourteen years old. My friend Marie came over—our assorted parents and older siblings were out on the town—for our first "adult" New Year's Eve, left to our own partying devices. The plan: Playing *Monopoly* and getting officially drunk. I find a bottle of generic whiskey in that bottomless liquor cabinet, and we get to work. Pass Go, collect $200 and gulp of whiskey. Buy a hotel, get a celebratory refill. It tastes as awful as I remember, but I am determined, whiskey is more potent than wine, and by 10 p.m. I am, at last, a girl of golden radiance, a soaring balloon girl, one of the great ones. I am in awe of my own exquisite depths, my multitudes. Now, I get it. This is a blast. By midnight we are crocked, thrilled with ourselves and delighted with our existence on this planet. We are both of us inspired, beautiful creatures; our friendship is the sacrament of angels. We sing, we giggle, we fall out of our chairs. No horses are killed in the making of this fabulous party. No imaginary lines are crossed, no one throws up in a gutter, there are no pink elephants, purple cockroaches, mice, or bats, and I win at *Monopoly*, buy hotel after hotel after hotel, gulp, gulp, gulp. This is a game I can win. This is a game I want to keep playing. Happy New Year, o life, I love you so very much.

My sixteenth birthday is celebrated at my favorite Thai restaurant, where all the adults order wine or cocktails, which I, Sarah T.–like, finish off for them while they smile indulgently, because I am full of sixteen-year-old ebullience, and adorable. By the time the pad Thai and satay are served, I have staggered to the bathroom, and then I am on the floor: Cold tile, a spinning sink, people pounding on the door. I call for Kathy, a friend of my mother's with whom I am not especially close, but it is her, for some instinctive reason, I want. She is allowed into the bathroom, where she repeatedly and expertly shoves her fingers down my throat (my instinct was right), holds my head and hair as I vomit, and cradles me in her arms. I do not remember eating any pad Thai, or how I made it home (I think they had to carry me out). I remember waking up the next morning to a pile of unopened presents, and my mother, on her way to work, giving me a slice of birthday cake she has proudly saved for me; I don't remember her saying a single other thing about any of it. Maybe she was simply glad I wasn't into drugs, wasn't shooting heroin. I sit by myself on the harvest-gold living room shag carpet, eat my slice of birthday cake, open my presents, and feel lonely and ill. I decide to adjust my attitude and view this experience as a positive ritual: It is my initiation into a complex, messy adulthood, and by making a spectacle of myself I have insisted on and offered evidence for my presence in the world. It is a Happy Sweet Sixteen.

At seventeen, Marie and I have brunch with my mother on a blindingly hot Sunday afternoon, gulp down multiple bottomless mimosas, then Marie and I decide to go see *Raiders of the Lost Ark*, which I have already seen three times, at the Cinerama Dome in the heart of seedy old Hollywood. We wait in line, the mimosas souring our mouths, roiling our bellies and brains, and the one-hundred-plus-degree sun sweating us out, when the heated world kaleidoscopes from orange to black, and when I come to, I am lying on the ground, ringed by happy tourists happily snapping pictures of the strung-out Hollywood chick on the sidewalk. I find this delightful: Let them think I am shooting heroin, sure: *Tara I: Portrait of a Complex Junkie Teen*. Marie, freaked-out and scared, wants to take me home, but *No way, I want to see the movie*, I insist, sloppily, aggressively, and so she drags me into the icy theatre, where my stomach and brain chill to lucidity and I enjoy *Raiders* in all its widescreen Cinerama Dome glory. Again, this is a blast. I do not consider the alcohol to have been sneaky or mean; it has done exactly its job, has giveth me the gift of a story for future dates and an insight into Indiana Jones's exploits I have hitherto failed to appreciate.

My seventeen-year-old high school boyfriend could pass for twenty-five, so perhaps he was the one to buy all the booze for those senior-year sunken–living room parties; perhaps we all filched from our parents' unmonitored supply. Perhaps they even bought it for us, believing, like my parents, that today's teens are going to have sex, drugs, and rock 'n' roll anyway, so better to do it at home where it's safe. I am nervous of this gorgeous, manly boyfriend, of my ability to transition from awkward-phase adolescent to an actualized adult woman, my teenage home life has become disorienting and destabilized, and alcohol, I have found, is a loyal, cheerleading friend. It whispers sweet everythings in my ear, unclenches my stomach, and enriches the iron in my blood. It doesn't *help the medicine go down*; it *is* the medicine. Most of my friends are drinking now, to varying degrees; we all seem to be on buddy-buddy terms with Sarah T. There is a year of glorious weekend beach parties fueled by teenage lust, arrogant incaution, many, many bottles of cheap red wine, and everyone just barely making it home with foggy, lurid brains, sandy underpants, and green teeth. Even at the time I am dimly amazed—as I still am—that none of us were killed or killed anyone else, that we drove home through those perilous winding canyon roads and made it through our senior year of high school half drunk, college-bound, and unscathed.

But why would we be scathed? Getting fall-down, whoop-ingly drunk needn't ring an alarm bell, be a trigger for family counseling or a trip to a hospital's dry-out ward. Drinking *is* so much fun, giveth so much, makes one so damned witty and adorable. Just look at Arthur in *Arthur*. Drinking even gives one an inexplicable but so-adorable English accent.[35]

Dudley Moore had already been delightful in Blake Edward's *10* a few years earlier, but if Bo Derek became my generation's iconic, top-scoring incarnation of beauty in that film (along with a symbol of cultural appropriation for those white-girl corn rows), in 1981's *Arthur*, Moore sealed his reputation as the archetypal and indelible Charming Movie Drunk.

And really, how cute *is* he, this diminutive, inebriated man-child? Arthur Bach is the fortyish wastrel son of a filthy-rich family, called upon to do nothing but enjoy himself, which, for him, means drinking himself into a riotously good mood and cracking himself up with his own nonstop wit: "Isn't this *fun*?" he rejoices, sloshed, in the backseat of his chauffeured Rolls Royce. "Isn't fun the *best* thing to have?" Yes, yes! He actually awakens himself in the morning—unhungover—by his own joyous cackle, and his laugh is the real soundtrack to the movie, thankfully drowning out Christopher Cross's awful theme song. Arthur plays with toy trains, overpays a hooker while sweetly

---

35 *Arthur* (Warner Bros., 1981): written and directed by Steve Gordon; with Dudley Moore, Liza Minnelli, John Gielgud, and Jill Eikenberry

calling her "darling," takes bubble baths while wearing a top hat. People around him either smile at his childlike silliness, his tipsy mal-apropisms and humorous stagger, or, if they disapprove—"He gets all that money, and pays his family back by being a stinking drunk? It's enough to make you sick," one guy disdains—are themselves made to look like assholes, disagreeable downers just looking to bum out this elfin charmer, and us.

The one thing he *is* called upon to do is marry Susan, daughter of another filthy-rich family. But Arthur has fallen in love at first sight with quirky working-class Linda (Liza Minnelli in the Manic Pixie Dreamgirl role, which she somehow nails while also being horribly miscast) and he balks. When his family threatens to cut him off without a cent, however, he reconsiders. As his butler/best friend Hobson (a deliciously, witheringly dry John Gielgud, who later insisted he had no idea the movie was a comedy) points out:

> HOBSON
>
> Poor drunks do not find love, Arthur. Poor drunks have very few teeth. They urinate outdoors. They freeze to death in summer. I can't bear to think of you that way.

Arthur polishes off a brown-bagged bottle of something while driving, and we are meant to find this madcap, completely unalarming, as his car swerves and careens across the bridge to Long Island. His father-in-law-to-be disapproves of his drinking:

> FATHER-IN-LAW-TO-BE
>
> I don't drink because drinking affects your decision-making.

> ARTHUR
> (slurring)
>
> You may be right. I can't decide,

but neither the asshole father-in-law-to-be, nor Susan, have any objection to Arthur's getting back behind the wheel of a car. At dinner,

Susan (Jill Eikenberry, amazing at oozing parodic sincerity) plays the loyal, understanding girlfriend card:

SUSAN

Arthur, don't you get it? You can get drunk.
You can throw up. You can forget to call me for
months. You can't lose with me. I know you too
well. I'm much stronger than you are. I know how
alone you are. I hate how alone you are. I've
cried because you're so alone. . . . Don't drink
anymore, Arthur.

ARTHUR

Susan . . . this is what I am. Everyone who
drinks is not a poet. Some of us drink because
we're not poets.

SUSAN

A real woman could stop you from drinking.

ARTHUR

She'd have to be a real *big* woman.

And because this *is* a comedy—comedy defined as disorder leading to order, according to Aristotle—it all works out just swell. When Hobson dies, after giving Arthur his changed-mind blessing to follow his heart, Arthur works up the nerve to dump Susan at the altar and give up his $750 million fortune to be with Linda (who has voiced no real objection to Arthur's little drinking hobby, no implying that her love will cure him, or need cure him, of anything), the gesture that persuades his grandmother to just go ahead and give him the money anyway. Arthur and Linda drive away in the Rolls, Arthur's still-drunken laughter playing them off.

Are we supposed to see Arthur's drinking as a response to soul-crushing emptiness, the existential despair of a man who has achieved nothing in life, and of whom nothing is expected? There are token hints: "I'd like to spend the evening with a stranger who loves me," he tells the hooker and, in a sober moment, shares that he hates to be alone. But isn't that true of most people? He is reliant on alcohol for the fortifying emotional crutch, yes; he doesn't want to face his father sober, and with good reason: "You're the weakest man I've ever known," his father tells him, "I despise your weakness" (again, the father is the judgmental asshole). There are sketch marks of an emotional arc; after Hobson's death, Arthur's chauffeur gently queries, "Would you like me to get you some Scotch, sir?" but Arthur says, "No, we'll get through this together," in what is meant to show growth toward a healthier, more self-aware maturity. But his sobriety lasts only a month, ending on the day of his scheduled wedding to Susan, and his drunkenness when he arrives at the church for the climactic scene is not presented as a failing but as an assertion of his true heart and will and self. And perhaps, in Arthur's comment that he drinks because he is *not* a poet, we are upending the narrative convention of the Tortured Artist with the bedeviled soul, in realistic favor of the Ordinary Everyman who must grapple with being no artist at all.

But writer/director Steve Gordon has no real interest in dissecting alcoholism as either moral failing or physiological addiction, or in subverting a romantic cliché; Arthur's simply having a genuinely good time in this happy comedic life of his, and we are invited to the party. His drinking is primarily an expression of a sweet childishness, not dysfunction, a Peter Pan–like reluctance to put away childish things. "Grow up, Arthur. You'd make a fine adult," a disapproving uncle tells him, and so raging alcoholism is merely a developmental phase thing to grow out of, like an addiction to Saturday morning cartoons or gobbling down the whole bag of Halloween candy at once. *Arthur*'s Arthur may be cinema's last innocent, unpathologized drunk; an attempt at a sequel a few years later, 1988's *Arthur 2: On the Rocks* (Arthur loses the fortune, Linda wants a baby, Arthur has to clean himself up to save marriage and money, blah blah blah) failed miserably—it gaveth stakes but tooketh away all the fun. We don't want our Arthur "in recovery"; he is charming exactly as is, and we see no need or have no desire for him to grapple with or recover from anything. Maybe because then we don't have to.

I see *Arthur* at seventeen, just as I am starting to worry about this little adaptive-technique hobby of mine. And I am counting; it is now well over fifteen months since that Happy Happy New Year's Eve. Has the scary "A" label taken hold yet? Where is that imaginary line, again, the Rubicon of addictive dysfunction? I seem to be doing just fine in my apparently normal, productive life, but I am also just beginning to question if all my fun, alcohol-infused weekends—and now those dinners out with my father, where I often join him in a glass or two or three of wine—are going too far, if I am out of control . . . or am I still leading the dance, here?

But I am so delighted and charmed by *Arthur*. Again, horses need not die, no sweaty convulsions need be had, the party and laughter needn't ever end or spiral downward to the sinful glutton's circle of hell. Arthur loses nothing, and gains it all: Money, attention, love, a hugely successful movie. No truly problematic problem, here. What could be more reassuring? Isn't fun the *best* thing to have?

- - - - - - - - - - -

Of course, my father did "abandon" us, this second family of his. He walked out of the house, sober, with nothing but his sculpting tools when I was thirteen, divorced my mother, quit his corporate job (echoes of Don Birnam, dismissing those poor fools who buy into the corporate ladder myth, telling his brother, "Most men lead lives of quiet desperation. I can't take quiet desperation"), and, again, never looked back. He defied the admonitions of his childhood; he did dream, of Something More. Of Something Else. Always, something else.

But: Unlike that first group of fatherless Wisconsin children in the nightstand drawer, he didn't abandon *me*. I never felt abandoned. He remained the loving, always-there-for-me father of our personal mythology. My father drives me to the airport in the middle of the night, I boasted to my friends for years. He still takes me for scary medical procedures and holds my hand. We regularly go out to dinner together—splitting that bottle or two of wine now—and talk for hours about meaningful, important things. My father would give me the last $20 in his wallet if I needed it, the shoes on his feet, would give me his blood, a kidney, without a split second of hesitation. This is all a given, still as sustaining and taken for granted as the very air. My father is always, will always be there for me, waving from his towel on the beach. Pouring me another cup of sake. Ordering me another glass of wine. We are a twosome, always. My father would never abandon me, not his final, most alike in temperament, most special and beloved child.

Alcoholics Anonymous offers a handy "Are You an Alcoholic?" self-test: twenty questions, Yes or No. Some of these questions are an easy No (*Is drinking jeopardizing your job or business, Do you turn to lower companions and an inferior environment when drinking, Have you ever been to a hospital or institution because of drinking?*), given that, by my late twenties, I have stumbled into a fun, successful career and enjoy a fun, full calendar of high-level friends and lovers and superior surroundings. I am having a blast. But every social event, five or six nights a week, has an accompanying alcoholic beverage— martinis for swing dancing at the Derby, sake with sushi, tequila at El Coyote, wine for everything else—and some of these questions get a Yes: *Have you ever felt guilt or remorse after drinking?* (Well sure, that drunken one-night stand with a groomsman after a coworker's wedding was probably a mistake . . .), *Do you drink to build up your self-confidence?* (Um, excuse me, everyone I *know* drinks to build up their self-confidence . . .), *Do you drink to escape from worries or trouble?* (Ditto.) According to AA, just one Yes is a "definite warning that you may be an alcoholic." *One?* Out of twenty? I decide this test is ridiculously punitive and restrictive. I create my own little tests: I will not drink at all for thirty days, I will have only one single glass of wine when I go out tonight, I will not drink at all when I am home alone. I pass these tests easily, and I am reassured.

I am also reassured that now that I am an adult, I can begin counting in years, not months; I have at least a decade before there is any actual peril here, before I might have to mumble those magic words, pin that scarlet letter *A*-for-*Alcoholic* to my chest. I am even reassured by my growing obsession/concern with the question of my drinking; surely a true alcoholic is not so self-aware, does not constantly "check in" with herself about this. As long as I keep asking myself the question, I reason, I can defy the Alcoholics Anonymous literature, the cinematic cautionary lessons, the conventional wisdom, and even, perhaps, the biological fact of genetic predisposition.

Alcoholics Anonymous serves as a supporting character in *Days of Wine and Roses*, Blake Edwards's 1962 searing, gold-standard depiction of the alcoholic's downward spiral, although this time it is a pair of alcoholics, an in-love couple trapped in a brutally codependent pas de deux.[36] Joe (Jack Lemmon) and Kirsten (Lee Remick) are not Tortured Artists, they are indeed Ordinary Everymen; Joe is given the gray-flannel-suit-man's frustrations with his corporate/PR job and the insecurities of his masculine role as provider/protector, and Kirsten is given an addiction to chocolate and daddy issues (he was always silent and withheld his affection). Initially it is Joe who sets off the alarm bells—from the start he is a Good Time Charlie, rarely seen without a drink in his hand—and Kirsten who is the prissy, bookish, every-hair-in-place killjoy, Lee Remick at her most elegantly refined. Her second line of the film is "No, thank you, I don't drink," and on their first date, Joe inquires:

JOE

What've you got against booze, anyway?

KIRSTEN

Oh, I just don't much see the point in it.

JOE

It makes you feel good.

KIRSTEN

I already feel good. Anyway, I don't like the taste. . . .

36 *Days of Wine and Roses* (Warner Bros., 1962): screenplay by J. P. Miller, based on his teleplay; directed by Blake Edwards; with Jack Lemmon, Lee Remick, and Jack Klugman

. . . a tiny issue that Joe overcomes by ordering her a Brandy Alexander (brandy, crème de cacao, cream: Chocolate as gateway drug). Mmm, yummy! She gets it now. By the end of the date she is all sparkling giggles and loosened glow—"You were absolutely right about that brandy thing! About it making me feel good! I feel wonderful!"—and after her disapproving father's tense first meeting with Joe, Kirsten announces, "You know what I'd like to do? I'd like to go to some nice place and have a drink." But we move on to happy marriage, a sweet baby, a fabulously art-directed 1960s apartment, featuring a fully tricked-out wet bar. The days of wine and roses have a shelf life, however. Joe's drinking gets him in trouble at work (*Is drinking jeopardizing your job or business?*) and he turns his frustrations on Kirsten: He blames her relative sobriety for their problems, given that she is no fun, that if she really loved him, she'd join him in his drinking, "So maybe we can have some laughs around here!" *Is drinking making your home life unhappy?*

And so Kirsten pours herself a real drink, some of the hard stuff this time—and thus begins her own perilous descent. Within a scene or two, Lee Remick's crystalline blue eyes (even in black and white, those blue eyes are radiant) lose their spark, her hair is in constant disarray, she is sprawled on the couch, clutching a tumbler, smoking, ignoring their screaming infant daughter . . . and eventually setting their apartment on fire. *Does drinking make you careless of your family's welfare?*

Joe loses his job (*Has your ambition decreased since drinking?*), a move to a ratty apartment, spiral spiral spiral, until a clarifying moment when Joe spots his disheveled self in a mirror:

```
                      JOE
   I wonder who that bum is! Look at you, you're
   a bum! We're both bums. You know why I've been
   fired from four jobs in five years? Booze! It's
   the booze!


                    KIRSTEN
   Oh, a couple of drinks. . . .
```

JOE

```
We have more than a couple of drinks! We get
drunk! And we stay drunk most of the time. I'm a
drunk. We should have done this a long time ago,
taken a good hard look at ourselves and realize
we've turned into a couple of bums!
```

They're going to get sober, he insists, not a drop. They have to make it work before it's too late! And they do, briefly. They stay with Kirsten's widowed father in the country, where the sparkle returns to smiles and eyes, hair is back in place, all is buttermilk and haystacks and sunshiny love in the uncorrupted, purifying air. All is so well, in fact, they have been *so good* that Joe decides they have been *too good*, they deserve a reward, just a little bit, a drop, and look, he has hidden away a few pints . . . and very soon, bottles are emptied, and Joe is out in the greenhouse, searching for another hidden bottle, smashing things and rolling on the floor, drunk and unhinged, screaming.

But the most disturbing moment so far is Kirsten's: She creeps into her father's bedroom—"Daddy?" she coos—and crawls into bed with him, draping herself around him, and pleading

KIRSTEN

```
Daddy? I'm plastered and I'm lonely . . . kiss me
good night, Daddy, kiss me good night!
```

And when her own little daughter enters the room, looking for her grandfather,

KIRSTEN

```
You get away from him!
```

she shrieks, jealously. (*Is drinking making you sexually inappropriate with your own father?*) He wrestles her off him and into the bathroom, pushes her into the shower, holding her close from behind while she writhes and cries out in what sounds like both agony and ecstasy. Ick.

Meanwhile, Joe is in the hospital, straitjacketed, hysterical, and succumbing to forcible sedation. Enter Jack Klugman as Jim, the sympathetic voice and face of Alcoholics Anonymous, offering wisdom, a supportive shoulder, and a recitation of the AA preamble/mission statement. Joe, knowing he has crossed that invisible line, is ready to accept Jim's help. Kirsten is not.

> KIRSTEN
>
> They must think you're a bum or something!

> JOE
>
> I asked for it. I must have needed help, I was in the hospital!

> KIRSTEN
>
> Well, you didn't belong there! . . . All right, you had too much to drink. It doesn't mean you're an *alcoholic*. You can go, if you want to . . . I am not an alcoholic, and I refuse to say I am. I refuse to ask for help for something that is just a matter of self-respect and willpower. I refuse to get up in front of a bunch of people and degrade myself. I know I can't drink, because it gets the best of me. I will just use my willpower, and not drink, and that's the end of it.

Joe wants to believe love is strong enough to save Kirsten, but Jim warns booze has been integral to their relationship, and now:

> JIM
>
> You're sober—it's no fun to drink around you. It's worse. Your sobriety would be an accusation to her. She'd be miserable. She's lost her playmate.

And points out how when Joe found that hidden bottle in the greenhouse, he didn't take it back to share with Kirsten—he polished it off all by himself:

```
                    JIM
There comes a time in the life of every alcoholic
when the bottle is God. Nobody, nothing matters
but the next drink.
```

Kirsten disappears on a bender of booze and promiscuity; Joe discovers her in a seedy motel, drunk, mean, sloppy, and lonely: "Have a drink with me, please?" she begs him. "What did they do to you in there? I'm a woman, can't you hear me calling you?" and continues to beg, plead, and belittle him until, in what he believes is a gesture of love, he pours himself a drink. *Noooo!* I want to yell, and the moment he raises that glass to his lips is heartbreaking because this time he has no illusions, he knows full well exactly where it will lead.

Which is straight back to the hospital. Joe is strapped down for another screaming, sweating round of alcohol poisoning, DTs and withdrawal, while Jim insists if he loves Kirsten, the only thing he can do, until she is willing to accept help, is to stay sober and set an example. Months later he is doing just that, holding down a job, raising their daughter alone, living soberly in an apartment next door to a blinking neon bar sign—constant invitation, constant warning—when Kirsten shows up, bedraggled and wan. She's been two days sober, she tells him: "I want to come home." Joe, still very much in love, wants nothing more than for them to be a family again. But she scares him, he tells her. She cannot come home if she continues to drink.

```
                  KIRSTEN
The world looks so dirty to me when I'm not
drinking. I don't think I could ever stop
drinking, not completely, not like you. . . . I
want things to look prettier than they are. . . .
I can't bear the thought of never taking another
drink.
```

Why can't it just be the way it was between them, she asks, back in the beginning, back when it was *fun*?

JOE

The way it *was*? It was you and me and booze. A
threesome. Do you remember? We were a couple of
drunks in a sea of booze and the boat sank. I
got a hold of something to keep me from going
under, and I'm not going to let go of it! Not
for you, not for anyone. If you want to grab on,
grab on. But there's just room for you and me,
no threesome!

Try it for just one more day, he pleads. Go look at their sleeping
daughter! Do it for her!

But "it's so dirty out there," she says, and leaves. She has made her
choice. Joe hugs his daughter. "When is Mommy coming home?" she
asks, in a sad, sleepy-child quaver.

JOE

Honey, Mommy is sick. And she has to get well
before she can come home.

DAUGHTER

Will she get well?

JOE

(pause) I did, didn't I?

And he gazes out the window at Kirsten's retreating back, the
looming bar sign blinking, blinking. It will blink for him forever, and
he knows that, and sees it, appreciates it, for the warning it is. But
despite his hopeful final line, it will always be a lure for Kirsten, an
irresistible, winking invitation to the devil's dance.

Jack Lemmon gets the most intensely dramatic scenes, here—the
sweating, screaming, straitjacketed writhing—and he is brilliant in
this role. Lee Remick is no less extraordinary, but her unraveling
is quieter, more subtle: Messier hair, dulled eyes, a steadily less
expressive face. But Kirsten's plunge is the more tragic, because her
denial dooms her; all our hope is for Joe and his determination to

keep ahold of something and stay afloat. Yes, he relapsed for love, but from that hellish fire forged himself into a stronger man, and—significantly—a better father. No such hope for Kirsten, the drowning, floundering bum.

Her story is also the more disturbing to me exactly *because* of its subtlety, the lack of unhinged histrionics; I cannot imagine myself smashing a greenhouse to bits or writhing in that "Hangover Plaza" drunk ward, and while I might really like that second (or third) glass of wine sometimes, I can still stop at one. I don't gotta ride Don's merry-go-round all the way, around and around. I'm no common whiskey-head, as Sarah's Therapist warns. I am still a soaring balloon girl, held aloft by ethanol-heated air. But Kirsten's *I can't bear the thought of never taking another drink* hits a little too close to home. My thirty-day self-tests seem disingenuous; sure, anyone can stop for a while, when you know you can celebrate at the end with a festive Kir Royale or two. I do want things to look prettier than they are—not all the time, I really don't desire to *get drunk*, or to *stay drunk most of the time*, as Joe says—but why wouldn't I, or anyone, want a soft-focus lens sometimes, the cinematographer's trick of good lighting, the flattering angle, the clever aesthetic touches to pretty up a scene? As Kirsten reasons, can't I stay back at Brandy Alexander level forever, where it is all sweet giggles and *fun*? That's still the best thing to have, right?

Kirsten also unnerves me, because here is a relatively rare, fully realized *Portrait of an Adult Woman Alcoholic*, in her full, start-to-bad-finish trajectory. Female drunks are a different cinematic animal from male drunks; we shake our heads at the Dons and Joes, we weep for them or bemoan their bad behavior, but when it comes to the drunk female character, some of our reprobation is gender-specific; the drunk woman has "fallen" in a uniquely ugly way, and our sympathy for her is more limited. Kirsten's father stresses how, before meeting Joe, Kirsten was such a "good girl" (we are persona-sisters, there) and there is no worse indication of how low she has sunk than her drunken promiscuity (like Sarah T. propositioning the older guys . . . like my own inebriated, less-than-smart sexual choices . . . ?) or, the greatest of her sins, her abandonment of her daughter. A woman who chooses booze over her role as a mother is an especial failure and deserves an extra heaping of shame; in *When a Man Loves a Woman,* Meg Ryan's neglect of her children is the final shaming straw that sends her to rehab (at which point the story turns, like Joe's, to a portrait of the fallout of codependency—*Is sobriety making your home life unhappy?*).[37] The drunk woman is a harridan, coarse and unseemly, there is a certain monstrousness in her fleshy, unbridled appetite; Elizabeth Taylor's Martha in *Who's Afraid of Virginia Woolf?* is a blowsy, emasculating virago, and while Richard Burton's George is equally pickled in booze, we can't help but blame her for his escape into drink.[38] Patty Duke's campy, nasty drunkenness in *Valley of the Dolls* functions in the same way: The drunk woman is a harpy who drives men to drink or just far, far away.[39] She deserves to be punished, abandoned, and alone. Jane Fonda is an aging actress in *The Morning After,* who, after an alcoholic blackout, wakes up next to a dead man, and her inability to remember what happened is a moral failing; her slatternly bad behavior has led to murder . . . one she possibly committed![40] Dum dum *dum!* All those drunken sorority party girls in raucous teen or college comedies, sprawled out sloppily in their lacy bras and panties in some upstairs bedroom, empty Solo cup in hand and vomit stains on the sheets, are dismissible as stupid and slutty, objects of ridicule, wholly to blame for any subsequent sexual abuse. When the alcoholic woman is not a nasty harridan, she is pathetic, slurring, and sad, a cause for our pity, not our empathy, such as Maggie Smith's lonely spinster in *The Lonely Passion of Judith Hearne* or Gena Rowlands's self-destructive dysfunction in *Opening Night.*[41] There really is no female equivalent to Arthur, a

---

37 *When a Man Loves a Woman* (Buena Vista Pictures, 1994): written by Ronald Bass and Al Franken; directed by Luis Mandoki; with Meg Ryan and Andy Garcia

38 *Who's Afraid of Virginia Woolf?* (Warner Bros., 1966): screenplay by Ernest Lehman, based on the play by Edward Albee; directed by Mike Nichols; with Elizabeth Taylor and Richard Burton

39 *Valley of the Dolls* (20th Century Fox, 1967): screenplay by Helen Deutsch and Dorothy Kingsley, based on the novel by Jacqueline Susann; directed by Mark Robson; with Patty Duke

40 *The Morning After* (20th Century Fox, 1986): written by James Cresson; directed by Sidney Lumet; with Jane Fonda

41 *The Lonely Passion of Judith Hearne* (Island Pictures, 1987): screenplay by Peter Nelson, based on the novel by Brian Moore; directed by Jack Clayton; with Maggie

female character who can carry a whole movie on her drunken charm; the closest might be Renée Zellweger in *Bridget Jones's Diary*, but her drinking, along with her smoking and overeating, is still symptomatic of single-gal desperation and neurosis.[42] We excuse Audrey Hepburn her tipsy silliness for a scene or two in *Breakfast at Tiffany's*, but then we excuse Audrey Hepburn absolutely anything.[43] Another rare exception: Karen Allen's alcohol-empowered Marion in *Raiders of the Lost Ark*, who can throw back shots with the best of them, indeed, can drink a guy twice her size literally under the table or use her macho mastery of booze to outwit a Nazi.[44] But Marion isn't a drunk, and again, her drinking is limited to two scenes; this tough chick has her head on straight. Faced with images of passed-out sorority girls, desperate spinsters, and ugly, lurching, bitter harridans, I realize I need to take special, feminine care when I drink: Pronounce your words carefully, make smart choices. Stay elegant, stay upright, refined. Stay in control. Do not let it mess up your hair or get the best of you.

And do not retreat into Kirsten's denial, her self-dooming *I'm not an alcoholic and I refuse to say I am!* As long as you stay self-aware, I tell myself, as long as you keep that honest logbook going, you're fine. As long as . . . maybe . . . you can say those magic words, you can stay afloat indefinitely, stave off the Something Bad forever.

So, fine, I'll say it: I'm an alcoholic. Well, maybe. (That is not denial, just scientific uncertainty—there *is* no quantifiable, definitive diagnostic test to earn that label, now is there?) Okay, that was easy. *Nothing hard about admitting it*, as Sarah T.'s Teenage AA Friend says, sure. *Except then you have to give up the booze.*

Smith; *Opening Night* (Castle Hill Productions/Faces Distribution, 1977): written and directed by John Cassavetes; with Gena Rowlands

42 *Bridget Jones's Diary* (Miramax, 2001): screenplay by Helen Fielding, Andrew Davies, and Richard Curtis, based on the novel by Helen Fielding; directed by Sharon Maguire; with Renée Zellweger

43 *Breakfast at Tiffany's* (Paramount Pictures, 1961): screenplay by George Axelrod, based on the novel by Truman Capote; directed by Blake Edwards; with Audrey Hepburn

44 *Raiders of the Lost Ark* (Paramount Pictures, 1981): written by Lawrence Kasdan, based on a story by George Lucas and Philip Kaufman; directed by Steven Spielberg; with Karen Allen and Harrison Ford

But why? Life is still going along fine. By now I've stumbled into a second wonderful career, I treasure my relationships with beloved family and friends, I still score an A or at least a B+ on any silly AA exam. At least I'm not into drugs; I'm not shooting heroin. I'm a drinker, not a drunk; I have never hallucinated a purple cockroach or flapping bat. I haven't thrown up on a bathroom floor since I was sixteen. If I lived in France, I joke, the amount I drink would make me a virtual teetotaler. I can "watch my drinking" just fine, just as I "watch my sugar" because of my high blood glucose. What's the difference? I can have it all, like Arthur. I am leading my own delightful comedy of a life, and I can stay on my tipsy, prettied-up side of that imaginary line forever.

- - - - - - - - - - -

"How long does it take to drink yourself to death?" Sera asks Ben in *Leaving Las Vegas*.[45] "I think about four weeks," he estimates, but he is already well on his way, much further down the alcoholic road than Don or Joe, so far past the imaginary line the line has dipped below the horizon forever. When the film begins, Ben (Nicolas Cage in his gifted, authentic heyday, all snaggletoothed and thinning hair), a one-time ultraslick Hollywood agent or producer or some such, has already downward-spiraled his way out of a job and friends; there is no loyal sponsor or girlfriend to be found. His wife has left him and taken their child, but

BEN

```
I don't remember if I started drinking because my
wife left me or my wife left me because I started
drinking. So fuck it.
```

He's done; the opening scene is Ben enthusiastically filling a shopping cart with every gleaming bottle of booze there is, dancing in the

---

45 *Leaving Las Vegas* (United Artists, 1995): written by Mike Figgis, based on the novel by John O'Brien; directed by Mike Figgis; with Nicolas Cage and Elisabeth Shue

aisle. He arrives in glittery, dizzying neon Las Vegas, chugging a bottle of vodka in the car, to a sometimes-tinkling, sometimes-desultory jazz score, with the last of his money and one final goal: To drink his way *out* of purpose, out of life. Gazing at a hot woman, he fantasizes about getting her drunk,

>   BEN
>   . . . so then I could fall in love with you,
>   because then I would have a purpose: To clean you
>   up and that would prove that I'm worth something.
>   . . .

Despite a hint of the self-loathing, tortured soul, here, there is little time spent on the *why* of Ben's alcoholism, on whether the self-loathing led to the drinking or the drinking led to the self-loathing. Fuck it; this is where we're at. Ben meets and falls in love with Sera, a prostitute with struggles of her own (Elisabeth Shue, a very fresh-scrubbed hooker), but makes it clear that her love won't save him; he is a man with a bigger mission, after all. She asks why he's a drunk, with an echo of Helen's belief that unlocking the mystery of *why* someone drinks (*There must be a reason why you drink, Don, the right doctor could find it!*) will serve as a life preserver tossed to a drowning man, but Ben dismisses that line of inquiry as irrelevant. Sera moves on to why he wants to kill himself, then:

>   BEN
>   I don't remember. I just know that I want to.

>   SERA
>   Are you saying that your drinking is a way to
>   kill yourself?

>   BEN
>   Or killing myself is a way to drink.

Again, fuck it—he's not interested in chicken-or-egging anymore. Ben's drunkenness is not about fun, or building self-confidence, or

even an escape, really, from existential despair; it is an engraved invitation to the devil to join him in the ultimate dance marathon, a final
selling of his alcoholic soul. In his end is his beginning. Sera falls in
love with him, too, despite, or perhaps because of, his alcoholism
having rendered him impotent, sexless; it is intimacy and connection she craves, and the rare moments they have together between
his drunken binges are painfully lovely, Ben at his most soberly lucid,
vulnerable, and tender:

> BEN
>
> I'm in love with you. But be that as it may, I am
> not here to force my twisted soul into your life.
> . . . We both know I'm a drunk. And I know you're
> a hooker. I hope you understand that I'm a person
> who is totally at ease with this. Which is not
> to say that I'm indifferent or don't care. I do.
> It simply means I trust and accept your judgment.

She asks him to move in with her. But wouldn't she get bored,
living with a drunk? he asks.

> BEN
>
> You haven't seen the worst of it. These last few
> days have been very controlled. I knock things
> over and throw up all the time. Right now I feel
> really good; you're like some kind of antidote
> that mixes with the liquor and keeps me in bal-
> ance. But that won't last forever. . . . What you
> don't understand is you can never, never ask me
> to stop drinking. Do you understand?

And she says she does, even buys him a hammered silver flask.
They head out to a happy-couple, wine-and-roses montage at a casino,
Ben consuming a staggering amount of booze until at last he throws
an alcoholic fit, becomes irrational and violent, and they are thrown
out; he awakens the next morning to full-on alcohol poisoning, shak-
ingly pouring vodka into a carton of orange juice before throwing it

right back up. Don Birnam never quite lost Ray Milland's suave sheen; Jack Lemmon had his happy clown face to balance out his own tragic mask, but Ben's alcoholism is as nakedly ugly as it gets. We can see the toxins seeping from his skin, we can smell the corrosion of his organs. It shrinks his liver; it pickles his kidneys. He drinks underwater in a swimming pool, he takes a bottle into the shower with him, he cannot keep food down. And Sera knows she is losing. She tries seducing him by making herself into a human cocktail, pouring whiskey over her naked breasts so he can lap it off, perhaps satisfy his need by drinking her in, but he falls, shatters a glass table, and the moment is gone. In the end, all Ben can do is lie there, choking, convulsing.

> SERA
>
> You're so sick. So pale. My love. You're my love.
> Do you want help? Do you want my help?

> BEN
>
> I want your help. You're my angel.

And they begin making love, for the first real time. But too late, time's up; the devil arrives to take his due. Ben's hand goes dramatically limp, and he dies.

Ben's death is not the saddest thing of the story; it is his retreat from Sera that is so sad, his rejection of the human connection she offered, the wasted potential for true intimacy. Whether that can "save" anyone or not, it is still the thing that makes us human and alive. It's watching Ben, scene after scene, as he guzzles, gulps, swallows, belts, transform from the clear-eyed, smiling, so-very-present-with-you-in-the-moment man, to a solipsistic solitude where nothing and no one else can exist. We all die alone, but Ben's alcoholism doomed him to live alone—when he didn't have to.

And now finally, I am afraid, and sad, for my father.

- - - - - - - - - - -

After divorcing my mother, my father set off to resurrect and follow his long-buried dream of being an artist. But like Don Birnam (at least up until that lost, ultimately epiphanic weekend) he could never quite bring it into being, although he did establish a successful career as a studio sculptor in the film industry. But that is realizing someone else's vision, someone else's dream. Despite his success, and a third marriage to a wonderful woman who supported and loved him, who made of their home a shrine to his beautiful sculptures, over the years of our wine-fueled dinners together I could see the Tortured Artist bitterness set in; *Fuck it*, he would often say, his way of dismissing realities he didn't like, distancing himself from people he deemed not sufficiently supportive or understanding of his rarified genius, as he poured himself another glass.

I could relate, in part; I was trying to be an artist, too, and I could identify with his frustration, his need for validation. My stepmother didn't drink, so my father and I drank together, and it set us apart, reinforced our special bond. We were both so far above the ordinary, yes, waving to the rest of the world down below as our balloon soared. We were a twosome of misunderstood Michelangelos, a pair of unappreciated van Goghs . . . although deep down I was concerned, despite some success as a writer (which, over the years, I would feel increasingly guilty about and downplay in my father's presence), that I was not nor ever would be one of the great ones, that I was just an ordinary person whose success was a sham, who just got a little lucky. I was also like Don, hearing that thin, clear voice like an E string of a violin as I tried to write, whispering *It's not good enough . . . how about a couple of drinks, just to set it on its feet . . . ?* And yes, great idea, what a difference that made! Shut the laptop down, take a break, have a glass of wine . . . and the brilliant writing I could envision, the tragic sweep of a great novel, beautifully proportioned! But then, yes,

DON

  . . . before I could really grab it and throw it down on paper, the drinks would wear off and everything would be gone, like a mirage. . . .

In 1999, my father traveled by planes, trains, and automobiles across the country to attend my MFA graduation out in the middle of Vermont's nowhere—of course he did, I proudly told friends. My father is always there for me. He arrived wafting fumes and a little stumbly, and my graduation weekend became the déjà vu of a clenched-stomach childhood; he drank steadily and sloppily for three days, he got showy and loud, unwitty and uncharming—the anti-Arthur—he steadily retreated from active, lucid engagement with me or anyone into a brittle narcissism, and I could hear the *tick-ticking* in my ear, feel the smoke going swirly and dark, the tension ulcerating my guts, and although there was no real "incident" (other than my embarrassment in front of my friends and professors), no eruption, no fist holes punched into my dorm room walls, I realized a lonely paradox: Only now, for the first time, during this special, extended time we had together, did I feel abandoned by my father. There was no unique, sustaining bond between us; we were not a twosome, not father and daughter together. Because my father's closest, most intimate relationship was to alcohol.

JIM THE AA GUY
There comes a time in the life of every alcoholic
when the bottle is God. Nobody, nothing matters
but the next drink.

The alcoholic cannot be truly present with you, the other human being in the room, because his absorbed, focused love is solely for the drink in his hand. It is a threesome, as Joe says, but a lopsided one; it is two people going at it, enthralled with each other, and one person left out and observing from the sidelines. And actually, no, his love is not even for the drink he has in his hand, because he cannot be even that present in the moment, in the room—it is for the next drink to come, and his mind and heart are fully absorbed by when will that be, where will he get it, will it be there, waiting for him, arms outstretched,

DON
So I know I can have it, if I need it . . . that's
the devil, that's what drives you crazy.

I remembered the time I spotted my father, through my bedroom window, creeping around the side of the house from the garage, where he had filled a red Solo cup with wine; he carried it so carefully, like a toddler with a sippy cup, rejoining a party in the backyard and obviously hoping he could pass it off as soda. His sad, transparent subterfuge. But we all knew he would make more trips to the garage during the evening (and he did), we could all feel his increasing disconnection from us, the obsessive, absorbing love affair blossoming in our midst.

When a drunken Don, drink in hand, tries to throw Helen out, she protests:

HELEN

Because I have a rival? Because you're in love with this?

And yes, she should be jealous—there is no contest. *Leaving Las Vegas* and *Days of Wine and Roses* are both love stories, but the most driving passion is, of course, for the bottle. That should be the number one question on that Alcoholics Anonymous Twenty Questions self-test, I think:

Does your love for alcohol render the supposedly beloved and treasured actual people in your life invisible?

A few years later, I arrived at my father and stepmother's one evening to find my stepmother alone in the den, the carpet and my father's Barcalounger covered in blood. She'd come home to find him on the floor, drunk, passed out, and bleeding, and she'd put him to bed. I asked if we should take him to the hospital, and she said No, she didn't think so. But she'd dealt with this for twenty years, and she wasn't going to live the rest of her life this way, she told me. She was throwing him out in the morning. *Poor drunks do not find love, Arthur.* She looked at me with both pain and defiance; I told her I completely understood (while I wondered, guiltily, where he would go, would he have to come live with me now, would I have to take care of him, live the rest of *my* life this way . . . ?). The next morning my father came into the kitchen to announce he'd looked up the local chapter of Alcoholics Anonymous and was on his way to a meeting.

- - - - - - - - - - - -

Whip Whitaker is a brilliant ace pilot, who, when his plane falls apart due to mechanical failure at thirty thousand feet, masterfully, against all odds, manages to set the aircraft down in an empty field, single-handedly saving 96 out of the 102 souls onboard. He is also a raging, full-on, beyond-the-invisible-line alcoholic, one whose addiction, in the film *Flight*, raises the stakes considerably: Unlike Don or Joe or Ben, Whip's self-destructiveness risks not only his own life but also the lives of hundreds of other people every time he walks out the door and goes to work.[46] The film is terrifying, and not just because of the harrowing crash sequence; it is terrifying to realize how easily Whip has gotten away with everything until now, thanks to his Arthur-like charm, Denzel Washington's handsomeness and charisma, and the dedicated, hard-working alcoholic's gift at deception, subterfuge, and lies.

Everyone—Whip's union representative and attorney, his flight crew, the besotted media, even the NTSB investigators—agrees the way Whip handled that plane "was nothing short of a miracle," that he is a true hero, that his talents as a pilot are beyond question. No one realizes his other talents: Showing up for work with a blood alcohol level of 0.24 after a sleepless night of drinking and sex with one of his flight attendants (throw in some pot and cocaine, too, although booze is his true love) and passing himself off as stone-cold sober; genially reassuring passengers during the turbulent flight while one-handedly (and unobservedly) unscrewing mini bottles of vodka and pouring them into a carton of OJ to guzzle in the cockpit; his manipulative powers of persuasion that he has no problem, that he can stop anytime he wants:

WHIP

I'm not drinking anymore. Take the fucking vodka
with you,

he tells his dealer (who offers him a drug-and-liquor care package in the hospital), and even when he is alone, getting rid of every single bottle and can in the house—a swimming pool's worth of booze

---

46 *Flight* (Paramount Pictures, 2012): written by John Gatins; directed by Robert Zemeckis; with Denzel Washington, Don Cheadle, and John Goodman

poured down the drain, trash bags stuffed with empties—he is able to manipulate *us*, get us feeling so hopeful about his so-believable resolve. This guy has learned his lesson, we think.

But that damn toxicology report. If Whip's drunkenness is revealed, he could face four counts of manslaughter and life in prison. The attorney is confident he can obfuscate, get the report thrown out on some legal technicality, but cocky Whip isn't even worried about that. His drinking had nothing to do with the crash, someone put him in a broken plane, he is adamant:

> WHIP
>
> Without me, there would've been 102 dead bodies, not 6 . . . ! No one could have landed that plane like I did. *No one.*

Perhaps his 0.24 blood alcohol level even *helped*, we are invited to think, fueled his bravado to stay steady while the rest of the crew and passengers were hysterical with fear. I think of all the times I sucked down a glass of wine before a scary, intimidating thing, that few bracing ounces of liquid courage. *Go where you want to go, be what you want to be!* His attorney counsels that until the upcoming NTSB hearing is over, Whip has to stay sober:

> ATTORNEY
> You *can't drink.* We can get you help.

> WHIP
> I won't drink. I can stop on my own,

but we recognize those words as the ultimate tempting-fate trigger they are, the cue for a jump cut to Whip on a full-on binge, bender, spree. His ex-junkie girlfriend, herself trying desperately to stay clean, invites him to an AA meeting, where the Speaker begins:

> BARRY THE AA SPEAKER
> Hi, my name is Barry and I'm an alcoholic. Are there any other alcoholics present?

Everyone raises their hand except Whip, who crosses his arms defiantly.

> BARRY THE AA SPEAKER
>
> ```
> I always love a meeting where we all need to
> identify at the top, because it forces me to be
> honest about who I really am. I never told the
> truth out there, I lied about everything. I was
> taught in these rooms that I would never get
> sober if I kept lying. But that's what I was best
> at. If I knew anything in this world, it was how
> to lie. Especially about my drinking. . . . My
> whole life became a series of lies. . . .
> ```

And at that Whip has to get the hell out of there and get himself to a bar. "You need *help*," his girlfriend pleads, "you need rehab!" But "I *choose* to drink," he says; he is his own, decision-making Higher Power; he is not a weakling, not the victim of addiction. He is special, distinctive. Whip's denial and self-delusion are the opposite of Ben's naked honesty about himself; he even tries to extend his web of lies to the surviving crew members, asking them to lie on his behalf . . . and they agree. Lies and manipulation, that's what Whip is best at, his true gift.

Whip spends the night before the hearing in a hotel room cleared of all alcohol, a babysitting guard in the hallway. He paces, eats a room-service steak dinner, drinks a lot of water. He discovers the door to the adjoining room is unlocked; he discovers the mini fridge, he opens it like a treasure chest to reveal the gleaming diamonds, sapphires, and rubies of vodka, gin, and whiskey bottles. He opens a bottle. He smells it. He sets the bottle down. The tension of the moment is excruciating, more stomach-clenched and nail-biting than the crash sequence—I can almost hear the theremin wail—because it is our last precious moment of hope in what we want to believe is true: Yes, he is strong, he is distinctive, it is a choice, and Whip will make the right one. We want to believe this, because it means we can be that strong and resolved as well—the idea of powerlessness over a bottle of liquid is so frightening.

But his hand grabs for that bottle; we and his attorney find him the next morning in a trashed room, littered with bottles and cans, vomit, blood, clothing. Whip is lying on the bathroom floor, bleeding, incoherent, rock-bottom. They call the dealer, he arrives with a restorative concoction of cocaine and nicotine, and they head off to the hearing, his attorney counseling Whip how to evade the most potentially dangerous questions.

WHIP

Don't tell me how to lie about my drinking. I've been lying about my drinking my whole life!

At least that is a confession, of sorts. Whip pulls himself together for a final tour de force, manipulative, deceptive performance (and a magnificent performance by Denzel, charming, and his face full of pouches and seams, all at once); the investigation has proven mechanical failure, and, led by the head NTSB investigator, everyone applauds Whip's heroism.

But we're not done. The questioning turns to those potentially dangerous questions:

NTSB INVESTIGATOR

Do you now, or have you ever had, a problem with alcohol dependency, alcoholism, or drug addiction?

WHIP

No.

What about those empty mini bottles of vodka found in the wreckage? Whip has a final choice to make: Attribute them to the reckless alcoholic behavior of the flight attendant he had a relationship with or claim them as his own. It is Whip's moment of moral truth, his last chance to either exonerate himself or accept responsibility. It is his story's climactic moment, what we paid our $14 to watch this movie for. "God help me . . . I drank the vodka," he says.

```
                         WHIP
    I drank the vodka bottles on the plane . . . I
    drank to excess. I was drunk. I'm drunk now. I'm
    drunk right now. Because I'm an alcoholic.
```

There we are, the magical, epiphanous incantation. Our resolution: Whip in prison, serving his four or five years' time, and storytelling to his fellow inmates at an AA meeting:

```
                         WHIP
    That was it. I was finished. I was done. It was
    as if I had reached my lifelong limit of lies.
    I could not tell one more lie. And maybe I'm a
    sucker, because if I had told just one more lie,
    I could've walked away from all that mess, and
    kept my false sense of pride . . . but at least
    I'm sober. And I thank God for that. And this is
    going to sound stupid coming from a guy locked
    up in prison. But for the first time in my life,
    I'm free.
```

And good for him, yes, Whip transforming tragedy into the art of instructive narrative, just as Helen had urged Don. Another happy ending.

Watching *Flight*, I am so proud of my father. After a year of AA meetings, my father had stopped going—he couldn't stand the God stuff, all that higher power crap, he said, and they were all a bunch of losers. Fuck it. And he didn't need it, he felt; he certainly *was* an alcoholic, sure, a label he now announced to anyone who would listen and wore with a pride I recognized as a self-professed form of distinction. But he could do it all by himself, he insisted,

```
                         WHIP
    I won't drink, I can stop on my own,
```

it would be just that easy, yes,

KIRSTEN
I will just use my willpower and not drink,

and for fifteen years we clenched our stomachs and held our breath, hoping he could stay afloat. But he did do it, all on his own. Not a drop, not a sip. Seeing Whip on the floor, bloodied and rock-bottomed, I am so relieved and grateful those gut-sinking, hold-your-breath days are over, that my father's final binge didn't involve the straightjacket or the convulsions, that he didn't kill himself or anyone else. That he was now, finally and for the first time, free.

But . . . I wonder . . . isn't Whip's sobriety *assisted*, eased, enabled, just a little, by his being locked up in prison? I'm sure it's possible to brew up some moonshine out of cafeteria raisins or something . . . but what will happen to Whip when he gets out? Into the world of liquor stores and parties and bars with blinking signs, dates with old lovers and a lifetime of habits, the betraying biochemistry of his own body? Is this *really* the end to his story? Is he really so free?

Because my father isn't. Now in his eighties, his body has betrayed him, imprisoned him; he can no longer sculpt with his shaking hands and he has fallen multiple times, not because of the alcoholic's *delirium tremens* but because of advanced Parkinson's disease. It is my turn now to sit by his hospital bed, to hold his hand. And he *has* abandoned everyone, in a way, all of us; he is still retreating from the world, from attempting authentic connection with the people who love him, although that is mostly due to the narcissistic solipsism of old age. But the bitterness of the Tortured Artist remains, amplified by the clock now *tick-ticking* out on his life. I know he is afraid of death, and I believe it is because he feels, when he dies, that without leaving the artistic legacy he once dreamed of, any record of his existence will simply disappear from the planet. Sometimes I wonder if his longing to be an artist, if his self-perceived failure,

DON
The reason is me, what I am. Or rather, what I'm not. What I wanted to become, and didn't . . .

was what led to his alcoholism.

Some of us drink because we're not poets.

Or did the alcoholism lead to his inability to bring that identity fully into being?

Or is it just an unlucky, predetermined genetic quirk, a question of biochemistry?

"Your father has started drinking again," my stepmother told me a few weeks ago. Twice, on two recent occasions—dinner out with friends, a party—had raised that glass of wine to his lips with his shaky hand, guzzled, gulped, swallowed, as the theremin wailed. Then another glass, and another.

Why can't he just stop at half a glass? my stepmother asked.

Because he's an *alcoholic*, was all I could say. One's too many, and a hundred's not enough.

And yet I still had to ask him: Why, Dad? After all these years?

He just shrugged. He didn't even like it the first time, he told me, he didn't like the taste, or the way it made him feel. So why the second time? He shrugged again.

Fuck it, he said.

I don't know—he doesn't know—if it will happen again, if we all have to get back on that merry-go-round, ride it round and round until that blasted music stops. And stops where, at what? The hospital, the holes in the wall—punched by his enfeebled, shaking fist—the smell of his shrinking liver and pickled kidneys, the bloody bathroom floor? At least he isn't lying anymore. But *One day it's going to kill you*, I think, and I am afraid.

And maybe I should also be afraid for myself now. I take after my father so much.

Last night I met my friend Theresa at a hotel bar for a few glasses of cheap Happy Hour house white—for me. She has been sober for twenty-four years and six months, is well-versed in the language of alcoholism. I presented her with the logbook of my drinking behaviors, my subterfuge and self-consciousness. Maybe I am my father's daughter after all, I tell her. Maybe I am a drunk, not just a drinker. Maybe I am destructive to myself and the people around me; maybe it's time I take a good hard look at myself and realize I'm turning into a bum. She wasn't buying it. Perhaps I don't warrant the actual label, I say, but can you at least acknowledge that I have a "drinking problem"? She agreed it was possible, and we parsed terminology—a "reliance" on alcohol, a "dependency," an "addictive habit." But she was more interested in *why*—not why I drink, but why am I trying to convince her? Why am I so insistent I have a problem?

And I am eleven years old again, fearing invisibility, hoping to be heard. Seeking the distinction and complexity of dysfunction and dark secrets. Hoping to seem deeper and more interesting than I am, to offer evidence of the Tortured Artist to fulfill narrative convention, something to add a justifying glamour to my story.

HOW TO
BE A
SLUT

THE CHOICES AND PRIORITIES OF A PROMISCUOUS WOMAN, AND NO, YOU DO NOT COMPLETE ME

Doctor Zhivago
Jerry Maguire
Annie Hall
Erin Brockovich
Norma Rae
Silkwood
Mahogany
Bridget Jones's Diary
Bridget Jones: The Edge of Reason
Bridesmaids
Fatal Attraction
The Devil Wears Prada
Working Girl
Up in the Air
Thelma & Louise
Looking for Mr. Goodbar
Dressed to Kill
An Unmarried Woman
Private Benjamin

oscow, 1913: An icy Russian winter, the crystallizing Soviet chill. Gorgeous seventeen-year-old Lara has been secretly sleeping with her mother's lover, Victor Komarovsky, an older, slimy opportunist—she has just introduced him to Pasha, her idealistic young revolutionary fiancé, whom she is still planning to marry. Now alone with Lara, Komarovsky is unimpressed:

> KOMAROVSKY
>
> ```
> There  are  two  kinds  of  men,  and  only  two,  and
> that young man is one kind. He is high-minded. He
> is pure. . . . There is another kind. Not high-
> minded. Not pure. But alive. . . . For you to
> marry that boy would be a disaster. Because there
> are two kinds of women, and you, as we well know,
> are not the first kind. . . .
> ```

Lara gasps, slaps him. He pays no mind:

> KOMAROVSKY
>
> ```
> You, my dear, are a slut.
> ```

> LARA
>
> ```
> I am not!
> ```

she says, horrified; it is clearly the ultimate insult, the worst thing in the world for a woman to be called. "We shall see," Komorovsky replies, ominously; he then rapes her, in one of those "she struggles, pummeling him with fists until her passion is aroused and she gives herself over to it" scenes, proving, I suppose . . . his point? Which is . . . ?

I'm not sure. I am nine or ten years old, at a revival showing of David Lean's epic *Doctor Zhivago*—my mother's way of killing a long afternoon with her children while still being cultural.[47] We are forty minutes into a three-and-a-half-hour movie and I am already feeling a little bored until this scene, this charged moment, this epithet spat out in Rod Steiger's sneery, staccato clip: *Slut*. I have a vague understanding of the word (*bad woman*), but it has never grabbed my attention this way. What exactly is he accusing her of? Is it that she has chosen to participate in this loveless sexual relationship because she is getting something out of it—power, money, access to Komarovsy's worldier world—and is thus a de facto prostitute? Or is it that she is indiscriminately promiscuous—that she actually likes sex, for the sake of sex? And to such a degree that she has chosen to compromise her "purity," her "high-mindedness," and therefore risk her reputation and her marriageability?

But I can't quite puzzle through the logic of this: If the opposite of a "pure" or "high-minded" man is one who is "alive," then isn't that what he is accusing her of being? A woman who is, simply, *alive*? Then why is she so upset? I will soon be distracted from this question by the blood of Revolution, the balalaika music, the widescreen expanses of yellow flowers and snowy steppes, but I'm pretty sure this movie wants me, like Komarovsky, to judge and sexually shame Lara with that word.

Slut.

However . . . on some subliminal level, I feel that label actually has very little to do with sex—and far more to do with a woman's choices and priorities. And who gets to determine what those are, or should be.

In my midtwenties, my friend Helen tells me she is becoming aware of her biological clock revving up; she is feeling an urgency to find the right guy and settle down. She believes the female body, at some point, *craves* being pregnant, *wants* to give birth, hence the simmering instinct to date, get married, create a family. I am skeptical— what about the influence of societal pressure, what about cultural

---

47 *Doctor Zhivago* (MGM, 1965): screenplay by Robert Bolt, based on the novel by Boris Pasternak; directed by David Lean; with Julie Christie, Rod Steiger, and Omar Sharif

convention and conditioning?—but she insists it is a physiological drive for all women, the female's instinctive rush to embrace her fertility at its peak. I feel resistance to the idea of being so biologically, hormonally, Darwinally controlled—as well as to her heteronormative vision, although I do not have that word for it then. But I have zero interest in "settling down," I try to explain to her, and I've never really imagined, for myself, a life of marriage and children—there was no little-girl dress-up as a bride, for me, no play-acted weddings, no couplehood crockery dreams, no pretend mommy-cuddling a pretend baby doll. She smiles indulgently; it is going to happen to me any time now, she assures, that desire, that need; I will hear my anxious eggs and empty uterus begin screaming for attention, and then I will understand. All right, I think. Helen is two years older than I am, so I figure she has the authority on this issue.

And the movies back her up, don't they? All those love stories I've spent a lifetime watching and being charmed or tearfully enthralled by are, in fact, so *goal-oriented*: Let's get this gal a Prince Charming husband, let's get this guy to realize his dream girl is right in front of him, let's get these crazy kids together! The romantic comedies, from screwball Howard Hawks, insightful Preston Sturges, witty Nora Ephron, adolescent-angsty John Hughes, even crudely sweet Judd Apatow, all scramble to keep the bantering, sparring lovers apart for two hours, due to contrived miscommunications or inconvenient logistics or the quirky character flaws of jealously or pride, until all that gets sorted out and apologized for and Harry and Sally are off to the domestic bliss of the Happy Ending, where they will banter and spar as a team forever. The dramatic romances tend to have bigger stakes—a war is in the way, or an illness, issues of honor, profound and problematic values, or large-scale sociopolitical challenges, see: *Casablanca, From Here to Eternity, The Way We Were, Out of Africa, Titanic*—but the end game is the same: These two meant-to-be-together people must realize their enduring love and create a home and hearth and progeny of their own. It is destiny. Or, if that proves impossible, well, what a tragedy, to deny this fated pair their pairing, what lonely half-lives they are doomed to live, wandering the earth in their existential solitude!

All of which is summed up in that one famous line:

JERRY MAGUIRE
You . . . you *complete* me,

he says to his sort-of girlfriend, Dorothy—and when gorgeous Tom Cruise says this to normal-pretty Renée Zellweger, we all collectively, dreamily sigh with romantic satisfaction.[48]

So it is only a matter of time, I suppose, before my own life settles into this narrative construct, or, at least, focuses on achieving it: The happily-ever-after pairing up of soul mates, this Noah's Ark template of adulthood. All right, then. One day, I will be *complete*.

But meanwhile, I am having a pretty marvelous time. I am having delightful or tortured affairs, thrilling sex, falling in lust all over the place: The English guy on a Greek island, the Italian guy in Paris, the guy I meet on the picket line during the Writers' Guild strike, the hungry, still-single groomsmen I meet at friends' destination weddings and invite back to my hotel for the night. All the hip bars and house music clubs, all the bubbling hot-tub parties, all the flirty meet-cutes in supermarkets and bowling alleys that Nora Ephron herself would applaud. I am the star of my own romantic comedy life, my own epic dramas of love: I lose my mind over a guy from high school who has transformed from the sweet nerd I knew in eleventh grade to now-arrogant asshole and breaks my heart; I become insanely infatuated with my best gay friend's best straight guy friend, who dumps me two nights before I am scheduled to have brain surgery; I fall madly in love with my best girlfriend and try to learn How to Be a Lesbian by watching a lot of dreadful movies that show lesbians as borderline-psychotics (*The Killing of Sister George*) or merely going through a developmental rite-of-passage "phase" (*Personal Best*) or show lesbian sex in the blandest, most boring way possible, as if sex between women has no more sweat or friction than gently brushing each other's hair or frolicking through a field of daisies (*Lianna*, *Desert Hearts*, and yes, despite the hotness of Susan Sarandon and Catherine Deneuve, *The Hunger*)—thankfully, I go on to sleep with a lot of other

---

48 *Jerry Maguire* (TriStar Pictures, 1996): written and directed by Cameron Crowe; with Tom Cruise and Renée Zellweger

women and erase those tepid or faux-lesbian images from my mind forever.

By my late thirties, however, everyone seems to be doing that hand-in-hand walk up the ramp to the Ark except me. I like my sexual adventures, the variety and challenge, the thrill of the chase, the delight of discovery—I am enthusiastically and discriminately promiscuous. But I also like having a boyfriend or a girlfriend; I like love. I like the mutual emotional support, the way sex takes on resonance and layers, the evolution of shared gestures and silly jokes. I like reenacting Annie and Alvy's escaped-lobster scene from *Annie Hall* and the sharing of candlelit intimacies in a bubbly tub scene from, well, every love story movie ever. I have the serial monogamy thing down. But I can never quite make that leap to a shared *life*, the ultimate commitment and dedication to "togetherness" . . . and as Alvy says:

ALVY SINGER

A relationship, I think, is like a shark. You know? It has to constantly move forward or it dies. And I think what we got on our hands is a dead shark.[49]

And thus I develop a track record—a reputation?—as someone who in her life is racking up quite a number of dead sharks. I look around, I see my friends' relatively happy marriages and longtime companionships, their bridal-shower gravy boats and their adoration for their vanilla- and vomit-scented babies, and I don't envy them a moment of their paired-up or family-based lives. What is wrong with me? I worry. Am I really just some impure, low-minded slut? Why aren't I looking to be *completed*?

Maybe it's that I don't have a lot of happy formative role models to look to; my own parents' marriage was hardly a model of positive communication or emotionally fulfilling contentment, and in the twenty-five years since their divorce, I have witnessed my mother's absolute terror at being alone lead to desperate and self-destructive

49 *Annie Hall* (United Artists, 1977): written by Woody Allen and Marshall Brickman; directed by Woody Allen; with Woody Allen and Diane Keaton

decisions. And all those movies about relationships, both comedic and serious, tend to focus on the *conflicts* of couplehood, of course, the sheer messiness of two people trying to reconcile their independent selfhoods—otherwise there would be no story. This is Screenwriting 101, I get that—keep the happy stuff off-screen; it is increasing conflict that fuels narrative momentum—but still, it doesn't exactly trigger a desire to emulate these characters' turbulent romantic lives. Who wants all that drama?

By my early forties, I realize that storied "instinct" to go through life as a team, as one half of a hand-in-hand collaboration or as the nurturing matriarch of my own little clan, has never, in fact, kicked in for me. I like being in a relationship, but I am not looking for a *partnership*. The thing I tried to explain to my friend Helen twenty years earlier is the simple truth: What I have always ended up craving, ultimately, even when involved with the greatest guy or the most wonderful woman, is to be left alone. With a dog, and my dear friends a phone call away, my smooth-sheeted bed to myself, a quiet, molecule-steady room of my own in which to knit and read and do the work I am passionate about, to find every single thing exactly as I have left it, and the gift of absolute and autonomous self-determination. I know a hundred delicious ways to cook one chicken breast; I also love taking me and a book out to a nice dinner. I love traveling to my own circadian rhythms, having an empty seat on either side and the bag of popcorn to myself at a movie. To quote another less famous line from *Jerry Maguire*:

DOROTHY
```
I've had three lovers in the past four years, and
they all ran a distant second to a good book and
a warm bath . . .
```

and *Yes*, I think. Not always, but often. And I have never, in my entire life, felt the slightest aging-egg desire or uterine craving to have or raise a child—it is too late now, anyway, I have pretty much reached the biological end point on that one. Yes, I understand I have missed out on what is probably the most profound experience a woman can have. And that is perfectly fine with me.

So, begin the psychoanalysis: I am a child of divorce, of an emotionally absent and alcoholic father, a grappling, emotionally desperate mother. Hence, I obviously have "intimacy issues," an inability to trust, and the resultant, connect-the-dots label: A "fear of commitment." Maybe a dysfunctional degree of emotional immaturity, a self-absorbed selfishness, perhaps some narcissistic personality disorder? Sure, why not? I've heard all these textbook theories—if not directly, specifically about me, then about unmarried-by-choice, childless-by-choice, sexualby-choice women in general. Even my dearest of friends have sometimes ... questioned how I have chosen to live my life. Aren't you *lonely*? they ask, with a hint of puzzled concern. What about your old age, who will take care of you? So, who are you dating *these* days, who are you sleeping with *now*? they ask, and sometimes that comes with a whiff of envy, sometimes with a tiny judgmental edge. (*Slut*.) Well, maybe I just haven't met the right person yet, I still sometimes find myself defensively offering. And I value every sexual or romantic experience I've had. Why is relationship longevity the goal, a marker of success, why is anything that falls short of a golden anniversary considered a failure?

Or hey, maybe I'm simply part of a larger anthropological or sociological continuum? Maybe I illustrate the vaster, more textured range of human experience? Maybe I am an evolutionary outlier? I understand my life does not look like most women's—but surely not everyone is meant to pair up or reproduce.

But other than myself and my own life, I don't have a lot of other real-life exemplars to back up my argument; recent studies may show the increasing rate of single-person households, but when I look around, they are still quite few and far between. So, of course, I look to the movies; there have to be plenty of emotionally well-adjusted, professionally accomplished, socially engaged, single, childless, sexually active female characters, right? For whom a shared home and hearth and children romping at one's feet are absolutely not a priority, not even some goal to be achieved, but nevertheless are happy as independent clams?

Well, there are the Heroines, often based on extraordinary reallife women who dedicate themselves to a Big Purpose: Erin of *Erin Brockovich* takes on the corrupt Pacific Gas and Electric in order to seek justice for a poisoned, powerless community; Norma Rae of *Norma*

Rae risks death in order to unionize her textile mill; Karen Silkwood will actually die trying to speak truth to power in *Silkwood*.[50] I see all these movies and am inspired by their lead characters' commitment and bravery; these are the pure and high-minded women who will risk everything to change the world for the better. I am also glad to see the men in their lives take a backseat as supporting characters; they might grumble about the trouble their leading-lady women are getting themselves into, but they will also take care of the kids while the women are doing so. And there you go—these women are also mothers, motivated in part by the selfless desire to improve their own children's lives. I admire these women, but I am no heroine; I wimp out at the slightest hint of jeopardy, I don't have the energy to take on the evil conglomerates of the world, and, without children, any positive impact I might seek to make or legacy I might leave behind is abstract, theoretical. (The kickass Action Heroines don't count as models, either—the Ripleys or Femme Nikitas or Sarah Connors are great fun but bear no relation to my life; I will applaud them from the safety and comfort and quiet of my couch.)

Then there are the Pathetic Career Women, the poor deluded darlings who seek fulfillment in their careers, their work. At eleven years old I adored the movie *Mahogany*, went three times to see the garishly costumed Diana Ross's Tracy fight her way to the top of the glamorous fashion industry, only to learn in the last ten minutes that

BOYFRIEND BRIAN

Success is *nothing* without someone you love to share it with!

as her boyfriend Brian had prophesized, practically threatened her earlier in the film.[51] Come on, success at something you have worked

---

50 *Erin Brockovich* (Universal Pictures, 2000): written by Susannah Grant; directed by Steven Soderbergh; with Julia Roberts; *Norma Rae* (20th Century Fox, 1979): written by Irving Ravetch and Harriet Frank Jr.; directed by Martin Ritt; with Sally Field; *Silkwood* (20th Century Fox, 1983): written by Nora Ephron and Alice Arlen; directed by Mike Nichols; with Meryl Streep

51 *Mahogany* (Paramount Pictures, 1975): story by Toni Amber, screenplay by John Byrum; directed by Berry Gordy; with Diana Ross and Billy Dee Williams

your entire life for is still *something*, still feels pretty damn good, doesn't it? But she at last realizes how desolate her life is; she walks away from fortune and fame to become *his* helpmate, a partner in *his* life, and *What an idiot*, I thought every time. Bridget Jones, for all her ostensible commitment to personal and professional growth, never wavers from her ultimate desire in life: Gaining Colin Firth's validating, sustaining love in *Bridget Jones's Diary* and then trying to keep it without going too nuts in *Bridget Jones: The Edge of Reason*.[52] And pity poor, damaged, self-defeating, all-alone, and clinically depressed Kristen Wiig in *Bridesmaids*; everyone is getting married or finding love or being beautiful or enjoying success except her.[53] A talented-but-failed baker, her tragic-ness is best illustrated in a long sequence where, in a burst of focused energy, with furrowed brow and deft fingers, she mixes, stirs, bakes, frosts, and decorates the most exquisite Georgia O'Keeffe-ish cupcake ever made: It is a work of art. And then she eats it, all by herself, her one single cupcake, a look of sad and lonely resignation on her frosting-smeared face. Oh my God, can't she be proud of that, can't she even enjoy her own damn cupcake? I want to protest. But, no: A cupcake is *nothing* without someone you love to share it with.

Sometimes these frustrated or misguided professional gals tip into Crazy Career Women: Glenn Close's iconic Alex in *Fatal Attraction* starts off promisingly enough: A successful, single, childless, sexually assertive editor in her late thirties . . . until she fixates on the married Michael Douglas as her savior from spinsterhood and the future father of her last-chance child, and the frenzied alarm of her biological clock drives her to murderous, psychotic rage.[54] Meryl Streep's Miranda Priestly in

---

52 *Bridget Jones's Diary* (Miramax Films, 2001): screenplay by Helen Fielding, Andrew Davies, and Richard Curtis, based on the novel by Helen Fielding; directed by Sharon Maguire; with Renée Zellweger and Colin Firth; *Bridget Jones: The Edge of Reason* (Miramax Films, 2004): screenplay by Andrew Davies, Helen Fielding, Richard Curtis, and Adam Brooks, based on the novel by Helen Fielding; directed by Beeban Kidron; with Renée Zellweger and Colin Firth

53 *Bridesmaids* (Universal Pictures, 2011): written by Kristen Wiig and Annie Mumolo; directed by Paul Feig; with Kristen Wiig

54 *Fatal Attraction* (Paramount Pictures, 1987): screenplay by James Dearden; directed by Adrian Lyne; with Glenn Close and Michael Douglas

The Devil Wears Prada is made figuratively, comedically satanic—the Boss from Hell—in her focus on her career; she isn't single, she is a married mother of twins, but her marriage breaks up and her children are feral little monsters, home and hearth destroyed by her coldhearted Queen Bee ambition.[55] Sigourney Weaver is another Boss from Hell in *Working Girl*, whose duplicitous single-woman villainy is also played for laughs—she is so focused on being the Alpha Female that she is oblivious to Melanie Griffith stealing both her career and her man right from under her nose; she is left with nothing at the end, and we cheer her comeuppance.[56] And I count *Up in the Air*'s Vera Farmiga as a Crazy Career Woman; initially we are intended to enjoy her character (also named Alex) as a female George Clooney, a professionally successful, sexually assured, wholly delightful woman as committed to a Don't Tie Me Down lifestyle as his character, Ryan.[57] But while Ryan's trajectory in the film is (ostensibly) toward emotional growth and maturity, culminating in his wanting to commit to a relationship with Alex—"I am lonely," he confesses to her, which she, tellingly, just laughs at— Alex is revealed to be a manipulative, duplicitous married woman with children, who, to my mind, borders on sociopathic. (A far more benign Nutty Career Woman would be Nurse Jenny Fields, from *The World According to Garp*, who realizes her desire for a child but not a husband makes her *A Sexual Suspect*—the title of her feminist manifesto—in the eyes of the world.[58] I applaud her defiance of convention, but she loses me for her antilust asexuality.)

There are also the films that showcase the Mysterious Woman in Power—think Joan Allen in *The Bourne Identity* series or Jodie Foster

---

55 *The Devil Wears Prada* (20th Century Fox, 2006): screenplay by Aline Brosh McKenna, based on the novel by Lauren Weisberg; directed by David Frankel; with Meryl Streep and Anne Hathaway

56 *Working Girl* (20th Century Fox, 1988): written by Kevin Wade; directed by Mike Nichols; with Melanie Griffith, Sigourney Weaver, and Harrison Ford

57 *Up in the Air* (Paramount Pictures, 2009): screenplay by Jason Reitman and Sheldon Tuner, based on the novel by Walter Kirn; directed by Jason Reitman; with George Clooney and Vera Farmiga

58 *The World According to Garp* (Warner Bros., 1982): screenplay by Steve Tesich, based on the novel by John Irving; directed by George Roy Hill; with Glenn Close and Robin Williams

in just about anything after she turned forty: Severe, shadowy women who run big, shadowy things . . . and that is all they do. It is nice to see powerful women in command, in positions of authority, but we have access to no other aspect of their lives. Do they ever get to sit on their couch and read? When do they knit? Go out to dinner with friends? Whom do they have sex with?

But it isn't always about women who misprioritize career; the women who prioritize their self-determination, especially sexually, must also suffer, be taken down a peg or two. Sometimes they have to die: In *Thelma & Louise*, the two women head off on a girlfriend weekend; Thelma flirts herself silly with some guy in a bar and is saved from rape by gun-toting Louise—who then shoots and kills the guy, outraged by his crude and cavalier ugliness.[59] I'm not excusing the killing (although we've seen male antiheroes blow guys away for a lot less without blinking an eye . . .), and Louise deserves to be held responsible for her actions. But as the two women try to evade capture, it is their refusal to conform to code (choosing to leave their men behind, casual sex with a hitchhiking Brad Pitt, an unwillingness to turn their destinies over to a system they believe is stacked against them) that both exalts and dooms them. In *Looking for Mr. Goodbar*, good-girl schoolteacher-by-day Theresa (Diane Keaton) rejects the boring nice guy offering her that conventional home and hearth (and also has her tubes tied: "Just fix it so I can never have children," she says to her doctor, which we are meant to find pathological rather than responsible) in favor of a lot of recreational sex with strange guys she meets in bars, a hobby that becomes increasingly dysfunctional and addictive.[60] In the end, one of them flips out and stabs her to death: Ah, the wages of a barren sluthood. Angie Dickinson must also pay a hefty price, in *Dressed to Kill*: She cheats on her husband with a steamy-sex stranger, discovers she's probably just contracted a venereal disease (dirty slut), and then is slaughtered

59 *Thelma & Louise* (MGM, 1991): written by Callie Khouri; directed by Ridley Scott; with Susan Sarandon and Geena Davis

60 *Looking for Mr. Goodbar* (Paramount Pictures, 1977): screenplay by Richard Brooks, based on the novel by Judith Rossner; directed by Richard Brooks; with Diane Keaton

with a straight-edged razor wielded by a self-loathing transgendered psychiatrist.[61] Even Lara, after leaving Komarovsky (she also tries to shoot him but misses), will be punished for the rest of the Russian Revolution and the remaining three hours of *Doctor Zhivago* for her deeply regretted choice of a sexual liaison for the wrong reasons, with the wrong man.

So where are they, the happy and identifiable models for me, the women who make choices about love and life and sex and work and independence I can relate to? *An Unmarried Woman* doesn't seem to offer that, to start: Wife and mother Erica (Jill Clayburgh) is devastated when her husband of seventeen years leaves her for another (younger) woman.[62] But by the end she learns how to be not just her own woman, but also her own person, how to reconstruct a life by herself, for herself: Her own apartment, a new job, new lovers. Offered the chance to pair up with gorgeous, sexy, famous, rich, artsy Alan Bates—which, it is implied, would require her to reduce herself to one half of a person all over again, in order to then become whole once more, to be made "complete" by a relationship—she demurs. She wants the relationship (Alan Bates, of course!), but on her own, I-am-already-complete terms; the final shot is a lovely, empowering one, Erica making her way down the street carrying the massive painting Alan Bates has given her, all by herself.

JUDY BENJAMIN

Did you see that movie, *An Unmarried Woman*? Well, I didn't get it. I mean, I would have been Mrs. Alan Bates *so fast* . . . ,

Judy Benjamin says just a few years later—*An Unmarried Woman* was such a significant cultural touchpoint that it is used as shorthand in *Private Benjamin* to illustrate how Judy views herself and her destined

---

61 *Dressed to Kill* (Filmways Pictures, 1980): written and directed by Brian De Palma; with Angie Dickinson and Michael Caine

62 *An Unmarried Woman* (20th Century Fox, 1978): written and directed by Paul Mazursky; with Jill Clayburgh and Alan Bates

path in life.[63] When Judy's husband, Yale, drops dead of a heart attack on their wedding night, this spoiled and dependent child-woman falls apart:

JUDY BENJAMIN

I mean, I don't know what I'm supposed to *do*, if I'm not going to be *married*!

she wails, and it's true: She has no identity whatsoever beyond pretty sweet daughter or trophy wife, has never needed to find one. So, she fecklessly joins the army (wackiness ensues, allowing us to overlook the promilitaristic politics); turns out she is surprisingly good at stuff, develops a sense of purpose and self-esteem, and has multiorgasmic sex with hot French gynecologist Henri (Armand Assante). But the army stuff gets complicated, and Judy decides to quit the hard, sweaty work of that life and go live with Henri in his gorgeous château outside of Paris, to marry him and become a Frenchified princess-housewife in designer clothing. He eventually reveals himself to be a controlling, lying, cheating jerk . . . but look what he is offering, is that *really* too much to put up with? (Even I would be tempted—look at that château!) But at the wedding, in her last moment before taking that vow, Judy flashback-reflects on who she once was, who she was able to become, and who she might still be able to be. Her choices, her priorities. And she walks out of the faux-fairy-tale château, rips off the white organdy veil, and marches off and away—a visual echo of *An Unmarried Woman*'s Erica, in this final shot—down her own path, all by herself, to the beat of her own independent, victorious, self-determined drum.

Melanie Griffith in *Working Girl* might also come close (despite the condescension of the title—she is thirty years old, for heaven's sake); she finally is rewarded with the professional success she has worked so hard for, and gets Harrison Ford, too, and a supportive best friend, a full and balanced life she gets to revel in without being called upon

---

63 *Private Benjamin* (Warner Bros., 1980): written by Nancy Meyers, Charles Shyer, and Harvey Miller; directed by Howard Zieff; with Goldie Hawn and Armand Assante

to make a *Mahogany*-style choice. But she is still happily shacking up with Harrison Ford at the end—and while the scene of their fumbling to slurp coffee from a shared mug and feed each other breakfast toast in their cramped kitchen cubicle is very charming, I cannot imagine doing that every morning for the rest of my life. I'm happy to have overnight visitors, yes—but I also like waking up alone. I like my solitary sun-dawning kitchen. I like my own cup of drip coffee, made with a No. 2 filter, and my single-serving bowl of oatmeal, all to myself.

There are other cinematic examples out there . . . there have to be. But I'm racking my brain to find one fully parallel role model for this, my singular life. Alone is not lonely, but, as other outliers know—racial, sexual, sociocultural—it can feel lonesome to have no cultural mirror in which to see reflected, and thus validated, one's true nature, one's essential identity. Movies love those big set-piece scenes of engagements, weddings, anniversaries, the birth of children—and I celebrate my friends' real-life versions of these events—but I have none of these markers in my own life.

However . . . if I have never quite seen my exact female doppelganger up there on the cinema screen, if a lifetime of movies has shown me how to be so many different things *except* my particular way of being a woman in the world, doesn't that mean I have, in fact, despite that societal pressure, that cultural convention and conditioning, defined this core aspect of myself all *by* myself? Constructed a life, like a beautiful flowery cupcake, all on my own from scratch? And that my carefully calibrated equilibrium of priorities and choices actually has created the most authentic me?

There are far more than your two kinds of women, Victor Komarovsky. You can keep your purity and your high-mindness. I'm happy to settle for just being genuinely, completely, alive.

HOW TO
DIE WITH
STYLE

TAKING ON TUMORS, ORCHESTRATING THE HAPPY END, AND WRITING IN THE DARK

Love Story
Dark Victory
Harold and Maude
Soylent Green
All That Jazz
Anne of the Thousand Days
I Want to Live!
In Cold Blood
Dead Man Walking
The Green Mile
Butch Cassidy and the Sundance Kid
Thelma & Louise
Gallipoli
Glory
Saving Private Ryan
Terms of Endearment
Million Dollar Baby
The English Patient

watched my first person die when I was six years old.

It was so beautiful, a lovely thing to see. And a loving thing, a moment of profound intimacy, honed by imminent loss. It was a love story, literally: My mother took me to see *Love Story* when it opened in 1970.[64] Erich Segal had famously written the screenplay first, then recycled it into a novel that went tear-jerking bestseller before the movie even opened, a novel my mother had wept her way through multiple times, as had all our mothers, the dog-eared, tearstained book ubiquitous on nightstands, tucked in beach tote bags and bathroom magazine racks. It's a very adult story with adult themes, she enthused on the way in the car, but such a beautiful story about a man and a girl who were in love, and then the girl tragically dies, and I was very mature for my age, and she couldn't get a babysitter, and she was sure I could handle it.

OLIVER VOICEOVER

What can you say about a twenty-five-year-old girl who died? That she was beautiful and brilliant? That she loved Mozart and Bach, and the Beatles? And me . . . ,

begins the movie, a morose, pretty young man thinking this while gazing upon a symbolically barren field of snow, and of course I can handle it, this adult story with adult themes. Rich boy Oliver "Preppie" Barrett (Ryan O'Neil, very pretty) falls in love with brainy, classical music–loving proletarian Jenny Cavalleri (Ali MacGraw, not as pretty as Ryan but looking like a real person with her thick unarched eyebrows and crooked tooth) at some college where it is always snowing, and they make snowy angels and bicker adorably in the snow. I don't really get the sociopolitical context of their

---

64 *Love Story* (Paramount Pictures, 1970): written by Erich Segal (screenplay first then, novel); directed by Arthur Hiller; with Ryan O'Neal and Ali MacGraw

bickering or the messy family dynamics (Oliver's father doesn't like Jenny, because why . . . ?), but there's some sweet closed-mouth kissing and a soft-focus sex scene that shows just the right, unfrightening amount of naked skin, and at their wedding they vow to "stick by each other as long as we live . . . to love and cherish until death us do part," and because I already know she dies, indeed *has* to die in the next forty-five minutes, I do understand this vow is meant to be tinged with extra bittersweetness. (One confusing thing, however— when Oliver apologizes for having said something mean during a fight, Jenny replies "Love means never having to say you're sorry," which makes no sense to me at all because isn't apologizing *always* the good and right thing to do, *especially* to someone you care so tenderly about in all that snow? Even at six I feel about this statement the way Ryan O'Neal will respond to it in self-parody a few years later in the film *What's Up, Doc?*: "That's the stupidest thing I've ever heard."[65])

And then Jenny, who has been unrelentingly vibrant with health, playing volleyball and prancing around in colorful tights, is deemed to be "malfunctioning" in a scene between Oliver and a Doctor:

DOCTOR

    Jenny is very sick.

OLIVER

    Define "very sick."

DOCTOR

    She's dying.

Again, we already know this (and my mother is already crying), but for the first time I am wondering *how* and *why* this "dying" is to happen, especially in light of Jenny's radiant, love-infused bloom. The Doctor offers no explanation, says only that her blood has been

---

65 *What's Up, Doc?* (Warner Bros., 1972): written by Buck Henry, David Newman, and Robert Benton, story by Peter Bogdanovich; directed by Peter Bogdanovich; with Ryan O'Neal and Barbra Streisand

tested three times, which is worrisome; to my child memory/mind, that means three scary trips to the doctor, three times that rubber strap is tied bruisingly, pinchingly tight around a tender upper arm, three rubbings with a harsh cotton ball, three hot steely punctures to look away from, and then three ruby tubes.

OLIVER

She's only twenty-four. Will it be painful?

DOCTOR

Hopefully not. . . .

And now I am truly, suddenly scared, because I haven't really thought before about *painful*. I have no memory of my parents ever "explaining" death to me, but I'm sure it was secular, uneuphemistic, and stripped of softening metaphor, no "going to sleep for a long time" or the vague "passing away," no haunting Grim Reaper with a scythe challenging you to chess, or hanging out with God in heaven and waiting for other dead people you know to show up for some fluffy fantastical reunion in the clouds. By now, at six, I understand that death is simply the final end of a thing, and the thing then disappears forever; I have flushed dead goldfish down the toilet without a second thought, have buried dead pet mice in the backyard with minimum ceremony. But I had no experience of their *dying*, and certainly no sense of *pain*, only the quiet simple stillness of death: Finding the mouse lying soundless and stiff in the wood shavings, the peacefully floating, mouth-agape fish. Pain is what frightens me; it is blood tests, yes, it is vaccinations, searing earaches and falls from playground jungle gyms and, memorized somewhere in my body if not my conscious mind, the dim cruelty of a spinal tap when I was two and a half. An adult in pain is even scarier, because they are supposed to be beyond and above that, brave and unflinching. Pain is for children, the thing for adults to kiss away and disappear, hold your hand through until the needle is gone, the arm unstrapped. Who is there to disappear an adult's pain?

One more brief snowy scene, Jenny watching Oliver ice-skate around, and then she sweetly asks to go to the hospital. Cut to the

Doctor telling Oliver she's refused some medicine that would "slow cell destruction" and result in bad side effects, and Oliver insists,

OLIVER
Jenny's the boss! Whatever she wants,

and of course, the dying person should be in charge, it's *her* death, her special day to celebrate, like a birthday. The dying person should get ice cream sundaes with extra nuts and not have to set the table for her last supper, be allowed to stay up watching age-inappropriate shows on TV as late as she wants. We finally enter Jenny's hospital room with Oliver, and my heart is beating, because what is it we will find here, in this scene of *dying*? I think of a mouse squealing, the little goldfish choking for a fish's version of air. I feel somewhere in my body a large but unseen needle in my spine and being told not to move, it's okay (but it isn't), it will be over soon (no, it takes forever. . . .) But Jenny is lying beautiful and unpained in a white lace nightie, her long dark hair fanned out on the pillow, her lips glowing red as if she's just come in from fashioning those angels in the snow. One arm is connected to a subtle IV, but that is our only visual cue that announces *hospital*, or *illness*, or *death*—we could be in a hotel room, one with tasteful appointments and flattering lighting, a bed awaiting a honeymoon intimacy.

JENNY
It doesn't hurt, Ollie, really it doesn't. It's like falling off a cliff in slow motion, you know? Only after a while you wish you'd hit the ground already, you know?

And I am so relieved—the idea of falling in slow motion is too abstract for me to grasp, but I do grasp *it doesn't hurt*. It is my father's deft removal of a splinter, the squeeze of a soothing, nonstinging antiseptic cream on a skinned knee, and yes, finally, everything is okay now.

JENNY

Would you please do something for me, Oliver?
Would you please hold me? I mean really hold me,
next to me.

So Oliver reclines on the bed beside her, the camera hovering respectfully above, gazing down upon this pretty young couple in a final but eternal moment of grace. What can you say about a twenty-five-year-old girl who died? That her death—*and* her dying—was beautiful, peaceful, a lovely and loving thing. My mother is sobbing, but for me, their last embrace, his anguish and her crooked-tooth beauty, are all wonderful, the perfect end; it is Jenny's tragic-heroine death, after all, that makes this tale bestseller special, creates a block-buster film, that makes a *story* of their pretty snowflake love.

My mother and I also watched *Dark Victory* on late-night television together—she was a crazy Bette Davis fan, and I'd already seen *Mr. Skeffington* and the duckling-to-lonely-swan *Now, Voyager*, had already fallen in love myself with those plummy, saucery Bette Davis eyes.[66] In *Dark Victory*, Bette is spoiled, fun-loving Society Gal Judith, who suddenly gets dreadful headaches, can't manage the hand-eye coordination to light her own cigarette or remember yesterday's bridge game. The handsome Dr. Steele (George Brent, who I get is meant to be handsome but has a silly pencil moustache) diagnoses her with a *brain tumor*, but I am as mystified by that phrase as I was by Jenny's unexplained blood problem. Judith is self-defensively defiant:

JUDITH

I'm well! I'm well! I'm young and strong and
nothing can touch me!

But Dr. Steele insists on surgery, the need to snip out this problematic thing in her head:

---

66 *Dark Victory* (Warner Bros., 1939): screenplay by Casey Robinson, based on the play by George Emerson Brewer Jr. and Bertram Bloch; directed by Edmund Goulding; with Bette Davis, George Brent, and Geraldine Fitzgerald

DR. STEELE

After all, the brain's like any other part of the
body. Things get out of kilter, and have to be
adjusted . . . Technically, it's called a _____
[word I can't catch, maybe not even a real scientific term]. It
is rather like a plant. A parasitic one.

The night before surgery, Judith is agitated and petulant, complaining about her dreary hospital gown and her biggest concern:

JUDITH

Will they cut off my hair?

DR. STEELE

Just a little bit.

JUDITH

I don't want my hair cut off.

DR. STEELE

(stating the obvious, yet reassuring) It'll grow
back. . . .

And after the surgery, it clearly was just a "little bit"—she now wears a series of small pointy beanies over her tumbling curls, which I suppose are meant to be both fashionable and cover what must be an infinitesimal brain surgery scar. But the pathological findings are bad; there will be a recurrence, perhaps as soon as ten months, and Judith is absolutely going to die.

DR. STEELE

A girl like that, so alive! So entitled to live!
And this thing, this *growth* comes along and puts
a period to it! Makes you almost wish it happened
on the table. . . .

Judith's best friend Ann is devastated, worried about the return of the headaches, about Judith suffering, about that "ghastly confusion." But Dr. Steele reassures her (and me):

DR. STEELE

No, she's not going to suffer anymore. That's all behind her . . . that's the freakish nature of this thing. She'll seem well and normal, just like everybody else.

BEST FRIEND ANN

How will it come?

DR. STEELE

Quietly, peacefully.

BEST FRIEND ANN

God's last small mercy. Will she have no warning? No chance to be ready?

DR. STEELE

There may be a moment near the end when her sight may not be quite as good as usual. A dimming of vision. Then a few hours, perhaps three or four. . . .

They agree she mustn't know, and this is bizarre to me, to *keep* something like that from the dying someone; I assume getting "ready" to die means tidying up her room and saying good-bye to people, but how can she do that if she doesn't know "some growth" is about to put a period to the end of her life? But meanwhile Judith and the doctor fall madly in love, and so when she does find out about PROGNOSIS NEGATIVE—the words leaping out of the file she snoops into, swelling up on-screen to meet us in an alarming font—she feels doubly betrayed, goes back to her old partying ways, and is generally bitter and bitchy until Dr. Steele confronts her:

DR. STEELE

Judy! I want you to find peace! We all have to
die. The tragic difference is that you know when,
and we don't. The important thing is the same for
all of us: To live our lives so we can meet death
when it comes, beautifully and finely!

Which convinces her, No, she "can't die like this! When it comes,
it *must* be met beautifully and finely," yes! She marries her handsome
doctor, and they live in Vermont for a few beautiful and fine months.
Then one bright sunny day Judith comments there must be a storm
coming, "Look how it's clouding up, getting darker by the second
. . . funny, I can still feel the sun on my hands . . . ," and she and we
realize the punctuation that is her grammatical moment of death has
come at last. She sends her doctor/husband away without telling him
she has gone blind in the past five minutes and gracefully, resolutely
climbs the stairs to her bedroom alone in her darkness, prays briefly,
then reclines, one arm glamorously extended above her head, looking
heroically beautiful, those now-dimming Bette Davis eyes as serene as
Jenny's. Celestial music swells, the angels sing, and the screen goes to
a soft blur, inviting us to identify with Judith's gentle, unraging exit
into the good night of her dark victory. Fade to black, the end, THE
END. My mother, again, is sobbing, and I realize it is sad, of course—"a
girl like that, so entitled to live!"—but I am again primarily reassured;
death is painless and glamorous, quiet and peaceful. A moment of
ultimate beauty and fineness, indeed.

Death is also something to be orchestrated, planned for: I see *Harold
and Maude* in 1971, when I am seven, and am intrigued by eighteen-
year-old Harold's theatrical faux-suicide tableaux (hanging, self-
immolation, etc.), his investment in death as spectacle; I am not a child
to act out, myself, but there is something in his seeking an insistent
affirmation of his existence by dangling his death in front of people—
especially his histrionic, self-absorbed mother—that touches me in a
way I feel but don't really understand.[67] I'm also delighted by perky

---

67 *Harold and Maude* (Paramount Pictures, 1971): written by Colin Higgins;
directed by Hal Ashby; with Ruth Gordon and Bud Cort

septuagenarian Maude (Ruth Gordon; please, please, let me be Ruth
Gordon when I am an old, purple-wearing woman) and the January-
December love affair with Harold (Bud Cort, angel-faced nerd), a relationship whose idiosyncratic tenderness engages me more than Oliver
and Jenny's formulaic quipping. And it is ultimately Maude's death
that stays with and inspires me; when Harold throws her a daisy-
decorated birthday party/marriage proposal, Maude is so moved:

                         MAUDE
        Oh, Harold. I am happy. I couldn't imagine a
        lovelier farewell.

                         HAROLD
        Farewell?

                         MAUDE
        Yes. It's my eightieth birthday.

                         HAROLD
        Well, you're not going anywhere.
                    (long confused pause)
        Are you?

                         MAUDE
        Yes, dear. I took the tablets an hour ago. I'll
        be gone by midnight.

                         HAROLD
                    (long horrified pause)
        What?!

He flips out. A screeching siren, an ambulance, Harold clutching
Maude's hand.

                         HAROLD
        Don't die, Maude! For Christ's sake. . . . Don't
        die! I love you!

MAUDE

Oh, Harold! That's *wonderful*. Go, and love some
more. . . .

and the last we see of Maude is her peaceful face, wizened and wise,
as she's wheeled off on a gurney, twirling a daisy. No writhing in pain,
no stomach cramped by those magically toxic tablets. This was a longtime plan of Maude's, hints dropped throughout the movie ("Well,
there's no question my body's giving out," she said earlier, "I'm well
into autumn. But it's all going to end this Saturday. . . .") Harold is
desolate, but if the infusion of passionate life energy that was their
love didn't change Maude's mind, we know it will change Harold
forever; the final moment of the film is Harold, after his final faux-
suicidal display of crashing his car off a cliff, dancing along, playing a
banjo while Cat Stevens reminds us all "if you want to live high, live
high! And if you want to live low, live low! 'Cause there's a million
ways to go, you know that there are. . . ."[68]

It wasn't just Maude's love that inspires Harold; her death is the
experience through which he will finally choose to embrace life. And
a death with such style! I want to live like Ruth Gordon, but I want to
die like Maude.

The best death, though, is in *Soylent Green*.[69] It's 2022, the water is
poisoned, our soil and atmosphere are polluted, the greenhouse effect
has created an unending heat wave, New York City has forty million
people, and while a very few of them live in fancy modular apart-
ments full of Lucite and dangly glass things, with access to real food
and water, the sweaty teeming throngs that are everyone else must
riot the streets in chartreuse-tinted air and have nothing to eat but
little crackers called Soylent Green. Charlton Heston is a cop named
Thorn, his best buddy Sol is Edward G. Robinson (his last film, he
died a few days after filming), who is old enough to remember real
food—they make a rhapsodic meal from an apple, scraps of lettuce,

---

68 "If You Want to Sing Out, Sing Out," music and lyrics by Cat Stevens

69 *Soylent Green* (MGM, 1973); written by Stanley R. Greenberg, based on the
novel by Harry Harrison; directed by Richard Fleischer; with Charlton Heston and
Edward G. Robinson

and a tiny piece of beef Thorne has filched from a crime scene. Thorne is investigating a murder linked to Soylent Industries, the megacorporation that controls everything, including food production; there is gunplay, scenes of rioters being scooped up and away by garbage trucks, a mild (again undisturbing to my nine-year-old eyes) sex scene, but the best part of the movie is the end; Sol, like Maude, decides he has had enough, it is time to wrap things up on his own terms, and this nightmarish futuristic society offers one perk, has made that an easy and pleasant option. Sol goes to a massive, well-lit complex, is politely asked a series of questions (favorite color: "Orange," favorite music: "Light classical"), led to a spacious private room by kind, Grecian-berobed attendants, given something tasty to drink, undressed, and invited to lie peacefully under a sheet on a cushiony bed. The lights dim to a burnished orange glow, light classical music plays, and there is a panoramic-screen mini documentary of Nature, what has vanished from this brutalized world: Flowers, deer, birds, rushing mountain streams, colorful undersea schools of fish. Sol is mesmerized by the beauty of his final moments; he is ecstatic to be "going home," as he has said in his good-bye note to Thorne, and he meets death, like Judith and Maude, so beautifully, so finely, and with such self-determined style.

Oh, and then his sheet-wrapped body is wheeled out and dumped in a truck, along with all the other bodies, and Thorne follows the truck to a Soylent Industries factory and realizes all the dead bodies of all the dead people get processed into those little crackers for the masses to feed on, and yes, "Soylent Green is people!" he screams, out into the annals of pop culture.

This does not dissuade me, however; Sol's death, like Maude's, while sad for the people left behind, the Olivers and Harolds and Thornes, is still wonderfully rational to me, the planning-ahead as sensible as the weeks my mother spends organizing the perfect dinner party. Soylent Green crackers aside (which, in 1973, I dismiss as pure unprescient "science fiction," a narrative twist meant to gross us out, one that could never ever happen . . . of course not . . .), I have no existential anxiety about what happens to me or my body after death—there is no worry of decomposition, or an afterlife, or any thought of an out-of-body spiritual redistribution of energy. There is no discussion of "the soul" in my family, there is no God, no heaven or hell, only a pragmatic ashes-to-ashes, death-is-a-part-of-life mentality. Flush the little goldfish, bury the dead mouse wrapped in a fistful of toilet paper, feel sad a moment, sure, then shrug. So these movie deaths are perfect to me: The angelic choir, the cinematography, the dignified elegance, the carefully constructed mise-en-scène. The lack of suffering, of distress, of pain. A beautiful, fine thing to aspire to. Exactly how you'd want a story, a movie, a life, to end.

That is how I am going to die someday, I decide.

My mother's most adored friend was Janie, who was also my parents' bookkeeper. I adored Janie, too—once a month, after dinner and writing checks for my parents' bills, she sat me on her lap and with a tobacco-smelling finger traced out words between my shoulder blades, the gentle lettering of *I love you* and *we are friends*. Her fingers were stained yellow from her cigarettes, but it was her ovaries, not her lungs, that turned against her; one day they swelled with rot and sent invader cells out to march through the rest of her body, demanding surrender. The doctors cut out bits of her, and then more bits, and then they resorted to poison.

Janie has *cancer*, my mother explains to me, and is very sick; we have not seen her for months, and I am being taken to visit her in the hospital to nurture in me a demystified acceptance of death. Or perhaps my mother couldn't find a sitter. I am nine years old. And I am entirely unconcerned—after all, I am mature for my age, I can handle any adult themes, any PG or old black-and-white or sci-fi movie about dying and death you care to throw at me. I know I was in the hospital myself when I was little, but I have only the vaguest and fleeting unmemory flashes of procedures and tests—and anyway, in this hospital they will not be doing anything to me. I reassure my mother I am fine, not to worry about me, as I always do.

Janie is sleepy and thinner and the yellow of her fingers has faded; there are tubes running in and out of her, the smell of alcohol and something else, a tapestry of green bruises on her inner arms, short black hairs on the pillow; she has some hair left but it does not fan or cascade like Jenny's. She will be bald soon, my mother had warned me, that's what the drugs do, so don't be scared about that, and I wonder if these are the "cell-destroying" drugs with bad side effects Jenny had refused. Maybe Janie should have refused them, too; she looks ungraceful and unserene. She looks sick, a kind of sick I have never seen, not like chicken pox or the flu. I am technically, at nine, not allowed to be visiting here, but I am so well-behaved (that means mute, I am too nervous to speak) the nurse smiles at my mother, gives an indulgent little nod. I have brought with me a short black wig my mother bought me once upon a time to play dress-up with; she had suggested it would be a nice gift for Janie, that very soon, when all her hair has finally gone, she will want to wear a wig.

Janie seems startled then pleased to see me, smiles at the wig. *Thank you, honey*, she says. I am unsure where to sit—Oliver lay down with Jenny, but surely even sitting on this narrow, stiff-sheeted bed would jostle her uncomfortably. My mother has no such hesitation, however, plops down, tilting Janie so the nurse must come to resettle her. I pull up a chair, perch nearby. I am reluctant to touch Janie—her skin looks thin and tender, the yellowed white of heavy whipping cream you decide to sniff first, or the kind of porcelain my mother calls *bisque*—but Janie reaches out a bony, spaghetti-veined hand and takes mine. She traces a heart on my palm, which makes me think of Helen Keller and Teacher. My mother chats about something and I try not to breathe in through my nose, so I can keep out the chemical and something-else-unpleasant sting. I had not expected a *smell*. I wonder if it is contagious, this *cancer*. I wonder if it will make me or my mother sick, if we will also lose all our hair. We leave when the nurse tells us it is time for Janie's chemo, which sounds like a Japanese cartoon hero.

I don't want to go back for another visit—this isn't mice or goldfish, this isn't Jenny or Judith or Sol or Maude. Nothing about this is beautiful and fine; it's horrible, and it smells. This isn't *death*, this is *dying*, for real, and it frightens me.

I try explaining to my mother that I am frightened, but she is unworried: "Janie loved seeing you; it's important you go," and I feel chastised for my selfishness. Each visit the bruises are darker, the veins more prominent, Janie's eyes brighter with something I don't understand. Where is the glowing orange light, the classical music, the madly-in-love and despairing lover? Where are the snow angels and daisies? The doctors finally decide to cease their relentless and redundant poisoning and send Janie home; on our next visit to her apartment, I am aware of an even worse smell, something sweetish, but in an unclean way. Janie is in bed, wearing an emerald-colored scarf on her head (I have never seen her wearing the wig), and insists my mother and I go through her jewelry box in front of her now. When I admire a pair of gold earrings, little rosebuds at their instant of unbudding, Janie gives them to me; my mother hesitates, then allows me to accept them, and I realize this means Janie will soon go from dying to dead, and I picture her lying at the bottom of a cage among wooden shavings, her sheet-wrapped body dumped into a garbage truck. Part of me hopes this will be the last time I ever see her—that she will *hit the ground already*, as Jenny might say—but we go back one or two more times: A weaker smile and translucent skin, sunken eyes, the green scarf revealing a hairless nape. Finally, my mother goes alone, because Janie has said she doesn't want me to see her like this. I never see her again, and I never wear the earrings. After my mother, crying, tells me Janie has died, my first thought is if someone will return to me my dress-up wig, but I sense that would be the wrong thing to inquire about, especially when my mother is so upset and needs me to comfort her. Anyway, I think, it probably has *cancer* on it. Soon I can't remember the feeling of Janie's finger tracing letters on my back, and it hits me this is the final end of Janie and Janie has disappeared forever; I will never feel those letters from her ever again, but I tell myself that is a silly and immature reason to cry, and anyway, my mother's crying is already very large in the house. Janie was thirty-four.

A girl like that, so alive, so entitled to live!

But who isn't "entitled to live"?

And why did the movies lie to me?

My next death is twelve years later and confirms for the adult me there is no last small mercy from God for anyone, no celestial choir, there is nothing beautiful or fine about death. My grandmother— one-time party gal like Judith, a tabletop dancer, a vibrant lover of song like Maude, a woman who laughed so hard at life she peed, and then laughed about that, and a lifelong pack-a-day smoker—had been breathlessly ill for several years with severe emphysema, osteoporosis breaking her body into porous, bony bits. By the time I was twenty she was barely able to get around the house, a portable oxygen tank trailing her like a spaniel. I leave home for a year to go to school in France, and by the time I come back she is bedridden, wheezing, exhausted, margarine-gray. I go see her the night my plane lands, and I lie on her bed with her, like Oliver, talking—or, me talking, her trying to between gasps—about the rupture and disarray of our family, her hope I might, somehow, disappear everyone's pain. That night my grandfather calls an ambulance; the next day, at the hospital, I get off the elevator at ICU to the loud sound of some odd mechanical dysfunction, the rattled choking of metal and rubber, of unoiled cogs or gears out of alignment: It is my grandmother down the hall in her hospital room, trying to breathe. I sit with her for a while; her eyes are dimming not with the imminent grace of release but with fear and agony and confusion, and my sitting there holding her hand cannot change any of that, any more than a parent can truly soothe or spare an anguished child from the absolute isolating loneliness of pain. Her death a few days later does not come "quietly, peacefully"; there is no lovely farewell, and I wonder about Janie's last days, last moments; when I cry for my grandmother, I finally cry for Janie, for her tender bruises and sweet lettering hands and death-bright eyes. But I do not have much time for that; my grandfather and my mother are now schism'd apart—my mother is especially distraught, having lost, essentially, both her mother and her father, and is now an orphaned child—and I need to double up my comforting and then split it in two. My grandfather asks me to select my grandmother's casket, arrange for deli platters and a reception, choose something to dress her in for burial; I choose an entirely inappropriate sweater I had knit for her a few years back.

At my grandmother's funeral—where she is slid into a mausoleum wall like a filing cabinet or something to be kept hidden away in a nightstand drawer—people tell me she "held on" until I came home, so she could see me once more before she died, and I feel a horrified guilt; does that mean if I had come home earlier, or if I had not left at all, I could have spared her all those months of suffering? And why was the suffering not "all behind her," like Judith's, at the end?

Couldn't someone have given her those magical tablets of Maude's? That science-fiction drink they gave Sol, some final Happy Hour elixir? Couldn't we, or anyone, *allow* her, arrange for her, a beautiful and fine recline on her own bed, a glamour-shot death?

Because that is what I want, for myself. I won't let dying happen to me as it did to Janie or my grandmother. Maude and Sol had the right idea; go out on your own, self-empowering terms. Go out with style. That is absolutely how I am going to do it, I reassure myself, die. Some day.

I get my chance six months later, when I make a grand mal seizure-spectacle of myself in a shopping mall, and, after a week in the hospital (procedures and tests, yep, but this time I absolutely refuse a spinal tap, which flummoxes, then infuriates my doctor, but this time I am an adult and he can't make me), I am finally diagnosed with a *brain tumor*. At twenty-two, I understand what this really means, the inherent drama and legitimate threat; the brain is not simply "like any other part of the body," as Judith's Dr. Steele would like to think, a tumor is not merely something "out of kilter," a thing "to be adjusted"—he was more on point in describing it as a parasitic plant, some venomous weedy growth in my left frontal lobe that must be pruned away. And yet the tumor looks so sweetly benign on the scans I am shown—an errant pinto bean, a lost little Raisinet—that I am almost surprised my doctor is so adamant about surgery. He is also adamant about using the words *biopsy* and *malignancy* and *chemo*, and I think *No, uh-uh, I'm not doing that*. I smell Janie's chemical rot, I see prognosis negative stamped in a file, I hear:

DR. STEELE

A girl like that, so alive! So entitled to live!
And this thing, this *growth* comes along and puts
a period to it! *Makes you almost wish it happened
on the table . . .*

and I think *Yes, what a* great *idea!* This is my big chance; for many months I had been trying to hide and ignore another kind of toxic weed in my garden-mind, an inexplicable depression that had taken flourishing, choking root and left me increasingly in a state of dull despair—I was anything but *so alive*. But now I get it into my tumorous head that I can will myself to die *on the table*; I can actually make that happen, and then it will all be over, the quiet wood-shavings stillness of an end without the suffering and decay and smell. Then it *would* be just like going to sleep for a long time. No bruising needlefuls of poison, no repeated operations to snip out metastasized, weedy bits. Just a graceful acceptance of the punctuated end to my life, a faint, sheer shine of the heroic, my arm elegantly extended over my head and then over with. *What can you say about a twenty-two-year-old girl who died?* they will ask about me, and I hope they will say I was *beautiful and brilliant*, or maybe at least pretty and smart. I'll be *well and normal, just like everybody else*, right up until the end. It is not a *tragic difference* that I know when I am going to die, it is a gift, a rare opportunity; if I can orchestrate the circumstances of my death, then of course I can be all ready, I can *meet it beautifully and finely*. For months I'd been feeling I had a life without the living; now I can have the death without the dying.

Of course, nobody orchestrates his own death—or choreographs, stages, *directs* his own death—as well or as literally as Bob Fosse in his semiautobiographical *All That Jazz*, inspired by his real-life heart attack while simultaneously editing the film *Lenny* and directing *Chicago* on the Great White Way.[70] Roy Scheider dances and sings as Joe Gideon, Fosse's alter-ego, a self-destructive, self-loathing, alcoholic, pill-popping film and theatre director whose death is brought to imagined, hallucinatory life as Broadway spectacle: A death with jazz hands and show-stopping musical numbers, death as the ultimate variety show, emceed by Ben Vereen, the finale a musical farewell to all the people in Joe's life—mostly women—he has done wrong:

JOE

Bye-bye, life! Bye-bye, happiness! Hello, loneliness. I think I'm gonna die. . . .[71]

---

70 *All That Jazz* (20th Century Fox, 1979): written by Robert Allen Aurthur and Bob Fosse; directed by Bob Fosse; with Roy Scheider, Jessica Lange, and Ben Vereen

71 Modified from "Bye, Bye Love," by Boudleaux Bryant and Felice Bryant

Starring in your own death might be a little self-indulgent, sure, but I can relate to Joe/Bob's perfectionist desire to turn death into performance art, to want that final editorial cut, to exercise that degree of aesthetic control—and who wouldn't want Jessica Lange as one's own personal, flirtatious Angel of Death?

Maybe I can't sing or dance like Joe/Bob, but I can still go out with style. I can still create my final tableau—like Harold, but with Maude's follow-through. So, I plan my going-away party, with all my family and friends, to be held two weeks hence, the night before I will return to the hospital to die tragically on the table during brain surgery. Party favors will be wispy snips of my long hair, tucked inside little brain-shaped lockets—like Judith, I don't want my hair cut off, that is my biggest concern, and I know they will not be cutting off "just a little bit"; they are going to shave my whole head, and so I may as well incorporate that motif into the mise–en-scène. I will blow up white helium balloons and draw sad unsmiley faces on them with a black Sharpie, draw little scars on their balloon-head tops. I will draw a large cartoony brain on the wall and we'll all play "Pin the Tumor on the Left Frontal Lobe." In France I'd played a Christmas game called *Le Tirage du Roi*, "Drawing the King," where a tiny porcelain baby Jesus is hidden inside a cake and whoever finds it in their slice is proclaimed King for the evening; we will play *Le Tirage du Tumor*; I will hide a tiny plastic tumor in a brain-shaped cake, and the winner will wear a pointy little beanie. I will bravely embrace everyone good-bye. *Go, and love some more*, I will say, holding a daisy as I take my lonely but brave exit. Like Maude, I can't imagine a lovelier farewell. *Bye-bye, life! I think I'm gonna die.*

My mother, who has needed an enormous amount of attention and comforting from me since my seizure and diagnosis, is horrified by all this planning, reduced to babbling helplessness and tears; I remember Harold explaining to Maude how he felt as an adolescent, what started his obsession with the dramatic power of suicide, when an accidental explosion at school resulted in his mother being misinformed of his death, how he was actually present to witness her reaction:

HAROLD

These two policemen came in, they found my mother
and told her I was killed in the fire. She put

one hand up to her forehead. With the other she
reached out as if groping for support. And with
this long sigh, she collapsed in their arms. . . .
              (crying)
I decided right then that I'd enjoy being dead.

The more collapsingly upset my mother gets, the more I feel she is co-opting my tragedy, and the more I take an odd, shameful satisfaction in my insistent, self-indulgent theatrics. There is something gratifying in being, for the first time in my life, a *problem*, an actual source of worry and distress; this acting-out is the extra nuts on my sundae, this feeling of being authentically, messily, three-dimensionally present in the room. This limelight death is all mine, and I am not going to share. Like Sol, I will be "going home" on my own terms. Like Jenny, I will be the boss, get whatever I want. It's my party, and I'll die if I want to.

But there is no party, no darkly victorious or spectacular climax. For two weeks I am so doped up and energyless on antiseizure medication I can do little beyond lie on my couch or stagger around my apartment. My doctor had not wanted me to be left alone, so my friend Michelle had come from across the country to stay with me, to be sure I didn't crack my head in a seizure-fall on the pavement or seize-drown in the tub. The night before surgery, after I have emptied out my refrigerator and finished writing instructions for my funeral (cremation, please, it is sensibly space-saving, and I realize I don't want to decompose, to become food for either worms or people) and good-bye notes to my friends, I start to cry. I cry and cry and can't stop. I'm scared to die, I am not ready, there is no getting ready for this no matter how much orchestrating you might try to do, and is this what *falling off a cliff in slow motion* is like, when you *don't* want to hurry up and hit the ground? I wonder if maybe there is a God (there are no atheists in foxholes), if maybe there is a heaven, and do I get to go there even if I didn't believe in it until my foxhole now? And will Janie and my grandmother be there, dancing on top of cloud-tables and lighting up their cigarettes like a pretumor Judith, and will they forgive me for not doing more? I feel like a baby, a frightened two-and-a-half-year-old clutching for some adult's hand, wishing for someone to disappear my pain. I feel like a failure, humiliated by my powerlessness and unglamorous fear. I feel a sudden warmth, and I realize Michelle has come to lie in bed beside me—I'd wanted her to *hold me, I mean really hold me, next to me,* but was afraid to ask, and she has done so without my having to ask, and I am so then-and-forever grateful. She holds me close for what seems like long sobbing hours until I am able to sleep.

The next day at the hospital—but before they shave my head—one final presurgery scan shows the tumor has not grown. A true, real, legitimate tumor should have grown a tiny bit, even in two weeks. Again, my doctor is flummoxed. Huh, he says. Maybe they shouldn't be so quick to cut me open, root around in there. Go home, come back in another two weeks, we'll try this again. This goes on for six stuporous months, my life on hold from week to shapeless week, a story that has lost its narrative structure, scrambling to figure out the perfect set piece to end Act 3. The doctors finally decide it is *not* a tumor, this out-of-kilter thing in my head; it is probably something called a *cysticercosis*. A worm, *a parasitic one.* (Dr. Steele was right about that, at least.) It will snack on my brain for a while, they tell me, then simply die, calcify, stay there forever as a little ghostly calcium dot but be absolutely no problem at all. Nothing to worry about.

And so, I realize, my life will not end as a tragic brain tumor drama; it is a shaggy worm story, a comedy with an anticlimactic punch line. It is just back to a regular, ordinary life, after all—there is no flatteringly lit, dying heroine here, struck down in her prime. I don't get to be Maude, in the end; I'm still just Harold, indulging in faux-death, playing around with a fantasy of non-existence. And I remember what Maude said, after he told her he'd *enjoy being dead*:

MAUDE

I understand. A lot of people enjoy being dead.
But they're not dead, really. They're just backing
away from life. Reach out. Take a chance. Get
hurt, even. But play as well as you can! Give me
an L, give me an I, give me a V, give me an E!
L, I, V, E, live! Otherwise, you got nothing to
talk about in the locker room.

All right, Maude. I will try. I will play as well as I can, I will dance along that cliff, plucking that banjo.

Because if I'm not going to die, then you're right—I will have to find a better way to live.

- - - - - - - - - - - -

For a long time I avoid dying-heroine or hero movies; I am a little annoyed by those sanitized, odorless, prettified portraits of death, and at the same time I feel ashamed for having gotten away *without* dying so easily—how many tragic heroines get a happy final-reel reprieve? Even Joe Gideon, in the end, dances only with death; the bleak final abrupt shot of *All That Jazz* is dead Joe zipped shut into a plastic body bag, reduced to prosaic procedure—you might hum the score on your way out of the theatre, but that's it folks, show's over, nothing more to see here.

But now that I have had the experience of "meeting death" (or the brief flirtatious tease of it, even if only in my own off-kilter'd mind), I find myself fascinated by "moment of death" scenes in movies, that final meet-and-greet we are all supposed to do so beautifully and finely, according to Dr. Steele. I'm drawn to execution scenes, in particular; we all generally go around in blissful ignorance of when the timer will *ding* on our lives, of the stopwatch's final *click* on our existence, so what must it be like to be aware of that actual inevitable moment as it ticks down? To await the noose or needle, to know the exact looming instant you will shift from present to absent, the split-severing-second between consciousness and oblivion? Would your last thoughts be profound, mundane, frozen-blank, and blinking like a crashing computer screen? Does everybody really get their own life-in-flashbacks video? How would it feel to breathe your last breath, knowing for absolute sure it *is* your last breath—wouldn't you feel the instinct to hold that breath, try to cheat death just a few extra stalling seconds, *wait wait*, by puffing out your cheeks or sneaking in a whiff of air through your nose? Having a scheduled *appointment* with Death (the formality of a planned rendezvous invites the capital D), having Death marked down in the Day Runner or red-circled on the wall calendar, creates movie scenes of unique ontological mindfulness: A character no longer struggling to live her life—that game is over—but instead strategizing how to die her death.

Anne of the Thousand Days: "Will it hurt?" Anne Boleyn (Genevieve Bujold, the best Boleyn ever, all French accent and pug-nosed, fiery snap) asks the Keeper of the Tower, where she awaits her beheading for an adultery conviction, trumped-up so Henry VIII, escalating into monstrousness, could kill this wife in order to marry the next.[72] The Keeper, distraught, assures her No, the executioner is very good, and she jokes about her little neck, reassures him: "I am glad to die." Is she? Is it a genuinely resigned acceptance of the inevitable or a martyr's impassioned embrace of defeat? She exits the Tower, pauses to appreciate the flowering Maytime trees, the chirping of birds—her moments-away death is thrown into poignant relief by the everywhere blossoming of life. She spots the raised scaffold, the waiting casket with the Tudor rose, the death-hungry spectators, and proceeds with a stately dignity. Word on the street is she used sorcery and seduction to rise above her station, but this is her final performance, her legacy for the ages, and they are not going to see her sweat; she is going to die like a queen. She mounts the steps, head high. She kneels upright in the straw, crosses herself, then raises her chin—there is no block, she has been granted the mercy of the more-noble beheading by sword, which the executioner now pulls from a pile of straw. And for the first time, her courage falters—she snaps her head to the side to look at him, Bujold's huge brown eyes made huger by sudden panic, this is the moment, the second before her death—is she questioning her choices, was she a victim of fate or agent of her own downfall?—wait, wait, will it hurt, that slice through my little neck, it is here and now, a blade away, and the vulnerability of her fear startles the executioner—"Distract her, she looks at me!" he barks, and someone does—she turns her head again and so doesn't see the final slashing sword. We cut away—no prurient shot of spurting blood or a severed head jiggling a basket—and so her death is hers alone to own, for us

---

72 *Anne of the Thousand Days* (Universal Pictures, 1969): screenplay by Bridget Boland, John Hale, and Richard Sokolove, based on the play by Maxwell Anderson; directed by Charles Jarrott; with Genevieve Bujold and Richard Burton

to admire but not gawk at, an elegant jump-cut final exit from this world. Brava, Anne!

I Want to Live!: The true-life story of Barbara "Babs" Graham, a loose-living, jazz-loving, hep-speaking, noir-heroine broad (a knockout Susan Hayward, oh, was my grandfather hot for her), convicted of the murder of an elderly woman in a home-invasion burglary gone wrong.[73] The movie is highly sympathetic to Graham's claim of innocence, but it is the slow psychological torture of Graham's start-and-stop path to the gas chamber that tugs the heart rather than the martyr's justified pathos. The "moment of death" here is actually the full second half of the movie: Numerous stays, appeals, new dates and times set for the execution, a drawn-out capital punishment striptease as Barbara is aroused, then calmed, then aroused again. We get the leitmotif of Time itself: The "death watch log" of Graham's final Death Row days, closeups of the massive clock on the wall with its slow-pirouetting second hand, everyone sneaking peeks at their watches. "Do I have time to dress?" Barbara asks, after the second last-minute stay (10:45), and she is told "Fifteen minutes," just enough time, yes, to put on her nice, look-like-a-lady suit, her fancy earrings; death is her final fashion statement, the single last thing this woman can control, and she fights to be allowed to wear her elegant pumps rather than meet death barefooted like some common two-bit slut. Barbara has ranged from quippy (jokes about cyanide eggs with her name on them, etc.) to defiant, and as she now begins her final runway strut, accompanied by a priest—"It's time," at last—she takes a final drag on her cig and heads to her rendezvous with her coiffed head held high. But mere feet from the chamber, the shrill ring of the phone, yet another stay, and she crumples, moans in anguish: "Oh, Father, why do they torture me?" We all wait together, including those cyanide eggs, wrapped in a white hanky and suspended by a chain above the waiting canisters of sulfuric acid . . . it is now 11:30, Barbara's chest is heaving—is there a chance, maybe, maybe . . . ?—and the phone screams again. *It's time*, for real this time. But her strength is gone; she asks for a mask, so she

---

73 *I Want to Live!* (United Artists, 1958): screenplay by Nelson Gidding and Don Mankiewicz, based on articles by Ed Montgomery and letters by Barbara Graham; directed by Robert Wise; with Susan Hayward

doesn't have to see the onlookers looking on, she needs the priest to support her as she walks in the already-dark. At the chamber door, she leans in—"Father, I didn't do it," she whispers, either one last protest or one final plea to be seen as victim and thus deserving of a martyr's grace. Perhaps both. She is strapped in to the chair, arms, legs, chest, a stethoscope attached. "When you hear the eggs drop, count to ten, take a deep breath; it's easier that way," an attendant murmurs. "How do you know?" she responds, in a voice all at once guttural, ragged, and so pissed-off—they are her final words, and indeed, how can anyone know, really, how this moment might feel, what "easier" might even mean? Do the nice suit, the fancy earrings, really make any difference? The door is closed, sealed; the eggs drop, her startled, strapped-in body giving a jerk. Onlookers peer. Fumes rise; the acid bubbles. The sound of her heart, beating, thumping, and my heart begins to thump right along in companionable rhythm. She clenches her fists, her head lolls: Is she breathing deeply, savoring the last of that life-sustaining oxygen, holding on, wait, wait—or hurrying to fill her lungs with gas, let's wrap this up already? Defiance or defeat? Resignation or embrace? Our final shot of Barbara is her fist going limp; we only hear the moment of her death, that thumping heartbeat slowing, finally, fin-a-lly, to silence. It takes mine a bit longer to quiet down.

In Cold Blood: The question of guilt or innocence is moot this time; Dick Hickock (Scott Wilson) and Perry Smith (Robert Blake) ultimately confessed to the killing of four members of the Clutter family, and we've seen the flashback of the killings in that remote Kansas farmhouse; there are six executions in this true crime story, and before Dick and Perry get their date with the noose, we are allowed to experience the terror of that family, tied up in separate rooms and ignorant of their fate until that first of four resonating gunshots: The father, then the son, then the mother, then the daughter.[74] And it is Nancy, the sixteen-year-old daughter, especially, whose countdown terror increases exponentially with each gunned-down death on the list; the end of her own life happens three shotgun times, I count along with

---

74 *In Cold Blood* (Columbia Pictures, 1967): screenplay by Richard Brooks, based on the book by Truman Capote; directed by Richard Brooks; with Robert Blake and Scott Wilson

her, she must die three times until it is her own turn: "No, no, please don't . . . please," she begs when that shotgun is at last pointed at her, it is her turn now, wait, wait, she is so young, there is Prom and horses to ride, boyfriends and cherry pie, and she turns her face away in that childlike, hiding-ostrich instinct: If I can't see it, it maybe isn't there; if it doesn't see my face, maybe my existence can stay a secret, stay mine, just stay . . . . No.

When it's Perry and Dick's turn, Dick, the cockier of the two, is led almost cheerfully to the gallows in shackles, but his cocky façade slips as he climbs the steps . . . and we cut to Perry, waiting, gazing out the window at the rain: "What time is it?" he asks, that most innocent, most existential question. *Tick tick tick.* We have always been allowed more intimacy with Perry, invited in to understand, or try to understand, the workings of his mind; Dick is the truly amoral psychopath, while Perry, the one who actually pulled that trigger those four times, is the broken, tortured soul, and he reminisces for us about his childhood, his broken and torturing father, his own cognitive-dissonant struggle with both love and hate. The rain-weeping window reflects as tears streaming down Perry's face—a gorgeous effect that spares us the sympathy-begging ploy of having him cry real tears for himself, and so allows us to empathize for him without being told to. Perry is not worried about shoes or hairstyles or the visual markers of ladyhood (not that Barbara or Anne's concerns are silly—these are the only props they are allowed, their femininity their only rhetorical tool); his final request is to use the toilet, for he has heard "when you hit the end of the rope, your muscles lose control. I'm afraid I'll mess myself," and it doesn't get more relatably, humanly vulnerable than that. He is marched out in his own shackled turn, rapidly chewing gum, panicked. "Anything you want to say?" he is asked, and he says, "I think maybe I'd like to apologize. But to who?" obliquely acknowledging his own execution of four now-absent innocents. His feet are placed on the trapdoor, tied together; the noose is slid over; and Perry swivels his head to see the Hangman, nods at him in fraternal recognition: They are killers both. The Lord's Prayer is read aloud—"Is God in this place, too?" Perry asks. The noose is necklaced around his throat, a black hood placed on his head, and through it we can see him shaking, see his mouth frantically working that sad chewing gum, we hear again the rapid heartbeat, *beat beat beatbeatbeat*. Again, my heart is beating, too, but this time I am jolted from its companionable thump when the trapdoor drops and we see the body fall and jolt, and we abruptly switch to an ethereal slo-mo swinging, soundless except for the last of Perry's still-beating heartbeat slowing down . . . is he flashbacking for himself right now, with the last of those oxygenating beats? About the Clutters, about his father, about Dick, about God? At what point does his strangled brain die of hunger and thirst, put that final period to thought?

Dead Man Walking: Matthew Poncelet (satanically bearded Sean Penn), on Death Row for the murder of two teenagers, has spent the film protesting his innocence, despite Sister Helen Prejean's (mascara-free Susan Sarandon) insistence that the only path to God, to grace, to any hope of redemption or meaningful context for his life, is to accept full responsibility for his crimes.[75] Minutes before his execution—again, the clock on the wall, the ticking down of time, of heartbeat, of breath—Matthew finally breaks down: Yes, I am guilty, yes, I am a rapist and murderer, yes. Sister Helen assures him that now, at last, he can die with dignity and no one can take that away from him, that he is a child of God. But for me his confession seems to be less about earning God's love than about earning Sister Helen's: "It figures I'd have to die to find love," he tells her. "Thank you for loving me." It is the human connection that humanizes him, not the spiritual; it is "Time to go, Poncelet," a guard booms, "Dead man walking!" and despite Sister Helen's reading the Bible aloud, or the priest who crosses him at the door to the death chamber, any meaningful context Matthew might now be creating for either his life or his death, to me, is not because God is with him; it is because Sister Helen is. He asks if she might touch him on this final walk; it is her approval that comforts him when he publicly confesses and asks forgiveness of the victims' parents—"I hope my death gives you some relief"—it is her loving face he seeks as his last living vision of this world. He is still terrified as he is strapped down, still shaking as the rubber strap is tied on

---

75 *Dead Man Walking* (Gramercy Pictures, 1995): screenplay by Tim Robbins, based on the book by Sister Helen Prejean; directed by Tim Robbins; with Susan Sarandon and Sean Penn

his arm and a thick needle slid into his vein, but this is ultimately a love story between two human beings, and how the experience of that love, especially at the moment of death, is perhaps the closest any of us might really get to not dying alone. Who will be with me when I die, I wonder. Whose is the last face I would like to see?

The Green Mile: The famous flames-and-screams, deliberately-botched-by-sadistic-guard electrocution occurs earlier in the film, but it is the final scene of "gentle giant" John Coffey (Michael Clarke Duncan) in the electric chair that serves as the creepy moneyshot death here.[76] "It be all right, fellas. This here the hard part. I'll be all right in a little while," he tells the guards as he is strapped into Old Sparky; he speaks of the two little girls he was unjustly accused of murdering, talks understandingly about the hatred the witnesses must feel for him. His death is all about his empathy for others, his intention to console; when a witness spits out she hopes his electrocution "hurts like hell," John responds with "I'm sorry for what I am." He is crying when a guard approaches with a hood, asking, "Please, Boss. Don't put that thing over my face. Don't put me in the dark. I's afraid of the dark." His head is sponged, the electrodes put in place, he sings "Heaven . . . I'm in heaven . . . ," echoing his earlier delight at a Fred Astaire film—indeed, he is all angelic innocence and child-like fear, none of that messy emotional complexity allowed Barbara or Perry or Matthew or Anne. Spike Lee criticized the depiction of John as the "Magic Negro," the black man whose one-note character exists primarily to serve as a catalyst for the white characters' illumination, and John's mysterious, magical life and climactic death serve the same function; it is head guard Tom Hanks's trauma at carrying out the execution (his "last one," he will tell us soon in the film's coda) that we are meant to feel and identify with when the switch is flipped. I feel for John, but at a distance—I can't quite enter into his conscious-ness, not because the circumstances of his life or death are so different from mine, but because it seems the filmmakers are not really all that interested in allowing us inside his psyche.

---

76 *The Green Mile* (Warner Bros., 1999): screenplay by Frank Darabont, based on the novel by Stephen King; directed by Frank Darabont; with Tom Hanks and Michael Clarke Duncan

Then there are the imminent "moments of death" brought about not by judicial execution, but by choice or circumstance, characters who know they are about to die, and it will be minutes, seconds from now, not in some hazy, safely distant future, and how are they going to go out? Butch (Paul Newman) and Sundance (Robert Redford), in *Butch Cassidy and the Sundance Kid*, may be reprobate outlaws, but their lithe, blithe beauty, their abiding bromance love, their willingness to risk death for each other, and their flair with screenwriterly quips, have won our hearts; now, at the end, they are trapped, outmanned, and outgunned in a Bolivian marketplace, wounded and fully aware that this is it, the closing credits of their story loom.[77] In their final moments they mock-plan and mock-bicker where they will travel together next—Butch pushes for Australia; Sundance is skeptical—while they load their final rounds, knowing without saying a word, in the intuitive intimacy of true love, that they are going to die, and right now, and they will go out together, guns blazing. Cut to their bursting outside, together, firing. A sepia-toned freeze-frame captures their final moment alive—the sound of the Bolivian army's gunfire mowing them down continues—and elevates them forever, in their death, to a victoriously stylish, iconic, antihero buddyhood.

Similarly, Thelma and Louise, in *Thelma & Louise*, are cinema's iconic outlaw gal pals, for whom a shared death is an expression of empowerment, newfound self-determination, and an unbreakable sororal bond.[78] Pursued by cops across the Southwest, after Louise (Susan Sarandon) killed a man threatening to rape Thelma (Geena Davis), the women find themselves trapped in their blue Ford Thunderbird at the edge of the Grand Canyon, a helicopter swirling above and an army of police with raised guns behind them. What to do? "I'm not getting caught," Louise says, although they already are. "Okay, then. Listen. Let's not get caught," says Thelma, gazing imploringly at Louise. "Go," she says. "You sure?" Louise asks, but they both already are. They smile. They kiss. They have each other. Louise floors

---

77 *Butch Cassidy and the Sundance Kid* (20th Century Fox, 1969): written by William Goldman; directed by George Roy Hill; with Robert Redford and Paul Newman

78 *Thelma & Louise* (MGM, 1991): written by Callie Khouri; directed by Ridley Scott; with Susan Sarandon and Geena Davis

it; they clutch hands and zoom in a cloud of thick orange dust off the edge of the world—another for-the-ages freeze-frame of that blue Thunderbird soaring into empty space above the Canyon, not quite yet beginning its parabolic fall. Unlike Butch and Sundance, Thelma and Louise had a choice—good cop Harvey Keitel had begged them to give themselves up peacefully and live—but they choose death as a liberation from both societal oppression and actual imprisonment, their final shared statement of Fight-the-Power sisterhood. I am angry at them—was that a cowardly choice? I cheer them on—I would love to have that kind of courage, the willingness to choose death over a compromised life.

The young Australian soldiers in *Gallipoli* have no real choice; they are pawns, cogs, peach-fuzzed cannon fodder in the failed Battle of the Nek against the Turkish army in World War I.[79] They huddle in the trenches awaiting their fate, the bodies of their already-butchered comrades sprawled inches above their heads. Their turn to die in vain is next. They are dazed, and they are so, so young: They scribble good-bye notes to parents and girlfriends, they take their last look at mementos, they share a last cigarette, a last recitation of the Lord's Prayer, they suck the dusty air into their panicking lungs, they embrace. Our young hero Archy, a former world-class sprinter, takes off his prized medal, hangs it from a bayonet driven into the dirt. Elegiac music plays. There is no spirit of bravery in this dirty ditch of a waiting room and certainly no question of beauty or fineness; they are terrified and powerless and doomed, shaking and trying not to, and perhaps having the "chance to be ready" is not always a gift. Perhaps at one time they thought they were fighting for honor; now they are dying simply because they are ordered to. And the order is given— *wait, wait,* perhaps they think one last hopeful, futile time—they climb obediently from the trench and over the dead bodies, they run blindly headlong into a faceless and brusque annihilation. Archy loses his gun but keeps running: "What are your legs? Springs. How fast can you run? Like a leopard. How fast *will* you run? As fast as a leopard!" he

79 *Gallipoli* (Village Roadshow/Paramount Pictures, 1981): screenplay by David Williamson, story by Peter Weir, based on the novel *Tell England* by Ernest Raymond and the book *The Broken Years* by Bill Gammage; directed by Peter Weir; with Mel Gibson and Mark Lee

had murmured to himself in the trench, his own version of prayer; maybe he *can* outrun those bullets, maybe, but no; the film's final shot is his body arched backward by gun blast at the instant of a pointless death, a truncated, eyeblink life, and I am left despairing and angry at this waste.

The soldiers in *Glory* are a different lot; this is the story of the first all-black regiment to fight for the Union in the Civil War, and while their white Colonel Shaw (Matthew Broderick) is almost as young as the soldiers at Gallipoli, these men are already seasoned veterans of a different kind of battle: Private Trip (Denzel Washington) and Sergeant Major Rawlins (Morgan Freeman), like most of the regiment, are runaway slaves, men who have chosen to live, fight, and perhaps die *"like men,"* Rawlins has vowed, with bayonets and guns in their hands.[80] When the Confederacy announces captured black soldiers will be immediately executed, the men are offered an honorable discharge; none of them accept. The regiment has primarily been used by the Union for show, and for free labor; in the campaign to capture a foothold in Charleston Harbor, they are given their first chance for actual combat, and it is a suicide mission—their real function is to clear the advance for the white troops who will follow, and they all know that. But they are recarving history, reforging the future, and they know that, also: "O Heavenly Father, we want you to let our folks know that we died facing the enemy!" says Rawlins, praying with his men the night before battle. "We want them to know we went down standing up! Amongst those that are fighting against our oppression. We want them to know, Heavenly Father, that we died for freedom!" In battle, they charge with ferocious, concrete purpose; there is no hesitation, no *wait, wait,* for the raw adrenalized power of their anger, honor, pride, and dignity overcomes fear. When Shaw is gunned down, Trip seizes the Union flag, exhorts his comrades to surge ahead, and they do. In the end: Dead bodies, a failed military campaign. Shaw's body is dumped in a mass grave by Confederate soldiers, Trip is tossed in

---

80 *Glory* (TriStar Pictures, 1989): screenplay by Kevin Jarre, based on the books *Lay This Laurel* by Lincoln Kirstein and *One Gallant Rush* by Peter Burchard, and the letters of Robert Shaw; directed by Edward Zwick; with Matthew Broderick, Denzel Washington, and Morgan Freeman

after him. And yet—the empowerment, the victory, was theirs, they created their own destiny rather than awaiting their fate. They went down standing up, and for something larger than self. I am awed, humbled, educated by their sacrifice.

Like *Glory* and *Gallipoli*, *Saving Private Ryan* portrays death on an epic scale: The wide-angle battle scenes, the countless massacred bodies, the use of fictional characters caught up in true events to create both validating historical relevance and dramatic narrative force.[81] *Saving Private Ryan*'s opening half-hour depiction of the WWII invasion of Normandy and the slaughter of American troops on Omaha Beach is horrifying but avoids numbing us out by skillfully personalizing the soldiers, many of whom are left dead in the bloody sand and sea, some of whom have the luck to survive, and whom we will follow for the rest of the story, hoping their luck holds out. But the most haunting scene, for me, comes two and a half hours into the film; a minor character, Private Mellish, a wise-cracking, gum-chewing, volatile Jewish soldier—he has pointed at himself and yelled "Juden, Juden!" at captured Germans, his proud, self-defining taunt—has found himself in hand-to-hand combat with an enemy soldier. They are alone and isolated inside a building, no one is coming to help, and there is an intense intimacy to their grappling, their bodies pressed together like lovers as they tumble and roll over the freshly killed body of Mellish's comrade. Mellish is able to draw his bayonet but the enemy soldier wrenches it away from him, and, now lying on top of Mellish and murmuring almost reassuringly in incomprehensible German, presses the tip of the bayonet over Mellish's heart. And Mellish's instinct at this moment—face to face with Death, it is his turn, now, after seeing the butchered bodies of his friends, and the maybe-guilty hope that maybe, just *maybe*, his luck would hold and he would get out of this alive, because don't their deaths somehow appease, fulfill a quota, don't they count as escrow monies for his life, *hasn't* he been alive, until now, isn't he *still* alive, this very second, so how can he possibly die?—is to protest, stall, try to freeze-frame this last second of his existence: "Listen, listen, *listen* to me," he says, "no, no, stop, stop!"

---

81 *Saving Private Ryan* (DreamWorks Pictures, 1998): written by Robert Rodat; directed by Steven Spielberg; with Tom Hanks and Adam Goldberg

He is being so reasonable, *listen*, can't we talk this over, *listen*, can't we work something out? *Stop*, just for a moment, please. But the German slowly drives the bayonet into his chest—"Shh, shh . . . ," he whispers soothingly. It is not a brutal stab, it is delicate and slow, so slow, it is a forever moment and there is no one to hold his hand, Mellish aware of Death's gentle, obliterating entrance into his body, of Death's indifferent victory, until it is over and he is still.

Wait, wait, I think, is it really the end, did he really die? Wait, wait, give me one eternal second more—forget meeting Death beautifully and finely, inviting it to come in and sit down and being a gracious host. Isn't the most honest, visceral instinct to slam the door in Death's face, bolt and barricade it, do whatever you can to keep Death out? Just a little while longer?

- - - - - - - - - -

My mother battled her weight her entire life; I remember, as a child, the acrid haze of Sweet'N Low in the air; I remember her visiting fashionable fat farms, trying every faddish diet and dieter's gimmicky trick, while things like reasonable portion size, healthy foods, and exercise were simply derided or dismissed, because, really, where is the fun or glamour in any of that? It wasn't entirely her fault—I've seen the butterball baby pictures. She was dealt a low card from the genetic deck, destined to fight unfavorable odds on the wheel spin of human metabolism; by her late forties her body had taken on a mind of its own and she gave up the fight, succumbed to a wardrobe of caftans you could paper walls with, and a diet of chocolate, cheese, and chicken skin. The pains and aches began, she increasingly struggled to walk and stand and breathe—and she grew angry with me when I tried to suggest, so helpfully, and so annoyingly, I'm sure, maybe a healthier lifestyle, maybe some exercise? Maybe speak with a nutritionist, maybe be more mindful of some basic biological cause and effect? But she was a frolicking grasshopper, and I was a killjoy ant. Her vertebrae began to fracture and compress, inflaming nerves and curving her spine forward into a frozen capital C, hindering an upright stance. Her blood sweetened and her joints swelled; her lungs clotted up with chronic obstruction, requiring the constant companion of portable oxygen, just like my grandmother and her spaniel-tank, and the last fifteen years of her life devolved into unremitting pain and immobility. Every system in her body was breaking down, prompting a debutante's complicated datebook of doctor's appointments, hospitalizations, and procedures. She had a cluttered Lazy Susan of medications and became a junkie on prescription pain pills; she kept "losing" those pain pills, and kept charming her doctors, somehow, into prescribing more. She had always been a charming woman, the life of the party, the grasshopper dancing away in careless denial and defiance of stark, wintery realities—leaving those realities for other people to deal with. But she was also emotionally fragile, emotionally voracious, and now, imprisoned in her failing body, she became even more so, reduced to an infantilizing dependency.

I did my best to help her. But I had been taking care of her for so, so long, my whole life, it seemed—who was the mother, who was the daughter, those roles had blurred and reversed long ago—and watching her suffer, I was torn between feeling afraid for her and the chilly path ahead; despair at my inability to make anything better for her; compassion-free resentment at having to take even *more* care of her, be even *more* responsible for her now; a self-righteous desire to blame her for many of her own self-inflicted woes; and incredible guilt: This is my *mother*, who loves me so passionately, I owe her my life, I owe her everything. So I did my best. I told myself I was doing my best.

One month before her seventy-sixth birthday, her breathing became so labored she called 911 and then called me; when I found her in the ER she was gasping for breath—my goldfish mother, terrified and choking for air—hooked up to a million machines while a reassuring doctor reassured me she would be perfectly fine, would probably just go home the next day. Three days later she was moved to an ICU ward, an ill-fitting oxygen mask clamped on her face like catcher's gear; she was miserable, it hurt, she wanted the damn thing off, get it off of her, and it was a battle to convince her it had to stay; she and her lungs needed that little oxygen boost right now, was all. I'm sorry, Mom, I said over and over, I'm so sorry. But she's doing fine, her doctors told me, she'll be just fine. Three days later—vague talk of pneumonia, maybe—they jammed tubes down her throat so she could both breathe and receive nutrients and moved her to some part of the hospital that was more intensively dire than ICU. She was crying nonstop, it was painful, she couldn't talk, couldn't eat, *Please, Tara*, she tried to mouth around the tubes, tried to scribble on a piece of paper, tried to letter-trace on my palm, like Janie so long ago: Please help me, it hurts, please do something, please.

I'm sorry, Mom, I'm so sorry.

Terms of Endearment is the ultimate mother-daughter story; Aurora (Shirley MacLaine) and Emma (Debra Winger) are caught up in a lifetime of love-hate, oil-and-water, emotionally consuming battle until Emma is stricken with some undefined malignancy.[82] She is in the hospital, she is dying, in pain (a pain we never really see—her final scenes, while heart-tugging, have an almost Jenny-like sanitized prettiness), and Aurora politely reminds a nurse that it is ten o'clock; it is time for her daughter's pain shot. The nurse, busy and distracted, assures her she'll get to it. And Aurora goes off:

> AURORA
>
> It's past ten; my daughter is in pain. I don't understand why she has to have this pain! All she has to do is hold on until ten, and it's past ten! My daughter is in pain, can't you understand that? Give my daughter the shot! *Do you understand me? GIVE HER THE SHOT!*

she screams, in increasing volubility and hysteria, at every nurse she sees. And they do, of course, they scurry to help, to give Emma that blessed pain shot, and it is all because of Aurora's power, her tiger-ferocious devotion and love; she cannot give her daughter any more life, but she is going to orchestrate this death, she is going to disappear Emma's pain, goddamn it, and will happily kill anyone who gets in her way.

I want to scream at someone. I want my Aurora-self to help my Emma-mother, *Do something*, I want to shriek at them to fix this, *I don't*

---

82 *Terms of Endearment* (Paramount Pictures, 1983): written by James L. Brooks, based on the novel by Larry McMurtry; directed by James L. Brooks; with Shirley MacLaine and Debra Winger

understand why she has to have this pain, I want to make it all better for her, and, in doing so, prove to her I am a good daughter, that she was a good mother, that I love her, that I am sorry she has to suffer this, I am sorry for any second of my life I have not done or given her enough.

Instead, I ask her doctor, trying to be polite and good-girl-like, to please tell me what is really happening, here, please, be honest with me: Is this *treatment*, a miserable but temporary thing she must endure and get through in order to get to the other side of this? Or are we simply torturing her, for no reason? Oh no, he says. She'll be fine. She'll go home, soon . . . although she will be in very bad shape, probably worse than before, she will need full-time care, and the nightmarish thought of that is no comfort—to *me*, for I am more focused in this second on my own pain and fear than my mother's: How will I manage full-time nursing care, I cannot quit my job because then how will I manage to live, how much money is left, and if we run out of her money, which will happen soon, and I spend whatever money I have saved, how will I pay for my own sick and pained old age when it is my turn, me with no daughter? Will I have to put her in a Medicare nursing home? Promise me, she had begged a few years earlier, Promise me you will never put me in a home! I promise I will do my best to keep that from ever happening, Mom, I had said, choosing my words very, very carefully, so as never to break a promise to her.

Meanwhile, we need to restrain her, her doctor is telling me. We need to tie her arms down so she doesn't rip out her breathing tube. Tell your mother, explain to her: If she rips out that tube, she will die. And they do, they tie her arms down while I watch and she cries, and I do, I explain to her very carefully, and she nods, nods, tells me she understands, and she does.

I'm so sorry, Mom, I tell her. Because that is what love means; you damn well tell the person you care about that you are sorry.

But a few days later, when I arrive in the morning, the tube is gone, her hands are free, and she is smiling. She is weak and exhausted, her breath rapid and shallow and her throat whisper-raw, but smiling, in victory and freedom and with exquisite pleasure in the applesauce I hurry to get her, the most exquisite applesauce she has ever eaten in her entire life. Somehow, sometime in the middle of the night, she had ripped out her tubes, and yet here she was: Smiling, eating applesauce, breathing (rapid and shallow), asking about her cat. For an hour we sit together and smile and marvel at the exquisite magnificence of the applesauce, and I marvel at her strength and steely, stubborn determination, and then her face goes into an abrupt and frozen twist, her eyes bulging and her mouth agape, and I go screaming for a doctor.

Million Dollar Baby's Maggie (Hilary Swank) is a thirtyish gal with steely, stubborn determination to box her way out of desperate, going-nowhere poverty with the help of grizzled trainer Frankie (Clint Eastwood).[83] And she has done so, risen to the cheering acclaimed top of the boxing world until an opponent's bad-blood blow breaks her spine, sentences her for life to a quadriplegic's bed and permanent life-sustaining machines. Skin ulcers, a gangrenous leg, an amputation, while Frankie rages in unaccepting despair that he will fix this for her, he is on it. But he can't, there is no fixing any of it, and so the thing she must ask of him is to do for her what her father had done, when she was a child, for the family pet: "I can't be like this, Boss," she tells him. She got what she needed in this life—"Don't let 'em keep taking it away from me." But he can't do that, either. And so Maggie chews through her own tongue—twice, two times she bites and chews and bloodies herself in a desperate effort to choke to death, the one single thing she can do to make that happen, to die on her own terms, and twice they stitch her up and then finally sedate her so she doesn't try it again. Frankie goes to a priest to see if maybe, maybe, he can help her as she wants, but the priest confirms, of course, that Frankie cannot do that; it is in God's hands.

FRANKIE

But she's not asking for God's help. She's asking
for mine. . . . What if it's a sin to keep her
alive?

---

83 *Million Dollar Baby* (Warner Bros., 2004): written by Paul Haggis, based on stories from *Rope Burns,* by F. X. Toole; directed by Clint Eastwood; with Hilary Swank and Clint Eastwood

Your mother can't do this on her own, the doctor tells me—an on-call doctor who has never met my mother before now—your mother's body just can't get enough oxygen on its own. I'm sorry. All I can do is put the breathing tube back in. But, she says, quietly and gently and meaningfully, If I put that tube back in, it is never coming out. It is your decision. It is up to you.

That Dr. Kevorkian is a saint of heaven, my mother would say, often and out of nowhere, my devout-atheist mother. Promise me you will not allow me to live on tubes in the end, she would ask me. Promise you'll never let that happen. I had made that promise to her, too, and at this moment, now, there is the one single thing I can control, can orchestrate for her, can make happen and make better. Maude's tablets, Sol's blessed cocktail. I wish I could have done this for her earlier, charged ferociously into the hospital and somehow spared her these last ten brutal and pointless days; that applesauce wasn't worth it. But now I am going to make sure it is as beautiful and fine as possible. I am going to make it a lovely and loving thing, this ending to our love story. I am not going to *wait, wait* her death.

We are done, I tell the doctor. Do not put that tube back in. And the doctor nods, gently and meaningfully. That is the right decision, she says, this most human and humane saint-of-heaven doctor. Don't worry, I will make sure she is very, very comfortable.

And so Frankie creeps into Maggie's room at night. "All right," he tells her. "I'm going to disconnect your air machine. Then you're going to go to sleep. I'll give you a shot and you'll stay asleep. My darling, my blood." He kisses her; she smiles in gratitude. He does what she asked, what he promised her, and she dies.

My mother grows sleepy. Her breathing thins. I comb her hair. I hold her hand and hope I am sparing her from an absolute, isolating loneliness. I tell her I love her, that her cat is doing just fine. I had called family members, and they begin to arrive; we stand around her bed and say sweet things to her and to each other, but her eyes have fluttered closed and I can't tell any longer what she is quite aware of or not. I cannot tell if she is flashbacking her life, or which subtle heartbeat or breath is her last. I whisper to her that I love her, and quietly, peacefully, it is finally the final end of the person that is Beverlee, who was my mother, and then the person that is my mother disappears forever.

"'My darling. I'm waiting for you. How long is a day in the dark? A week? The fire is gone now and I'm horribly cold . . . we die, we die'," Hana (Juliette Binoche), the nurse in *The English Patient*, reads aloud.[84] She has holed up in an abandoned Italian villa to devote herself to taking care of that mysterious, unnamed English Patient, a man with a hidden backstory of wartime love and betrayal and pain, now burned by fire to a leather husk. Hana has nursed him tirelessly, has been benevolent with the morphine needed to keep him from excruciating pain. But he is done; he is ready for his story to end. As Hana preps an injection— breaking open a glass ampul, readying the needle—he reaches out a raw, leathered finger, tips over the box of ampuls, pushes them toward her. She sees his face, the imploring, wordless request. She has been determined to keep him alive, but now he sees her purpose shift, her determination acceding to his. "Thank you," he whispers. She nods, briefly, the tears coming as she loads the needle for the last time. After the injection he asks that she read him to sleep; she lies on the bed beside him, and reads aloud the letter written by his lover, Katharine, whom he had been forced to abandon to a lonely, solitary death in a desert cave:

HANA/KATHARINE

```
"We die, we die. We die rich with lovers and
tribes. Tastes we have swallowed. Bodies we have
entered and swum up like rivers. Fears we've
hidden in, like this wretched cave. I want all
this marked on my body. . . . The lamp's gone
out, and I'm writing in the darkness. . . . "
```

- - - - - - - - - - -

I don't know how I will die, of course. Stylishly, I hope. But, still: Will I meet death head held high, like a brave, misjudged queen or convict? A weeping martyr, or a murderer offering himself in expiation

---

84 *The English Patient* (Miramax Films, 1996): screenplay by Anthony Minghella, based on the novel by Michael Ondaatje; directed by Anthony Minghella; with Ralph Fiennes, Juliette Binoche, and Kristin Scott Thomas

of a confessed guilt? Will I be an old, purple-wearing woman, well into autumn or a stark winter, ready to go home? Will I be pretty and cherry-lipped in a white lace nightie, protesting that *I am young and strong and nothing can touch me*, or a bald baby bird, my body wasted and riddled with pointless poison? Will it be the malfunctioning blood, or the tumor I cannot get away with a second time, the bullet I do not see coming, the proverbial, Tara-numbered bus offering a jump-cut exit, the peaceful slip into an angel-assisted sleep? Will I have the dignity of self-determination, or will I mess myself, be left to lie in my helpless body like a helpless infant? Who will be there with me, if anyone? Will anyone be there to hold my hand? Will I have a karmic reincarnation as higher consciousness or insect, will there be that heaven or that God after all, a reunion with those who have gone before me, my goldfish swimming eternally in a bright clear bowl, my little pet mouse happily running forever on that rickety wire wheel?

Will I have lived a life that makes me ready to meet death beautifully and finely?

Or will I fight to the last, try to barricade that door, claim every last second, last breath, last beat of my heart before it is the end of the thing that is me, and the thing that is me disappears forever?

I don't know. I am writing, as all of us do, in the dark.

HOW TO
BE
MRS. ROBINSON

SEDUCTIONS, TRYSTS, AND
THE INEXORABLE TICKING CLOCK

The Graduate

Class

Notes on a Scandal

The Reader

Summer of '42

My Tutor

The Roman Spring of Mrs. Stone

The Last Picture Show

40 Carats

White Palace

Something's Gotta Give

How Stella Got Her Groove Back

Don Jon

Harold and Maude

Texasville

```
                    BENJAMIN
    Mrs. Robinson, you're trying to seduce me . . .
    aren't you . . . ?
```

Benjamin Braddock so famously says—accuses? hopes?—in *The
Graduate*, having been lured from his college graduation celebration
by the elegantly lupine, well-coiffed, and much-older Mrs. Robinson,
who, indeed, is intent on seducing this feckless younger man.[85] We
glimpsed her earlier, at Benjamin's parents' house, her appraising
Cleopatra eyes following him across the room, the predator tracking
her prey; she has manipulated him into driving her home and by
now has forced a glass of bourbon on him, put some groovy music
on the hi-fi, tossed out an intimate question or two, and announced
her husband will be home *quite late* . . . . She has this depressed and
adrift young man exactly where she wants him, is batting the nervous
mouse around in her well-manicured paws: "Well, no, I hadn't really
thought of that," she responds coolly to his question, "I feel very *flattered* . . .", laughing as though oh-so-delighted this young man would
even *think* she would even *think* of such an outrageous thing.

```
                  MRS. ROBINSON
    Benjamin, you've known me all your life . . . !
    I'm nearly twice as old as you are . . . ,
```

she protests disingenuously, as she disrobes down to a leopard-print
demi-bra and slip—one more strategy to unnerve him, make him flus-
tered and mortified and thus more malleable. And she is good, this
Mrs. Robinson; when she finally flat-out confirms her intentions:

---

85 *The Graduate* (Embassy Pictures/United Artists, 1967): screenplay by Calder
Willingham and Buck Henry, based on the novel by Charles Webb; directed by
Mike Nichols; with Anne Bancroft and Dustin Hoffman

> MRS. ROBINSON
>
> Benjamin, I want you to know, I'm available to
> you. And if you won't sleep with me this time, I
> want you to know you can call me up anytime and
> we'll make some kind of *arrangement* . . . ,

Benjamin, terrified, flees the house—but he will soon nevertheless seek her out, unable to resist this magnificent older woman's
proposition.

And how could anyone resist the magnificent Anne Bancroft? At
thirty-six, she was actually only six years older than Dustin Hoffman
(who was playing twenty), but her mature, stylish sexuality is a glorious thing: See the poise with which she orders a martini in her
leopard skin (again) coat, assures Benjamin in her butterscotch voice
he needn't be so *nervous*, snaps on the harsh overhead light when she
enters the hotel room for their first rendezvous—this confident woman
has no need of softening shadows—and suggests he watch while she
gets undressed. Benjamin is a nervous wreck, but she is the epitome
of seductive, in-control self-assurance. I love this Mrs. Robinson, all
the electricity she brings to the screen; later, when Benjamin shifts
his attentions to her plastic-pretty young daughter, Elaine (Katharine
Ross, beautiful, yes, but so neutral, so blank), Mrs. Robinson retreats
to the background of the story, and she takes all the charged-up sexy
fun with her.

But Mrs. Robinson's character also changes (or is changed?) significantly over the course of the film. As her affair with Benjamin
continues, we learn more about her—a shotgun marriage that ended
her college career, a chilly and sexless life with her husband—and
she grows more realistically multidimensional; director Mike Nichols
allows her the vulnerability of a woman at a certain age for whom life
is a gilded-cage disappointment, determined to seek out and hold on
to whatever small or visceral pleasures she can, while she can. And
when Benjamin arrives at the Robinsons' to take Elaine out on their
first date—which a jealous Mrs. Robinson had desperately sought to
prevent—the camera creeps close and rests on her face, now stripped
of makeup, dry-lipped, lined, defeated, her hair careless, an afghan

draped old-lady-like across her lap. She is no longer glamorous; she is simply sad, and she hurts my heart.

But Nichols isn't done with her. As Benjamin and Elaine "fall in love" (quotations mine, to indicate my eye-rolling rejection of this superficial "relationship"), Mrs. Robinson's vulnerability turns vengeful; by the film's end, when Benjamin rescues Elaine at the altar of marriage to some plastic Ken-doll guy, she has become a desperate shrew, the caricature, if not the prototype, of the shrieking, scorned, unstable older woman. She is easy to ridicule and dismiss, exactly as we are meant to.

I have no idea when I first saw *The Graduate*, but I was young enough to feel awed by the early Mrs. Robinson, impressed by her glamorous self-possession: This is the type of in-charge woman I wanted to become and to be. However, I was also young enough to feel comfortably distanced from the horrible wretch she devolves into: How pathetic she is, this older woman. No, she is no longer an *older woman*; she is just *old*. She is all done for, by the movie's end; no more Benjamins await her, no more erotic interludes. Time to pack up your animal-print lingerie and bourbon and bag of seductive little tricks, Mrs. Robinson, sorry—that's all over for you, now.

Nine months before my fiftieth birthday, I am sexually propositioned by a thirty-three-year-old young man (and he is a "young man," to me; he seems so Benjamin-boyish), and the first thing I think, and blurt out in response is "What, *why*?" Why *me*, is what I mean—he knows exactly how old I am, he has his choice of moist-skinned, lustrous-haired twenty- and thirtysomethings, and I am flummoxed by his forthright interest. The next thing I think, delighted, is *Well, here's to you, Mrs. Robinson.* I think of martini assignations in hotel bars and black lace garter belts with sheer stockings, of shared, soaped-up showers and steamy gropings in cars. I think of the delicious word *tryst*. I think of how long it has been since I strolled naked and sex-sated across my bedroom in the morning light before someone's watchful eyes . . . and then I think of how long it has been since I worked out, of the dusky circles under my eyes I now feel compelled to cover with makeup, of the failed promise of that expensive new collagen-boosting moisturizer. I laugh with what I hope is elegant, glamorous style—and I tell the young man how *flattered* I am, of course, but I could not even *consider* such an outrageous thing. I send him on his way, and then I start to think some more.

It's been a while, is what I think. My twenties and thirties were so *busy* with dating, and sex, and love, my oyster world of boyfriends and girlfriends and a seemingly endless supply of romantic partners and scenarios, all those tequila shots and couch cuddles, all that sweaty lace. But I had also become a little weary of the stale loop of first-date stories, the *So, where is this going?* third-month conversations, and all the overwrought drama of mismatched vulnerabilities and priorities and needs revealed by the tempering of sexual heat. All the inevitable complications and compromises. And for a while now things have been, yes, gloriously peaceful, satisfyingly calm.

But I realize my last actual date—and by that I mean sex, my last invitation to a sweaty tryst—has been much more than *a while*, has in fact been over five years ago; it was as if I awakened on my forty-fourth birthday to an erotic wasteland, a sexually barren landscape (and the sudden need for reading glasses in every room). Where did everybody go? Or . . . is it my appeal that has withered, expired, slipped away? Have I aged out of a romantic career, been retired from the game? Is it just the anthropological reality of a woman my age, the inevitable fade into sexual invisibility? Something I should simply accept with resigned grace—get rid of the lingerie, get out the afghan? Is it my turn to be *done for*, is it really all over for *me* now?

Perhaps not—for here is this adorable young man, charmingly nervous as he tries to explain just why he finds me so irresistibly hot, making me feel so alluringly self-assured, offering me, well, what could be the perfect *arrangement*, as Mrs. Robinson would say (the early glamorous Mrs. Robinson, of course, not the horrid later one). And I remember the thrill of this long-lost feeling: Being desired. The ability to quicken someone's pulse and feel my own begin a responsive sprint, the smell of someone's blood-heated skin, the dizzying myopic high of it all. And the young man keeps pursuing me—delightfully, flatteringly—and I finally think: Why would I turn down this opportunity? One that has become, I have realized, so increasingly rare? How much longer *do* I have, to offer my no-longer firm and young flesh, to tempt in this way? Shouldn't I seek out whatever small or visceral pleasures I can, *while* I still can?

And then I decided to stop thinking about it all so much, and simply say *Yes*.

The older man/younger woman pairing in films is beyond cliché or trope—it simply *is*, has always been: Art reflecting a double-standard fact of life. The actors age into distinguished gentlemen, the Carys and Clints and Harrisons and Seans, while the ingénues, once they've lost their ingénue-ishness, are replaced by a fresher, up-and-coming array—and, if they're lucky, age-morph from playing the enticing lover or eyelash-batting girlfriend into wife and mother and grandmother roles, or divorced or still-single career gals, distinguished primarily by their anxiety.

There are far fewer cinematic models for the older woman/younger man arrangement, and they generally aren't very happy ones. If the younger man is still technically an underage boy, the older woman tends to exhibit a dysfunctional neurosis or all-out pathology. In 1983's *Class*, prep student Andrew McCarthy has a passionate affair with roommate Rob Lowe's mother, Jacqueline Bisset, who turns out to be an emotionally damaged, alcoholic loon.[86] *Notes on a Scandal*'s Cate Blanchett "yields" to the precocious advances of a fifteen-year-old student, replaying her own seduction as a young woman by an older teacher and shredding two families in the process.[87] In *The Reader*, Kate Winslet seduces yet another fifteen-year-old boy and is revealed to be a murderous, unrepentant Nazi.[88] Or, the alternative narrative is the nostalgia-fantasy of a boy's initiation at the hands of a loving and sensitive "teacher," as in *Summer of '42*, with soldier's wife Jennifer O'Neill introducing young Gary Grimes to seaside, soft-focus

86 *Class* (Orion Pictures, 1983): written by Jim Kouf and David Greenwalt; directed by Lewis John Carlino; with Andrew McCarthy and Jacqueline Bisset

87 *Notes on a Scandal* (Fox Searchlight Pictures, 2006): screenplay by Patrick Marber, based on the novel by Zoe Heller; directed by Richard Eyre; with Cate Blanchett

88 *The Reader* (The Weinstein Company, 2008): screenplay by David Hare, based on the novel by Bernhard Schlink; directed by Stephen Daldry; with Kate Winslet

sexual love, or the surprisingly tender *My Tutor*, where mature blond Caren Kaye "tutors" high schooler Matt Lattanzi in French, and oo-la-la, so much more, that lucky, lucky *jeune homme*.[89]

At thirty-three, my young man certainly isn't a child: The seventeen years' difference between us might make me old enough to be his mother (ouch), but there's nothing criminal about it. But even in movies about two legal and consenting adults, the older woman is rarely anything other than a figure of sad despair or unhinged desperation. And even gloomier than the ugly downward spiraling of Mrs. Robinson, I remember, is *The Roman Spring of Mrs. Stone*, one of those old afterschool Afternoon Movies on television I channel-surfed into at twelve or thirteen—and this one, I was so happy to find, starred Scarlett O'Hara![90] I'd been a *Gone with the Wind* freak since reading it at nine years old, had seen the movie countless times, and was madly in love with Vivien Leigh and her green-eyed siren's song, could not wait to see that dazzlingly beautiful face again.

But here is no vixenish, dimpled Scarlett; she is now forty-eight-year-old Vivien Leigh playing Karen Stone, a wealthy, newly widowed actress who has, in fact, aged out of a career as a romantic leading lady:

> SCORNFUL THEATERGOING WOMAN
> My God, what's happened to Karen Stone?

> SNIDE THEATERGOING MAN
> Well, you know, there comes a time when Mother
> Nature catches up with you old gals.

> SCORNFUL THEATERGOING WOMAN
> Oh come now, she can't be *that* old!

---

89 *Summer of '42* (Warner Bros., 1971): written by Herman Raucher; directed by Robert Mulligan; with Jennifer O'Neill and Gary Grimes; *My Tutor* (Crown International Pictures, 1983): written by Joe Roberts; directed by George Bowers; with Caren Kaye and Matt Lattanzi

90 *The Roman Spring of Mrs. Stone* (Warner Bros., 1961): screenplay by Gavin Lambert and Jan Read, based on the novel by Tennessee Williams; directed by José Quintero; with Vivien Leigh, Warren Beatty, Lotte Lenya, and Coral Browne

SNIDE THEATERGOING MAN
Well, she's *forty-five!*

And while she is still *Vivien Leigh*, for heaven's sake, still a movie-star-beautiful woman with her feline bones and her dancer's posture showing off her Balmain-designed pencil-skirt suits, that beautiful face has changed; the cat eyes have dimmed, the delicate features have slipped a bit and settled into harder, more angular lines—I never imagined Scarlett O'Hara could *age*. As an adolescent, I am taken aback to see Vivien Leigh this way; it is the opposite but equally disorienting effect of seeing old photos of your grandmother, back when she was full-cheeked and glowing with a sexual spark you never imagined her—this now-ancient woman—to ever possess.

Karen has decamped to Rome, hoping to lead "an almost posthumous existence," a Voiceover announces; Karen herself tells a friend she feels her life may as well be over, that "three or four years is all I need . . . after that, a cut throat will be a convenience." She has stumbled into a culture of pretty Italian boys offering companionship to lonely moneyed women of that *certain age*; a ragged, angel-faced kid lingers hopefully below the window of her fabulously appointed apartment, haunt-stalking her literally and symbolically for the rest of the film. But Karen's casual friend, the vague "Contessa," has something else in mind for her: Karen is "only beginning to find out what loneliness is," she says to Paolo, the young stud she is planning to pimp out (played by twenty-four-year-old Warren Beatty, unctuous, indolent, and toothy). Paulo is a suaver version of the street urchin; he knows just how to pose in a well-cut suit, how to lean in attentively to a carefully-groomed woman over the candle-lit dinner table and murmur how *alike* they are in their lonely drifting. Karen is no fool; she knows it's all a hustle, an act, and she is happy to play along for the diversion and amusement this delicious young man offers—as long as there is no greater cost than those at-arm's-length dinners. She isn't one of those sad, self-deluded women, of course not.

But she is embarrassed when confronted by her cynical friend Meg:

> **MEG**
>
> ```
> Isn't it odd how women of our age suddenly start
> looking for beauty in our . . . well, our male
> partners. . . .
> ```

Meg warns Karen to be careful of what she might become—or even what she might be perceived to be:

> **MEG**
>
> ```
> A figure of fun. The stock character of a middle-
> aged woman crazily infatuated with a succession
> of young boys. . . .
> ```

Karen scoffs . . . but as Paolo manipulates her emotions, keeps her alternately ego-stroked and insecure, she becomes swoony and inflamed. When he rolls out a sob story about a buddy swindled out of money and now in dire need of "help," she knows she's being tested—and decides to test him back:

> **KAREN**
>
> ```
> When the time comes when nobody desires me for
> myself, I'd rather not be desired at all. . . .
> ```

And she retreats to her bedroom, steps out of her Balmain suit, slides between the sheets of her bed in her modest slip, and waits. Paolo does what he must; the deal is sealed.

And voila, Scarlett is, briefly, back: Karen gets a flirty new smile, a becoming new haircut, and a vivid red suit—strolling down the street, a girlish lilt to her step, she literally stops to smell the flowers. But it is only one scene later that the bickering tug-of-war begins: Karen is needy and clingy, Paolo huffy and petulant. She anxiously studies her face in the mirror, snaps on a bright table lamp to get a better look—and gasps, horrified and afraid. *Tick tick tick.* She offers to buy him new clothes; he accuses *her* of using *him*, whines their relationship is *special*, so unlike all those other arrangements: "This is different, we *love* each other," he insists, mock-insulted, Warren Beatty chewing that Italian accent hard. There is such naked longing on her face—*does* he desire her for herself, really and truly? *Is* she that special to him? Paolo is playing her, of course—or is he? We are meant, briefly, to share Karen's self-deluded hope—when he gazes into her searching eyes, I believe his protestations of love, too. But then we are invited to laugh at her, just as Paulo and the Contessa do, exulting in their inevitable payday . . . because, after all, how could this beautiful young man possibly love or desire this fading woman, really and truly, no matter how beautiful she once was?

The tabloids trumpet their affair, and Karen becomes an object of pitiable ridicule, just as Meg warned; Karen begs Paolo to reassure her she is not like all those other pathetic women: "I'm not an old fool with nothing but money to give you!" She has so much to offer him . . . doesn't she? But he is finally fed up she has not followed through on her implied promise of riches; "What are you, *fifty*?" he sneers, and walks out, cutting his losses, abandoning her.

And it hits her she has become exactly the thing she most feared: That stock character, that figure of fun—and it's too late to become anything else, to play any other role in this life. We hear the voices echoing in her head: Paulo telling her *this is different, we* love *each other*, followed by that stab of *What are you, fifty?* Her own voice, *three or four years is all I need, after that, a cut throat will be a convenience.* . . . All she can do now, at last, is toss her keys down in invitation to that ragged, angel-faced street urchin; her "posthumous existence" will be living with the death of dignity and hope.

I remember feeling so sorry for Karen; how sad, to be so old, so unalluring! She might as well be dead, sure. But now—what am I, *fifty*, ouch—with my own impassioned young suitor, my condescending pity shifts to an uncomfortable identification with her. Am I a Karen, is my young man a Paolo? Am I self-deludedly trying to convince myself I am not self-deluded, that I really am still an object of genuine desire? Older women, after all, everyone knows, are so hungry and grateful for the slightest loving or erotic caress . . . am I being manipulated? Am I just an easy lay, a gullible mark for some insidious, insulting purpose? Am I being used?

No, of course not. This is not some 1960s melodrama, I am no wilting and broken Tennessee Williams heroine, my young man is no oily gigolo, and unlike Karen I have no unsettling doubt at all that my beautiful male partner desires me *for myself.* I still might wonder about the *why*, but I do not doubt the sincerity or intensity of his attraction to me—his lack of guile is almost quaint. And if he actually *is* just using me for sex . . . well, good Lord, I tingle to think, how thrilling is that, to be deemed usable, at my age, *for sex?*

But it also seems, surprisingly, a little more than that. At least for him. We have virtually nothing in common—food and sex can just about carry us through an evening, but . . . —and I have assumed this will be the briefest of carnal flings, a one or two or three nights' stand, maybe a couple of weeks (which is fine, I tell myself, three or four weeks *is all I need*) and then the thrill—of novelty? of conquest?—will fade. But months pass, and he makes clear he considers this a "relationship," that what we have is "real"; he wants dinners and movies and that cuddling on the couch, he abjures the idea we are mere fuck buddies or friends with benefits. He uses the language of emotional intimacy, of lovers, of boyfriend-and-girlfriend, and I am bemused by his earnestness.

Nevertheless, I am clear this "relationship" isn't going to go anywhere or last very long, as I insist to my friends, the few friends I have told the story of this young man—I am both proud of and embarrassed by this little arrangement, have found myself, in response to a teasing slew of "Mrs. Robinson" jokes, repeatedly asserting that *he* pursued *me*; I am no leopard-skin predator. (At the same time stressing that *seventeen years'* difference between us—that number has become magically arousing to me, a geometric proof of desirability, an erotic math.) I announce that I am simply carpe diem–ing for a while, indulging in an amusing and diverting experience. One friend congratulates me for finding a boy toy, another wants explicit details of the raunchy sex with my "young dude," another refers to him as my "new puppy," and I chuckle along. They all seem a little envious, which pleases me; I am no sad stock character, no ridiculous, pathetic figure of fun.

But my friends, at the same time, also express concern that I will wind up getting hurt—and this I find annoying. Why assume *I* am the vulnerable one in this, that I will be the one to suffer, to pay some price? Is it just a given that an older woman, at some point, cannot possibly hold the sexual interest of a younger man? Is that *tick tick tick*ing so predestined? Can't my story be different? Am I not hot enough, am I not special enough to defy a supposed biological imperative, to beat that anthropological clock?

I'm certainly no poor Ruth Popper, right?

The Last Picture Show, like *The Graduate*, seems like one of those films I have never not seen—but, as with *The Roman Spring of Mrs. Stone*, I find my perspective on the story and my investment in the characters has changed over the years. . . .[91] At one time I identified, or wanted to identify, with Jacy (Cybill Shepherd), the nubile blond number in this desolate 1950s Texas town whom all the boys—and men—want. But the storyline that now both fascinates and disconcerts is the relationship between eighteen-year-old Sonny (twenty-year-old Timothy Bottoms, sad and child-eyed) and older housewife Ruth Popper (Oscar-winner Cloris Leachman, also sad-eyed, forty-five but playing forty). I had only ever seen Cloris Leachman as the nutty and narcissistic Phyllis from *The Mary Tyler Moore Show*, and it was a bit shocking to see her in this role—she is timid and matronly, all clumsy movements and stammering speech, hair in a prim twist. Sonny has been charged by the high school football coach to drive his wife, Ruth, to a doctor's appointment; afterward, she invites Sonny in for a soda, "If you can stand me a few more minutes . . . ," then weepily apologizes for taking up his time. She is the anti-Mrs. Robinson, the opposite of Karen's chic sophistication, poor plain dear.

But there is something there between them, timid housewife and despondent teen: They are both living, as Paolo once manipulatively alluded to, a life of lonely drifting, and they recognize that in each other's sad, sad eyes. They begin an affair that is painfully poignant in its awkwardness, both of them so terrified they can barely manage to undress. Their first sex is quick and unsatisfying, and Ruth weeps again with . . . what? Fear? Relief? Disappointment? Hope?

---

91 *The Last Picture Show* (Columbia Pictures, 1971): screenplay by Larry McMurtry and Peter Bogdanovich, based on the novel by Larry McMurtry; directed by Peter Bogdanovich; with Cloris Leachman, Timothy Bottoms, and Cybill Shepherd

                              RUTH

        I'm sorry I cried. Just scared, I guess . . .
        scared I could never do this, I guess. I can't
        seem to do anything without crying about it. How
        could you like me?

                              SONNY

        I like you.

                              RUTH

        I'm glad. . . .

As the relationship continues, it is less about lust—it was never
really about lust, anyway, unlike my relationship with my lusty young
man—and more about a domestic companionship, a nourishing balm
to their loneliness; they have both been reawakened to an emotionally alive life. Ruth serves Sonny cookies and milk, brushes his hair,
dreams of buying "them" a new quilt for "their" bed, her face aglow
with tenderness, with purpose. And while she has become happily
maternal (which I am decidedly *not*, in my lusty feelings toward my
young man), she also seems younger than both Ruth's age and Cloris
Leachman's actual older age; her bliss and the black-and-white cinematography have softened the contours of her features, making her
delicately beautiful. She is genuinely in love. But while Sonny has
also grown attached to their intimacy—another sweet young man
with no guile, he has never wanted anything from her but herself—
he nevertheless abandons Ruth the moment the manipulative Jacy, in
a pique of petulant boredom, invites him out for a burger and fries
and a makeout session with her firm young body . . . leaving poor
Ruth Popper sitting on "their" new quilt on "their" bed, all dressed
up pretty and waiting for her young man, who will never come again.

    Until the end of the story. Jacy dumps Sonny, his buddy Duane
heads off to Korea, his friend Billy gets hit by a truck and killed, and
Sonny is once again living a posthumous existence in a dying town,
aimless and emotionally numb. He shows up at Ruth's door, asks if
he could have a cup of coffee with her—she is stunned to see him,
embarrassed by her disheveled hair, her frumpy robe. She seems

emotionally renumbed as well, back to looking her sad-eyed age; she
looks even older than Cloris Leachman's actual older age. She apologizes for her robe, allows him in, tries to pour some coffee, her hands
shaking—and then hurls the cup against the wall, allows herself the
release of anger:

RUTH

Why am I always apologizing to you, you little
bastard? Three months I've been apologizing to
you, without you even being here! I haven't done
anything wrong. . . . You're the one made me quit
caring if I got dressed or not. I guess just
'cause your friend got killed you want me to
forget what you did and make it all right? I'm
not sorry for you. You'd've left Billy, too, just
like you left me! I bet you left him plenty of
nights, whenever Jacy whistled!

I guess you thought I was so old and ugly you
didn't owe me any explanation. You didn't need to
be careful of me. There wasn't anything I could
do about you and her, why should you be careful
of me? You didn't love me. . . .

You shouldn't have come here. I'm around that
corner now. You've ruined it. It's lost, completely. Just your needing me won't make it come
back.

He can only gaze at her, a lost, wordless little boy. He takes her
hand, and that one vulnerable touch—the infant clutching at his
mother—erases all her hurt and jealousy and rage. She puts his hand
to her cheek,

RUTH

Never you mind, honey. Never you mind . . . ,

she murmurs soothingly. This is it, then; he needs her for something,
and she'll take it. Whatever it is—comfort, friendship, mothering,

maybe sex, maybe not, maybe just being another body in the room, another clutching hand and lonely beating heart. But she's right; whatever reinvigorating, revitalizing thing they once shared—love?—or that he brought into her life, *is* ruined now. It is lost, completely, and has taken the last of her reawakened hope and faith with it.

I'm not going to become a sad Ruth Popper, not ever, no.

- - - - - - - - - - -

O ne night with my young man, I speculate how our "relationship" will come to a close, as if raising this question will illustrate my lack of anxiety, my sophisticated expectation that this little arrangement of ours will, of course, end. I casually mention, chuckling, that my friends worry I will get hurt—a notion he rejects, because he is sure some "distinguished gentleman" with far more to offer will come along and sweep me away. I do not point out the dearth of distinguished gentlemen lining up at my door, but he has a point: They once did, my own Carys and Harrisons and Seans, and I once liked that. ("You're used to being the young one, aren't you?" my young man had said, smiling, when we swapped some of our romantic and sexual histories.) I had always liked older men, yes, was happy to trade bloom for worldliness; I liked the empowering yet kittenish feeling their interest gave me, that faint echo of my Lolita days. Indeed, my last relationship, six years ago now, was with a man almost twenty years my senior. But as my stepmother, fourteen years younger than my father, once said to me: *Honey, at some point, an older man just becomes old*, and she was right.

So is it my turn now, to feed off this young man's carefree vitality, his boundless, unsullied energy? Passion offers a heightened awareness of and sensitivity to life, but also a blinding, consuming distraction from whatever existential terrors one is stalked by—I think of the vampiric Countess Bathory of legend, who bathed in the blood of virgins for the collagenlike infusion of their youth; am I her metaphorical contemporary, trying desperately to halt or turn back the clock, mute the ominous *tick*ing, stave off age, decay, death? Because that soak-up-their-essence ploy is not just figurative or the stuff of myth, I've learned—that stuff *works*. I *have* been revitalized by this young man's fresh pulse. I am working out, eating my veggies, breaking out the lacy lingerie once again, bothering to put mascara on, giddily gathering roses. I do feel reawakened; I must admit to myself that I have absolutely become emotionally invested in this, yes, *relationship*. I am, I realize, genuinely in love.

Not that I am in love with this young man. For all his adorableness, his sweet-and-nasty sexual skill, despite the genuine affection we feel for each other, this is not a love affair, for either of us—we barely know each other. But I am in love with the experience he can create, or re-create for me; the truth is, this relationship is all about feeding my aging ego, bolstering my saggy sexual self-esteem, assuring me I am still oh-so-damn hot. And I find myself feeling a bit ashamed and guilty about this. Am *I* just using *him*?

But that is also a reassuring thought, offering me the illusion of control, here . . . because I *am* getting anxious. That ticking clock is increasing in volume, getting so intrusive, so distracting. I'm feeling sexually empowered, sure—oh my, did that twenty-five-year-old barista just *flirt* with me?—but I am also, paradoxically, feeling more insecure than I ever have in my life. Do you not see the crepey skin of my throat, I find myself thinking when my young man and I are trysting. Do you not notice my Shar-Pei belly, the spider veins on my thighs, that old hag chin whisker I always forget to pluck? Are you unaware of how I always strategize to be seen in the kindliest, most low-wattage light? Do you not see the calcium tablets in my medicine cabinet, my posthysterectomy prescription for estrogen? Do you see all this and not care? Does it inspire your tenderness toward me, your pity? Is it fetishistic for you, a source of arousal, a form of *gerontophilia*—sexual preference for the elderly—or *anililagnia*: the "atypical" sexual attraction of a younger man to an older woman? Am I just some new experiment in kink?

But this doesn't have to end with my being rejected or getting hurt, I remind myself; there are some happy models for this. A few. The older woman isn't *always* a vicious Mrs. Robinson, a vulnerable, defeated Karen, a sad sack Ruth. In *40 Carats* (1973) Liv Ullmann stars as a forty-year-old divorcée, who enjoys a rapturous one-night fling on a Greek island with twenty-two-year-old Edward Albert; they rediscover each other back in New York City, and he pursues her relentlessly until, overcoming her anxieties, she succumbs to his adoration and they go prancing back off to Greece together.[92] *White Palace*'s twenty-seven-year-old James Spader is fixated on forty-three-year-old Susan Sarandon, and their age difference is played up as transgressively erotic, whetting the "Oh, we can't *possibly* be together!" forbiddenness of their pairing.[93] *Something's Gotta Give* has late-thirties Keanu Reeves falling madly in love with fifty-seven-year-old Diane Keaton—until she rejects him for "age-appropriate" Jack Nicholson; forty-something Angela Basset gets her *Stella*-groove back in the coconut-oil arms of twentysomething Taye Diggs.[94] Thirty-two-year-old Joseph Gordon-Levitt, in his 2013 *Don Jon*, is finally able to overcome his addiction to online porn and his inability to experience true intimacy with the help of fifty-three-year-old Julianne Moore.[95] And the gold standard, of course, of the happy older woman/younger man love story is 1971's *Harold and Maude*, which my young man and I watch together one night (he had never seen it, maybe never even heard of it, ouch . . .), the ironic humor of which I did not appreciate until halfway through; Harold, eighteen, and Maude, eighty, are blissfully, anililagniacally in love, until the end when she, well, dies.[96] (She was eighty, after all.)

But other than Harold and Maude or the so-rare example of a Diane Keaton giving up a young Keanu for a paunchy Jack, we do not see how these older woman/younger man relationships actually work or

92 *40 Carats* (Columbia Pictures, 1973): screenplay by Leonard Gershe, based on the play by Jay Presson Allen; directed by Milton Katselas; with Liv Ullmann and Edward Albert

93 *White Palace* (Universal Pictures, 1990): screenplay by Ted Tally and Alvin Sargent, based on the novel by Glenn Savań; directed by Luis Mandoki; with Susan Sarandon and James Spader

94 *Something's Gotta Give* (Columbia Pictures, 2003): written and directed by Nancy Meyers; with Diane Keaton, Jack Nicholson, and Keanu Reeves; *How Stella Got Her Groove Back* (20th Century Fox, 1998): screenplay by Terry McMillan and Ronald Bass, based on the novel by Terry McMillan; directed by Kevin Rodney Sullivan; with Angela Bassett and Taye Diggs

95 *Don Jon* (Relativity Media, 2013): written and directed by Joseph Gordon-Levitt; with Joseph Gordon-Levitt and Julianne Moore

96 *Harold and Maude* (Paramount Pictures, 1971): written by Colin Higgins; directed by Hal Ashby; with Ruth Gordon and Bud Cort

eventually end; there is nothing beyond the climactic What the hell, let's throw societal convention to the wind and just *be together*! Of course we almost never see how any love story "ends"—the Jane Eyre "Reader, I married him" (and then Mr. Rochester got his sight back and we had a kid and we really, really are living happily ever after in the burned remains of Thornfield Hall . . .) type of coda has gone out of style. But we know in our hearts that crazy Scarlett and Rhett are going to work it all out, that Mr. and Mrs. Smith will stop assassinating people and go buy a nice dinette set and raise beautiful children, that Tom Hanks and Meg Ryan will grow cozily old together in matching cardigans. We subconsciously extend the narrative beyond *happily ever after*, invest in the mythology of true love's longevity after the *The End* of the standard rom-com.

There is a subliminal bittersweetness, however, to the older woman/younger man love story, because, yes, that anthropological ticking clock is so damn loud—we can hear it over the closing credits. We know on some level this misaligned pair are not going to grow old together, that their mutually enthralling passion has already peaked; let the wane of lust begin. One of these two is going to grow older, and one is just going to grow old, and guess who is going to leave whom?

Nothing shows this more literally and visually than *Texasville*, the 1990 sequel to *The Last Picture Show*, set in 1984, thirty-odd fictional years after we last saw Sonny, Jacy, and Ruth.[97] Sonny/Timothy is now middle-aged (Timothy, thirty-nine, ineffective makeup trying to age him to fifty), but Ruth/Cloris (sixty-four, effectively playing seventy) is now an old woman, edging toward shriveled crone—forget about their being together now (they aren't, and their storyline is minimal), the thought of them ever having *been* together borders on distasteful, creepy. What does Sonny/Timothy think, if anything, when he looks at Ruth/Cloris now, I wonder? What does she think back on, when she looks at him? "He loved me once . . ." Ruth says, and I cannot tell if that is gratitude in her voice, or longing, or regret.

---

97 *Texasville* (Columbia Pictures, 1990): screenplay by Peter Bogdanovich, based on the novel by Larry McMurtry; directed by Peter Bogdanovich; with Cloris Leachman, Timothy Bottoms, Jeff Bridges, and Cybill Shepherd

SNIDE THEATERGOING MAN
Well, you know, there comes a time when Mother
Nature catches up with you old gals.

Everyone worries about losing a lover's love, of course; the fear of
rejection is present from time to time in all relationships. I have been
rejected, and I have been the one to reject: Hurt, heal, move on, repeat.

But this time the fear feels different; this young man has brought
into my life a thrilling reminder of my body's most euphoric function,
a validation of my visceral presence in the world; I have my groove
back. And I fear, this time, when that unabashedly lustful gleam fades
from his eye—when Karen's harsh table lamp inevitably snaps on,
when he leaves me sitting alone on my bed like Ruth—he will take
all of that with him. And that without that last-gasp bloom he has
reinspired, I will have little to offer—or, like Karen, I will try to offer
whatever I have left, but will find no sincere takers. And then what?

PAULO
What are you, *fifty*?

Yes, Paulo, I am. I will soon no longer be an older woman; like Mrs.
Robinson, I will simply, at last, be old. Will I become that caricature,
then, that

MEG
. . . figure of fun. The stock character of a
middle-aged woman crazily infatuated with a suc-
cession of young boys,

tossing my keys to some cute baby barista guy? Is that how the story
of my sexual life will conclude?

"What's with all the hand-wringing?" my friend Theresa says.
"You have plenty of options, just go out there and find someone! You
don't have to be alone!"

But it isn't a partnership I crave. I'm not afraid of being alone—
that's my comfort zone. I'm afraid of losing something else from my
life: The thrill, the steam, the primal heat, the divine pulsing spark

of desirability. I have heard older women describe the fade of their sexual allure as liberating, but I fear, when that is extinguished or lost, that my own posthumous, invisible, dismissible existence will begin. And I cannot shake that fear, I can't stop thinking about this, I can't fake out Mother Nature or stop the clock or control any of this, and the anxiety is not doing my crow's feet or worry lines any favors.

So I tell my sweet young man that our time together has come to an end. That he's lovely, but this no longer works for me. That I wish him all the best: *Go, have fun,* I say.

Because this feels like the last elegant, self-assured, self-protective thing I can do. Older skin is thinner, more delicate. I bruise easily these days. This is the one way I can have any control at all over this narrative. It is the only way I can know how this part of the story will end—the only way I can sit on my own quilt, on my own bed, by myself, by choice.

And he protests just enough to satisfy, for a moment, my hungry, fragile ego, and then he goes. His options are unlimited, after all. He has all the time in the world.

HOW TO
BE A
WRITER

THE BEACH HOUSE, THE BATHROBE, AND SAVING THE WORLD

Julia

The Shining

Rich and Famous

Reds

Doctor Zhivago

Sophie's Choice

The World According to Garp

Sunset Boulevard

The Big Picture

Barton Fink

Sullivan's Travels

Wonder Boys

am, in my beginning, a plagiarist.

As a kid I was effortlessly good at a little bit of a lot of things. Which was fine, but complicated by having benevolently enthusiastic and supportive parents: Twirl a bit, and *You can be a ballerina!* Swim a few laps without gulping water into your lungs—*Aim for the Olympics!* Nurse that baby bird back to health—*You'll be a brilliant doctor some day!* No future occupation was beyond my casual grasp, thanks to my obvious if gestational talent. One day, when I was around six or seven and feeling bored (or perhaps terrified) by all my looming potential, my mother suggested I go into my room and *write something*. A poem, a story, a song. I liked the sound of that. I retreated behind my closed door, armed with pencil and paper, to go *write something*. To go be a writer. I sat on my bed and waited for the easy *en pointe* twirl, the smooth glide through waves, the robust flap of tiny wings.

Nothing came, except for panic. A fear of failure. The blank, dun-colored page of my school tablet glared.

This wasn't easy—but the concept of labor required for victory seemed inelegant, even absurd. I waited for achievement to come, magically—and I didn't know how long a writer should take before coming out of her room with a poem, a story, a song. But I couldn't come out without having become a writer. Without having *written something*.

Or—here was a way out—without having *something written*.

I pulled from my shelf an old book of poems for children, took it into my closet, crouched on the ground next to my Mary Janes, and copied out, word for word, in deceptively bold little-girl block letters, a poem I found there about a little girl and an apple tree. Something about apples, and maybe some baskets to fill. A couple of rhymed quatrains, most likely an *apple/dapple, tree/free* type of scheme. And presented it with a nervous flourish to my mother. I awaited judgment. The proclamation: A whole poem, you *wrote* this, it's brilliant, my God, you'll be a writer some day, you *are* a writer, *now*, already, a fine, fine writer. Go, write!

Six years old, I'm told I'm a Writer, and it's an abrupt joy to me, a rush, suddenly the coolest, most crucial thing in the world to be. It obliterates the pallid pastel ballerina in my mind, scoffs at the meager dangle of a gold medal around my neck, burns from my nose the medicinal scent of doctorhood. I don't know why this identity, this label—*You're a writer*—hits me so hard, but it lures. It sounds both private and exhibitionist. Adult, yet redolent of mud pies, of popsicle stick creation. It smells of fresh-sharpened Ticonderoga pencils and beloved, transcendent books. And how easy it was! (And I want the victory of it badly enough to ignore the crunch of the lie in my gut.)

I wanted to be a Writer long before I ever wanted to write.

What do you want to be when you grow up?

Kids see this question in primary colors, in the rub-a-dub-dub nursery-rhyme world of butchers and bakers and candlestick makers. Kids generally don't proclaim a desire to become systems analysts or data processors; they have to be able to *see* what people do or make, and *see* people doing or making it. In my childhood world, my friends and I looked to our mothers and fathers and step-parents, to our immediate experience of going to school, getting booster shots, playing with the family dog, and then we latched on to the corporeal, easily identifiable idea that people become teachers or doctors or veterinarians. Of course, there were also movies and TV to look to, so we also planned to become actresses, ballerinas, and rock stars.

But I didn't know any *writers*. There weren't any down the street or at friends' houses or school. Both of my parents were readers, which helped, which breathed the printed word out into the daily air and atmosphere—ubiquitous books were used for coasters, makeshift forts, notepads, and tantrum-inspired missals, and gift certificates to B. Dalton were the favorite Christmas, Hannukah, and birthday presents. I was wildly fortunate that books were a quotidian part of life. But there weren't any *writers* to see, to watch, to look *to* or *at*. The posed author photos on book jackets didn't count; I studied those faces for their writerly secrets, but they just looked like ordinary frozen-in-a-pose people. Even in the movies or on TV, I just didn't see any writers around, doing their writerly thing.

So, six years old, and not only do I want to be a writer, I'm supposed to already be one. I can see the product of writers everywhere, the thing the writer makes, and I love the scent of it, the feel of the paper, the pussy-willow corner tips of worn hardbacks, the fanning flip of paperbacks, the look of pages stuffed thick with print. But I can't see The Writer anywhere, the doing of the writing, the action itself, the model. And I know, of course, that it *is* a lie, my being a Writer, my first dirty little secret, first fraud, that book of children's poems buried under shoes in my closet, and my stomach twisting when I think of that, and I know I better find out, fast, how to be a real Writer, before the world is on to me.

The first movie about a writer I ever saw was *Julia* in 1977, when I was thirteen.[98] I was still supposed to be a writer, which is easy when you're a child—kids can say they're going to be whatever and don't need to provide supporting evidence for it. So, aside from that one purloined poem, I never actually produced any writing—I was waiting for the writing to just *appear*.

Then, *Julia*. Opening credits, then a lovely twilight shot of an isolated clapboard beach house lit from within, and the sound, the *sound* of typing—the crisp, old fashioned *clack clack clack*, the kind you know is generated from a tinny, antiquated manual typewriter before you even see it, and, sure enough, we enter the beach house to find Lillian Hellman typing away, in a chenille robe, her hair rumpled, the toughening touches of a cigarette dangling at her lip and a tumbler of half-drunk amber liquid nearby. It's 1934 (calendar with Roosevelt on the wall), and she's writing, writing away. I have no idea who Lillian Hellman is, but here is a *Writer*, that much is clear. The first living, breathing, moving image of a Writer I've seen. I suddenly want

---

98 *Julia* (20th Century Fox, 1977): screenplay by Alvin Sargent, based on the memoir *Pentimento* by Lillian Hellman; directed by Fred Zinneman; with Jane Fonda, Vanessa Redgrave, and Jason Robards

that chenille bathrobe, I want that forehead attractively creased up in thought. She stops stabbing at the keys and peers at the page; the typewriter ribbon is black and red, and I vaguely remember my grandfather owning a typewriter like that, one you didn't plug in, one that didn't respond to a whisper of touch but that you had to jab at, hard, with your unaccustomed fingers, the firm left-handed push needed for the carriage to drop down a line, and how you hit a certain key to raise the red strip of ribbon up to type in crimson ink for emphasis. I remember what effort it took to type anything, the conviction you needed with each single letter or number or punctuation mark, each decisive punch. I realize I never saw my grandfather actually use that old manual typewriter, and I wonder what he kept it around for—was he, in fact, a writer? Did he type away on hidden novels at night, is there a secret stash of poems and plays? Is being a writer actually in my genes, my blood? I used to play on that typewriter when I was a kid, and I make a mental note to find it; maybe my parents have the thing stashed in the garage.

Lillian doesn't like what she sees on the page—she tears the sheet from the typewriter's grip, throws it in a trash can full of crumpled pages, and goes to the window; outside a worn-faced but handsome man is heading up from the ocean's edge with a bucket, where he has obviously dug them a dinner of clams. The first line of dialogue, I remember so clearly:

> LILLIAN
> It's not working again, Dash! It's falling apart
> again.

I recall feeling that in-the-closet kind of frustrated panic, and watching Lillian confirm this idea is comforting; writing *is* effort—it wasn't just me and my stupidity!—it *is* work, it's something you have to build and then have to watch fall apart. It's a rickety city of warped wooden blocks, a sand castle precariously close to sea. But she's a Real Writer, so surely there are tricks to get you by, secrets to be learned. Maybe it's just the effort of that manual typewriter that's necessary, and then the rest is graceful ease.

I begin taking notes.

Dash—himself the Real Writer Dashiell Hammett, though at thirteen, I have no clue—tells her to put on a sweater and drink some whiskey, he'll build a fire, and they'll have dinner. We cut to her sitting before the fire, wearing a lumpy cardigan (I want that sweater), drinking the whiskey, and moping.

<pre>
                    DASH
    If you really can't write, maybe you should go
    find a job. Be a waitress. What about a fireman,
    huh?

                   LILLIAN
    I'm in trouble with my goddamn play and you don't
    care!
</pre>

He suggests she go to Paris to work on the play, or Spain, there's a civil war going on there and maybe she can help somebody win it. Maybe she can visit her friend Julia there. She's barely listening.

<pre>
                   LILLIAN
    I can't work here!

                    DASH
    So don't work here. Don't work anyplace. It's
    not as if you've written anything before, you
    know. Nobody'll miss you. It's the perfect time
    to change jobs.
</pre>

Okay, I tell myself; so she *isn't* a writer, not really, not yet. No wonder she can't do it. No wonder she's struggling. Perhaps that's why it's so hard for her; she isn't the Real Thing.

<pre>
                   LILLIAN
    You're the one who talked me into being a writer,
    Dashiell. You're the one who said stick with it,
    kid, you got talent, kid! You soft-soaped me with
    all that crap. Now look at me.
</pre>

DASH

> If you're going to cry about it, go stand on a rock.
> Don't do it around me. If you can't write here, go
> someplace else. Give it up. Open a drugstore. Be a
> coal miner. Only just don't cry about it.

She certainly should just give it up, I think. Why work so hard? In my mind, of course, that doesn't mean she can't still be a *writer*, at least in name. Just keep telling people you are one.

We retreat to Lillian's childhood memories of her beloved friend Julia, where Young Lillian is unformed, bewildered and intimidated by this worldly, glamorous girl. They grow up; mature Julia is brilliant, idealistic, wholly committed to social justice and willing to fling herself into a crowd of marauding Fascist thugs. I don't understand most of her politics or philosophies, but she's clearly a muse for Lillian, with her lacy blond hair, her passion for an engaged life. There's clarity and enlightenment in her very blue eyes. She's damn intoxicating. I fall under her spell, too:

JULIA

Work hard! Take chances! Be very bold!

she calls back to Lillian as she leaves for Oxford, and I realize those are the very three things I've never done, I don't know how to do, and they aren't really necessary, really, are they? But if Julia wants me to, perhaps, perhaps . . . I feel inspired, emboldened. I want to earn Julia's approval.

Lillian visits her later and mentions she isn't writing much; Julia urges her to get involved with people who are really "doing something" to change the world, *then* Lillian will know what to write about.

I will! I will! I make an italicized mental note of this: *I will change the world!* I feel raring to go. I will take up my mighty pen and do battle! As soon as the movie is over.

Lillian goes to Paris to write, as per Dash's advice and on his money; she holes up in the charmingly crummy Hotel Jacob, for seven seconds of typing among scattered plates of bread and cheese and fruit and half-drunk glasses of red wine. By now I'm looking hungrily for such images, taking notes on the Writer Writing, so I can see the Working Hard, the Taking Chances, the Being Very Bold. It all looks marvelous. Lillian is wearing a white linen blouse, and I love bread and cheese and fruit, I'm sure I'll love red wine some day, but it's seven seconds, that's all. A tease. So, how do you get from the cheese and the bread to saving the world? And what is she writing? Does that matter?

Lillian sees oppressed workers marching for their rights outside her window, and retreats, frightened—she's no Julia. Julia is the one doing something; Julia has been fighting those thugs on her mission to stop Mussolini and Hitler, and Lillian finds her beaten to a pulp in a Viennese hospital. Soon afterward, Julia mysteriously disappears, and Lillian decides to go on home.

We're back to the beach house and the bathrobe. A sandwich, a bottle of beer, and more thrilling but fleeting images of Lillian writing, images I scrutinize for their secrets. Is that how you sit, is that how you bite into bread, is that the pace one types at? (And what the hell *is* she writing?) She screams in frustration; she hurls the typewriter out the window. Then, a quick later, a proud smile as she types THE END five times at the bottom of a page. It's an orgasmic fulfillment, an achievement of enormous weight. We never did learn what Lillian was writing, what she found that was so important to write about, but no, it doesn't matter; the work is done and it took only a minute, even less. The Saving the World can begin.

Now Dash is seated in an Adirondack chair on the porch, reading the pages. Lillian watches him read, and my heart starts to pound . . . because it *isn't* finished, it isn't all over. Someone must now *read* those naked, fuzzy, black-ink words. I remember awaiting my mother's judgment, the proclamation of victory or defeat. This is horrible. I see Lillian's anxiety, but I'm sure it will be fine for her—she's done all the right things, hasn't she? She's in a beach house, she's in Paris, in a chenille robe, in a linen blouse, she used a manual typewriter that demanded firm conviction. And Julia is her dear friend, believes in her, told her to be bold and work hard and take chances, and I'm sure she did, she's actually *written*, we *watched* her do it. So she's a writer now, right?

Then:

```
                         DASH
   You want to be a serious writer. That's what I
   like, that's what we work for. I don't know what
   happened, but you better tear that up. Not that
   it's bad. It's just not good enough. Not for you.
```

Again, still no idea what she actually wrote, only that *it's not good enough.* I would be devastated, I'd fall apart, dissolve into tears at such lacerating dismissal, and I'm sure now she'll walk away, become a fireman or a waitress. But I'm stunned by Lillian's impassive face, by the fact that she doesn't crumple; I'm even more stunned by the immediate return to *work*, by the black-and-red typewriter ribbon sent on its jerking, scrolling way, by the late-night and early-morning attacks on the keys intercut with more walks on the beach and chopping an onion and gazing at the ocean through a clapboard window . . . then back at the desk, always, back to work. I'm amazed by this; it rivals, in my mind, Julia's foolhardy courage and her subsequent beating. I don't understand how Lillian has survived Dash's brutal attack; I don't get her willingness to hurl herself back into a crowd of thugs.

But, I console myself; it's only thirty seconds or so of screen time, no real sweat. She still looks elegant as hell.

Dash reads the rewritten pages, while Lillian paces on the beach, tries to smoke a cigarette, tries not to watch. He finally walks over to her, an agonizingly slow walk.

```
                         DASH
   It's the best play anyone's written in
   a long time.
```

(Ah, a play, she's been writing a play . . .)

```
                        LILLIAN
   Are you sure?
```

<pre>
                    DASH
I'm positive.

                  LILLIAN

                 (A beat.)
But are you sure?
</pre>

Cut to: Success, acclaim, opening night at Sardi's, where Lillian is overwhelmed by *Brava*s and applause. "They think I'm wonderful," she babbles on the phone to Dash, "I'm the toast of the town!" Later, back at the beach house, she tells Dash that she likes being famous and fantasizes about what to do with the royalties pouring in—a sable coat? Or should she give it all to Roosevelt?—and Dash reminds her:

<pre>
                  DASH
It's only fame, Lily. It's just a paint job. If
you want a sable coat, go buy one. Just remember:
It doesn't have anything to do with writing. It's
only a sable coat and doesn't have anything to
do with writing.
</pre>

Who cares? She goes off on a fancy tour of Europe, bejeweled and lipsticked, wearing her sable coat and hanging out with Hemingway and Dorothy Parker and Cocteau. She dances, she's feted, she's now staying at the Ritz. But a friend of Julia's mysteriously appears (Maximilian Schell, soft-voiced and gentle), with a request from Julia that Lillian carry money into Berlin—they need cash to smuggle out Jews and political prisoners. Even I feel the sudden shame of that sable coat; Lillian feels obligated and guilty, and I don't blame her. One play! Written in mere seconds of screen time, and now look at all that jewelry—doesn't she owe the world more than that?

Work hard. Take chances. Be very bold.

What a failure she is, I think. What a fraud. How will she ever face Julia again?

But Lillian agrees to do it; she gets on a train to Berlin, wearing thousands of dollars stashed in a fetching fur hat (I didn't really want the sable coat, but I wanted that hat), and passes the time in reverie about Julia. Passing through Customs at the German border, Lillian is questioned by a Border Guard, a Central Casting Aryan, who raises an eyebrow at the Jewish-sounding "Hellman" and asks:

> BORDER GUARD
>
> What is your occupation?

> LILLIAN
>
> I'm a writer.

> BORDER GUARD
>
> A *writer*?

> LILLIAN
>
> Yes.

> BORDER GUARD
>
> So . . . (menacing pause) you would write of Berlin?

> LILLIAN
>
> Oh, no, I wouldn't.

> BORDER GUARD
>
> Perhaps your impressions, you would write?

> LILLIAN
>
> My impressions? Yes, I would, write my impressions. . . .

She's just a *playwright*, for heaven's sake, I think—what's all the fuss? What in the world is so threatening? I'm surprised and confused that this is what causes the stumble, rather than her Jewishness. I don't understand the threat—it's the money in the hat that's dangerous, isn't it? Why does her being a writer disconcert?

But I'm thirteen; I'm too busy being thrilled by the answer to *Occupation* and how seriously that's taken. For the first time I imagine some stranger asking me that, my filling it out on a form, the public declaration of that identity. I feel the same thrill I felt at six, the same rich whiff of paper and pencil and ink.

And this is the end of the Writing. Lillian makes it safely to Berlin and, in a clandestine café meeting over caviar, delivers the money to Julia. It is their farewell scene; Julia is murdered soon after, and Lillian spends many scenes trying to find out how and why and in despair at the loss of her friend, her beloved mentor and muse.

But Lillian gets to have it all, do it all—the beach house, the bathrobe and the sable coat, and saving a little bit of the world, too. And if we never heard a word of her writing, or even what she was writing about (*did* she write her impressions of Berlin?), it doesn't matter. I'm even more profoundly, delusionally in love with the Writer, not the Writing, with the beach house, with Paris, with the bread and cheese, with walks on the beach, with the sound of that typewriter, with being loved and feted by glamorous, brilliant, vivid-eyed friends, with the identity.

This is what I decide I like: The paint job. This is what I decide to work for.

I graduated high school, I went off to college, I kept very busy trying to become a Writer without doing any Writing. This wasn't too hard—I could still pass as a writer, mostly thanks to other people's assumptions; I was terrible at math, and if you're terrible at math but possess a basic verbal competence, it can get balanced out by appearing that you're gifted at words; I turned in good reports because my father, in the guise of helping me with homework, rewrote my school papers word for word, and then he'd get the As; I loved to act in school plays, thus receiving a cross-genre benefit (somehow, liking to be in plays helps people assume you must like writing them); and because I genuinely loved to read, and if you carry a book everywhere, you easily get labeled as a writer as well as a reader. At college I declared myself an English lit major, because all the reading involved in being an English lit major would be good preparation for when I magically became a Writer. I even started writing my own papers, without my father's help; I still got As, but that wasn't real writing, that was just fulfilling assignments, rote, formulaic, Discuss the Symbolism of the White Whale assignments, and I didn't flake out on assignments.

A friend and I went to see *Reds*.[99] I'd been looking for other images of writers in movies since *Julia*, the way I stayed alert for glimpses of sex. *The Shining* had a novelist, who holes up for the winter in an abandoned hotel with his wife and kid.[100] He writes, literally, like mad; lots of shots of Jack typing, in a growing frenzy, wildly productive, until it's revealed his accumulated pages are the output of a diseased mind; we/his wife discover the thick sheaf of paper contains only one sentence over and over, in varying layouts: ALL WORK AND NO PLAY MAKES JACK A DULL BOY. Lots of fun, but Jack wasn't a real writer, and the lesson here is clear: When someone works too hard at writing, that someone will go insane and run after loved ones with an axe. (i.e.: Writing is unhealthy.)

Better when writing is all *play*. *Rich and Famous* had two writers, a Serious Writer and a Trashy Writer, neither of whom we ever see either write a word or evince any desire to Save the World—all I remember is Jacqueline Bisset, as the Serious Writer, flying to New York to see her editor and having sex on the plane with a handsome guy, which seemed like a pretty cool lark; Jacqueline meeting her editor at the Algonquin for drinks, which seemed like the most sophisticated thing a person could ever do; and Candice Bergen, the Trashy Writer, living in yet another house on the beach.[101] Paint job, paint job, paint job.

But *Reds* offered a three-and-a-half-hour beehive of writers, journalists, poets, and playwrights, arguing politics in cafés, wearing fabulous late-Edwardian clothes—and also, again, frolicking in a clapboard beach house. They drink a lot. Their explicit aim is, like *Julia*, to Save the World, but also, in the midst of an epistolary rant about Socialist politics and liberating the oppressed American worker, John Reed interrupts himself to explain to his girlfriend, Louise Bryant, that he's unhappy with the rhyme scheme of his in-progress poem

99 *Reds* (Paramount Pictures, 1981): written by Warren Beatty and Trevor Griffiths; directed by Warren Beatty; with Warren Beatty, Diane Keaton, and Jack Nicholson

100 *The Shining* (Warner Bros., 1980): screenplay by Stanley Kubrick and Diane Johnson, based on the novel by Stephen King; directed by Stanley Kubrick; with Jack Nicholson and Shelley Duvall

101 *Rich and Famous* (MGM, 1981): written by Gerald Ayres; directed by George Cukor; with Jacqueline Bisset and Candice Bergen

about lilies, that he must change it as soon as he can. Flower poems and revolutionary action are placed on a par. What does one have to do with the other? I wonder. How can you liberate an oppressed worker with a lily poem? That's hardly the stuff of sneaking money across Nazi-thick Europe.

Their politics don't intrigue me as much as their sex lives; Louise is the focus of beach-house passion for both John Reed and playwright Eugene O'Neill, and, when that's young Warren Beatty and young Jack Nicholson, well, that's deserving of admiration. But she is more than that; she, too, is a writer. Or, she's often asked, *So, Louise, what do you do?*, but her insecure peep of a response—*I'm a writer*—gets lost in the crowd. She keeps trying to assert this identity, but it vaporizes, it's brushed aside. We never see her write; even John berates her for this, that she says she's a writer, she wants to be a writer, wants to be taken seriously as a writer, yet she doesn't write much, or write about anything *serious*. This strikes me as incredibly unjust; he, obviously, takes his ode to the lily pretty damn seriously. And we don't see him write much, either, so why does he get all the respect? We never actually see *anybody* write; they talk *about* writing, they argue about the meaning and the goal of it, they put on their plays for each other, they make literary love. But dramatizing politics and sex is more, well, *dramatic* than the static shot of the writer at work; crowds of the proletariat marching for their daily bread, and riots that draw swords and blood, and tortured romantic triangles, naked moonlit romps in the ocean, all this is easier to act, direct, film, offer for visualization. It's a movie jam-packed with writers, all of whom have more important and, yes, interesting things for us to watch them do than write. I learn how to manage a messy triangular love affair and rabble a crowd to over-throw a tsar—and this is fine with me, for now; all I want is the beach house and the literary sheen of love affairs with brilliant, literary men. And I learn calling yourself a writer really does seem to get the job done, especially for a woman—nobody may take Louise seriously as a writer or a revolutionary, but it doesn't matter, she's still the object of fascination and desire, she still hangs with the writing crowd, she's still the star of the show.

The writers in *Reds* are actively trying to save the world, but Dr. Yuri Zhivago, in *Doctor Zhivago*, is trying to avoid it; he is a writer, yes, but he's far more often shown in his capacity as a doctor, fine and admirable, rushing to stitch up bloody Muscovites trampled by tsarist cops.[102] But his girlfriend, Tonya, really loves him *because* he's a writer—she's teasingly asked at a party if she'd ever marry a doctor and replies only if it were a doctor who wrote poetry, too. Writers, clearly, are hot.

But Yuri has the bad luck of being a poet and apolitical in Revolutionary Russia—his work gets him in trouble, not because it's revolutionary, but because it isn't. We don't really know what he writes about—the poetry of this up-and-coming Russian poet is never quoted or read aloud—nor, again, do we ever see him write, at least not for the first three hours of the movie. But there's a clue when his half brother, a minor Revolutionary official, comes to warn him that he's in danger, that his poetry is "not liked." Zhivago is bewildered (I feel the pang in my heart for poor Yuri, who seems far more stricken than Lillian did) and is told it's because his writing is considered "petty, bourgeois, and personal." Once again, the writer is a threat; but while Lillian, at least, could write her impressions of Berlin and thus, perhaps, reveal certain things the Nazis don't want revealed, if this writer's work is indeed petty, bourgeois, and personal, then why the hell would anyone care? I don't understand where the danger lies.

And Yuri is not a dynamic kind of guy—he means well, but as a movie hero he lacks the drive to make things happen, he lacks the John Reed/Louise Bryant/Lillian Hellman anxieties and energies. It's immaterial to him whether he doctors for the Reds or the Whites; he has no Big Cause, other than doing what he can for the patient in front of him. He doesn't want to fight, all he wants is to be left alone (with either his wife or his lover, Lara, whichever woman he happens to be with); he tells his half brother he admires him for wanting to create a new and better world, but that meanwhile, people have to *just live* while that's happening. To my mind, that makes him boring. Too passive. I bet he writes petty poems about snow and borscht and all those yellow flowers, and this is not the kind of writer I plan to be. We

---

102 *Doctor Zhivago* (MGM, 1965): screenplay by Robert Bolt, based on the novel by Boris Pasternak; directed by David Lean; with Omar Sharif, Julie Christie, and Geraldine Chaplin

spend a lot of the movie watching him watch what's going on around him—I suspect Omar Sharif was cast for the size and liquidity of those big brown eyes. I don't buy the idea of Red officials being "after him" because of his writing—this man is strikingly insignificant, the very definition of small potatoes.

But there is one scene, late in the movie: Yuri and his lover, Lara, in the dead of winter, have fled to the icy ruin of a *dacha* while awaiting their fate, where they wear great turtlenecks and make love and eat hearty meals that materialize out of nowhere. One night, Yuri, unable to sleep, finds pen and ink and leaves of paper and sweeps dust from an escritoire. The balalaika music swells; he dips the pen in the ink and draws LARA in elegant Cyrillic letters at the top of a page. He glances back at beautiful Lara, asleep, then furiously begins to write. It's the first and only time we see him write, a rare burst of Zhivago-passion, and we immediately cut away. Lara awakens in the morning to find the floor littered with inky, balled-up, abandoned pages, and one perfect sheet of paper with a perfect LARA love poem resting on the table.

It's a beautiful, romantic image—yet he's still no hero to me. So he wrote one poem, and a *love* poem, at that—where's the sword, the glorious battle, the noble death, the contribution? I like the writing at dawn, the wolves howling on the steppes, and those Cyrillic letters are pretty—but it's clear to me that Dr. Zhivago is far more vital, effective, revolutionary, *heroic*, as a doctor than as a writer. At least that way he saved a few people's lives.

A t college, I heard if you had a Creative Writing "emphasis," you were excused from courses in both Chaucer and Milton, neither of whom I found comprehensible. But you had to submit "original creative work" to get into those writing courses. You can do this, I told myself. On your own, without stealing or stealth. Writing something "creative" can't be worse than reading *The Canterbury Tales*. I sat at the IBM Selectric my grandfather bought me for college (his old manual typewriter had long since disappeared, alas) on which I tapped away my English lit papers at two in the morning and waited. I got a drink of water, a cup of tea, a bottle of beer. I got up to pee several times. Perhaps the Selectric was at fault; I found lined paper and experimented with a series of pens (expensive fountain pen I'd been given as a high school graduation present, a felt-tip that looked too intimidatingly like permanent marker, a Bic ballpoint whose scratchy letters looked too frail), a variety of pencils (No. 2 Ticonderogas were too soft, harder leads wrote too thin and faint). Chaucer and Milton loomed and smirked. I got up and put on a linen blouse. You're Lily, you're Louise, I told myself. Make Julia proud. Prove yourself to John and Eugene. Write a silly lily love poem, how hard can that be? I waited for the montage, the thirty seconds of typing that would Save the World.

I can't remember the moment of writing. I know I didn't plagiarize another *apple/dapple* poem—I wasn't that stupid, these were college professors, not my gullible love-blind mother. I suspect I tricked myself, told myself this was not a "submission of original creative work," it was just another school assignment not to flake out on. But I must have written something, cobbled together some meaningless anecdotes into a story, strung iambic phrases into a poem, because I wound up in enough writing workshops to become, emphatically, a Creative Writing person.

I wrote the bare minimum I could show up and get away with, to lessen the risk of being exposed. A sentence took forever to compose; I was floored by the casual flood of pages and pages and pages my fellow students seemed to generate with ease. I tried to pay attention in these workshops, but I was too scared to reveal my idiocy, my fraud, by commenting much on other students' superior, real, earned work or engaging much in the theoretical discussions of *craft*. I did learn something about narrative arc, and the definition of *aubade*; I learned the difference between a metaphor and a simile, and that adverbs were lazy; I heard somewhere that Sylvia Plath used to read thesauri like dime-store novels, so I took to doing that, too, and highlighting obscure polysyllabic words with a shriek of fluorescent yellow. I learned a writer needed to create one's own *writing space*, something like an altar, I supposed, with sacred objects on one's desk like a rock or shell and quotations by Virginia Woolf and Flannery O'Connor pinned to the wall, so I did that, too. I kept sneaking into the club; the bouncer kept waving me in. Each time I was accepted, there was the relief, then the fear—now that I'm here, I *have* to write. And, having written, the judgment will come, the exposure. Dash will tell me *It's not good enough*. The people in charge of running the world will tell me I and my work are *not liked*. Perhaps I was no longer a plagiarist (my mother wasn't going to show up on campus waving that unearthed book of children's poems), but I was still going to be found out, any second now. I took to writing my paltry short story and poetry assignments one hour before they were due, which left me a loophole: Of *course* it's terrible; I wrote it in only forty-two minutes! Better you try to fail—you're more assured of victory. Effort wasn't just inelegant, it was terrifying; it left you vulnerable, your soft naked underbelly exposed to the blow.

At least I had my professors to look to, this time—they were actually Real Writers, with many real and written and published books, the first writers I'd ever met, dazzling in their mere existence. But I was far more curious about their lives than their writing. One professor was an Irish writer of beautifully rendered novels I wouldn't come to appreciate until ten years later; another was a charismatic local guru, an earth mother to the Los Angeles community of fiction writers who offered writerly pearls to us students but whose only advice I latched on to at the time was the importance of sending thank-you notes to everyone you meet on engraved, writerly looking stationery. She also insisted that to be a writer, you must write at least five hundred words every day. She was adamant about this one, but I hoped my nice new stationery would get me past the Border Guards.

For our final class with the Irish novelist, he invited us to his home in Malibu; our workshop trooped out to find, yes, a *house on the beach*, lunch laid out for us on the brick patio, ham and baguettes and wine and cheese, a house with overstuffed white furniture and honey wood floors and charcoal sketches on the walls by, I assumed, famous artist friends of the writer, and shelves, shelves, shelves of books. We all drank a lot of wine on this most perfect, inspiring afternoon; the Pacific Ocean, the saline breeze, the halfhearted wine-infused literary conversation, the honey ham and honey wood floors, and the whisper in my ear: *This can all be yours, this is the writer's life.* Of course it was— just look at Lily and Dash, at Louise and John and Eugene. They're out there, strolling the sand. The sex and the wine and the consoling ocean rush and crash, the smell of salt, the floor-to-ceiling books making a fortress of your home. Such an alluring lesson. So apparently possible.

But my two professors, between them, had written well over two dozen books. They must have each written at least five hundred beautifully rendered words a day for years; they'd earned it. I'd written, for all intents and purposes, nothing. And *tick tick tick*, I wasn't a kid anymore, whose wild fantasies are endearing; at some point soon I was going to have to offer evidence. Real evidence. I was going to have to write.

Write what?

> JULIA
>
> People in Vienna are really doing something to change the world. You must come. Then you'll know what to write about.

Maybe that was it—I just couldn't write *right now*. Because I hadn't found anything to write *about*. Maybe writers really must go away somewhere, like Dash and Julia told Lillian, like John telling Louise she needed to run off to Moscow with him; writers must pack up their bags and wander off into another world, a foreign world, for focus, inspiration, adventure. Jack Nicholson went off to the mountain hotel, but took along his wife and child to go crazy on; perhaps you have to go further away from the familiar, be a stranger in a strange land, escape from your own insular little world and be absorbed into the more important world of others. Be both alone and, at the same time, with a cast of strangers.

Sophie's Choice proved it.[103] Young Stingo, at the beginning of the movie, is a fresh-faced Southern boy on a bus to somewhere, and we hear his inner thoughts:

> STINGO VOICEOVER
>
> I had barely saved enough money to write my novel, for I wanted beyond hope or dreaming to be

---

103 *Sophie's Choice* (Universal Pictures, 1982): screenplay by Alan J. Pakula, based on the novel by William Styron; directed by Alan J. Pakula; with Meryl Streep, Kevin Kline, and Peter MacNicol

a writer. But my spirit had remained landlocked,
unacquainted with love and a stranger to death.

(I note that he doesn't say he wants to *write*; he wants *to be a writer*.
I find this very comforting.)

Stingo wanders into foreign-to-him, post–World War II Brooklyn
to write his novel and meets up with Sophie, a gorgeous Polish refugee, and her brilliant boyfriend, Nathan, in their big pink Victorian
boarding house. He's a stranger in their strange land, with a small
pocketful of cash to finance the writer's voyage of discovery and a
case of Spam to live on. We await the arrival of love and death. Sophie
and Nathan accept him immediately as a Writer, giving him a book
of Whitman to welcome this "young novelist from the South." Stingo
does write for us (manual typewriter, rumpled clothing, furrowed
brow, slow-growing stack of pages), but it's another mere montage of
writing, a musical interlude intercut with Sophie and Nathan's com-
ings and goings, and the trio hanging out together. It's another writing
striptease, the appealing appearance of sweat without the strain of
sore muscles or psyche.

Sophie and Nathan's blind, unjustified faith in him is splendid.
"You will move mountains," Sophie assures him. Stingo is slightly
uncomfortable with this.

STINGO

You don't know if I'm really talented. You haven't
read anything I've written.

SOPHIE

Well, I don't ask you about that work, what it's
about, because I know a writer, he likes to be
quiet about his work.

Which launches Stingo into confession:

STINGO

It's about a boy, a twelve-year-old boy.

> SOPHIE
>
> So it's autobiographical.

> STINGO
>
> Well, to a certain extent, maybe it is. It takes
> place in the year his mother dies.

> SOPHIE
>
> Oh, I didn't know your mother died.

> STINGO
>
> Yeah, when I was twelve.

At least we know what he's writing about. So, clearly, he didn't need to go away from his own life to find material; he only needs his spirit awakened.

Nathan pressures Stingo to let him read the novel, but Stingo protests—he promised himself when he started he wouldn't show it to anyone until it was finished.

> NATHAN
>
> You mean you're terrified someone won't like it.
> What's the worst that can happen? I might dis-
> cover you can't write.

Even as a joke, this makes fear cramp my gut. Nathan absconds with the precious pages, then later takes Stingo, Sophie, and a bottle of Champagne on a moonlit jaunt to the Brooklyn Bridge; Stingo is in a panic, like Lillian, awaiting judgment. Nathan climbs a streetlight and offers an elaborate and inflated toast:

> NATHAN
>
> On this bridge, where so many great American
> writers have stood and reached out to give
> America its voice, looking toward the land that
> gave us Whitman . . . from this span for which

> Thomas Wolfe and Hart Crane wrote . . . we wel-
> come Stingo into that Pantheon of the Gods, whose
> words are all we know of mortality. To Stingo!

The music rises up, Nathan flings his glass into the Hudson, Stingo's face is glazed with joy, and I think, *Yes! I want to give America its voice, too!* The lure of the beach house is gone—give me the writer's penury and a can of Spam, if only I can be toasted on the Brooklyn Bridge, reach out and join the Pantheon of the Writing Gods. I'm madly in love, too—not with Stingo or Nathan, not even with the writer or with the writing, but with this kind of affirmation, this promise of glorious and eternal contribution. All I need to do, clearly, is go somewhere to awaken my spirit, to experience love and death (and write), and such riches can be mine.

Unfortunately, Nathan is also a paranoid schizophrenic, and it isn't long before he becomes suspicious of Stingo's friendship with Sophie and turns on him:

> NATHAN
>
> Baby Southern artiste, you have not fooled me,
> young Stingo. Since you so graciously allowed
> me to read your magnum Southern opus, your
> puling adolescent self-pity for your poor dead
> mother. . . .

We've been sucker-punched; here is that awful blow, the club in the hand of the thug. At least Dash offered Lillian the renewing, inspiring admonition of her talent; at least John Reed and Eugene stayed in love with Louise. Stingo, like Zhivago before him, is stricken; this is the most painful moment of the movie, for me, this crushing, annihilating pronouncement.

Which is odd, because this movie is *not* a story about Stingo the young writer, of course, not really—it's about Sophie, and her horrific life in Poland, in Auschwitz, her struggle to survive in the face of evil. Stingo's just a subplot, the film's storyteller of someone else's more important story. Sophie's the one who suffers real pain, real loss; the annihilating moment of the movie is intended to be the moment she's forced to choose between her children, a situation horrific on a scale beyond the ability to imagine. Sophie doesn't save the world, she isn't even able to try—her struggle is to save herself, and her children, and she ultimately fails at both. Stingo only tries to save Sophie, and fails. So he's ultimately unheroic—his writing couldn't save her, and, really, who *would* care about that self-absorbed mess of a puling adolescent book when people with real problems everywhere are dying like flies? How ridiculous to just write about your mother dying when you were twelve—who cares? Novels and Nazis; there's no contest. All Stingo's writing comes down to is the thing by which he is judged and found worthy of love or disdain. It's ultimately meaningless, and I can't forget Nathan's annihilating blow.

But neither can I forget Sophie's loving assertion of faith. (*You will move mountains.*) Or that moment of Champagne on the Brooklyn Bridge. And perhaps, after the movie, Stingo went on to finish his novel (and we can sort of assume he does, given the Styronic narration), and perhaps it became something very bold. Perhaps, now that he's had his adventures, become acquainted with love and on intimate terms with death, he went on to move a mountain or two. Perhaps he saved someone, I tell myself.

I tried. I went away, to have adventures; I'd lived a sheltered, landlocked life, too, and maybe I needed that shock and grope we experience when stripped of our context. What the hell had I experienced? What real experience had I even seen? I lived in France for a year, ate the bread and cheese and drank the red wine, hoping the babble of another language would send me scurrying back into my own. I traveled a lot, Italy and Russia and Greece, sat for hours in cafés thinking profound thoughts, pen frozen in hand, as everything ticked away. I berated myself for wasting time, for being a big lazy adverb of a person. I did write stacks of cheery, chatty postcards and voluminous letters, about food and hairstyles and the latest fresco or fountain I'd seen, the latest guy I'd slept with, the magnificent inspiration with which I was constantly being suffused—five hundred words a day was easy, as long as they weren't intended to be five hundred words of *real writing*. I tried to meet Sophie or Nathan or revolutionaries, people with bigger stories I could learn from, but it was mostly other American students with backpacks looking for adventures of love and death to write about, too. Everywhere I went I bought blank books— charming French schoolchildren's notebooks, Florentine hardcovers with bargello or marbled designs—that I was too scared to stain with my puling adolescent self-pity or insignificant observations. I amassed a large collection of them, lugged them around from country to country, and waited for border guards to menacingly ask me what my *occupation* was and would I write of my *impressions*. I took good care of those empty, hopeful books, because I hoped one day I'd open them and find them magically full of words.

Because, I realized, I still had no clue where those words came from. Not only did I have nothing to write about, I couldn't even get past the mechanics; I couldn't translate real thought out of myself and into the written word and onto the page. I was full up on images of the Writer at Work, the montage of typing and drinking beer, the European wandering. But I wasn't getting how words—real words, serious, written-down words—take shape to form people and pictures and tales that burst Athena-like out of your brain. Even if I found something to write *about*, I still had no idea how to make the writing *happen*. I'd learned all I could about How to Be a Writer; but without the writing, I was nothing. I stopped telling people I was going to be a writer. It was too late. If it hadn't happened by now, it never would.

What a failure. What a fraud. How would I ever face Julia again?

It's difficult to capture and depict the internal creative process visually. Movies about painters or dancers can show us how early daubs of paint evolve into Art on the canvas; the dancer straining to stretch at the barre can suddenly break into graceful grand jetés. We can watch the dance; we can gaze at the painting. Movies about musicians might show us Mozart or Beethoven in the messy, cacophonous act of composition, but then we get to *hear* the magnificent opera or concerto; a sculptor's lump of clay or block of marble becomes the Pietà or Camille Claudel's famous foot. Perhaps we can't touch, but we can still study and appreciate the product, not just the process.

We can watch a writer write (or eat a sandwich or stretch or gaze out the window), but you can't visually depict the inner workings of the writer's brain, the translation of cerebral electricity to language, the actual transformation of thought, image, theme, emotion, character, into mere words on a page. Thank God movies show us writers doing battle and making love! You can see the product only at a remove—that book on the shelf, that one perfect page of a Lara poem, perhaps a scribbled line or two of text—and you can't see the process at all, not really.

Then, *Garp*. I saw *The World According to Garp* in 1982, and for the first time I truly saw a writer writing.[104] Young Garp announces he's going to be a writer in order to impress young Helen, who is a reader, not a writer, but announces she'll only marry a writer, and a real writer at that. (Helen echoes Yuri's Tonia, here—Garp, a wrestler, asks if she'd ever marry a wrestler, but Helen replies only if it were a wrestler who's also a writer, a real writer.) Garp immediately tells her he spends a lot of time imagining things—it's part of his training as a writer, a real writer. Later, when a different girl he's sleeping with asks Garp how he knows he's going to be a writer, he replies with enviable assurance:

> GARP
> It's just something you know.

> GIRL
> What are you going to write about?

> GARP
> My life, once I've experienced enough.

I expect we will now see Garp go on to have meaningful experiences, but we just cut to Garp, sitting in his room, facing the typewriter. I'm waiting (yawn) for the archetypal montage—the eating of a sandwich, the seconds of typing, the bottle of beer, the pacing. Perhaps

---

104 *The World According to Garp* (Warner Bros., 1982): screenplay by Steven Tesich, based on the novel by John Irving; directed by George Roy Hill; with Robin Williams, Glenn Close, and Mary Beth Hurt

he'll throw the typewriter out the window, he'll bemoan (yawn) how it's all falling apart again. I dully wonder what he possibly has to write about—even he knows he hasn't experienced enough. All those generic, fleeting images of writers have gone flat and mystery-less for me. Garp looks out his window, through the slats of Venetian blinds; he blinks and sees his neighbor playing jazz; *blink*, the memory image of his playing as a child at his grandparents' beach house (!); *blink*, he sees himself wrestling; *blink*, he's running across a field with Helen, trying to recapture hundreds of loose, escaping pages whirling about. It's the oddest beginning to a writing montage I've seen, and I perk up, just a bit.

He goes for a walk in the city; movers are trying to get a grand piano into an upper-floor apartment window; there's a couple getting out of a cab and arguing; there's a glove lying in the gutter. We're suddenly back with Garp at his typewriter, and suddenly the couple are in his head, fighting about their relationship; the man is then hovering four flights overhead, playing the hoisted, dangling piano; the woman is begging him not to jump; the man tosses down to her a glove as a token of love, and it symbolically lands in the gutter. Garp is taking these bits and pieces of life and weaving them into a story; we're inside his head, we're *seeing* him do this. It's the first visual depiction of the writing process I've ever seen; it's like snapshots of cerebral impulses, clicking the pictures he sees in his mind. It doesn't involve words, it *can't*—this is a movie, we're here to watch images, not to read—but it's a quilt of impressions, a weaving together of images stitched into narrative. It's Rumpelstiltskin; it's profoundly generative; it's photosynthesis, gleaning nourishment from the very air.

This is writing, I think! This is what a writer does, how he does it. I get it, for the first time, and I feel hope. You don't need to go to Europe or have wild adventures or tap the lifeblood of a mysterious and suffering stranger's soul—just look out the window, look around you, observe the glove in the gutter and fancy how it got there, speculate on the strolling couple in crisis. Create experience out of that; insight into the human condition is just seeing, then connecting the dots. And being able to witness this excites me—it has finally morphed in my mind from theoretical discussion to tangible process and form.

Garp's first book confirms he's a Real Writer; he and Helen marry, buy a house (not a beach house—no need for a beach house, not for a *real writer*!), and all is well, but: Garp's mother, Jenny, has also written a first book, which becomes an enormous cultural phenomenon, and from this point on the writing's over; we're suddenly back to the paint job, to the quandary about sable coats. Garp becomes increasingly concerned with his mother's fame at the expense of his own. "Nobody is buying my book!" he complains, "I'm starting my second and the same nobodies are going to line up not to buy that one, too," while his mother's book is being translated into Apache. Helen tries to console him—he's an artist, Jenny is merely a cult of personality, but:

GARP

I don't want reviews! I want an audience!

And we never see him write again. The movie turns cloyingly domestic: Taking care of kids, extramarital affairs, hanging with a transgender buddy. I'm disappointed in him. He has one more writing flurry—a book about a young traumatized girl, and writing becomes, briefly, an explicitly political act. My admiration for him is refueled; he is compelled to tell the story of this one girl because she cannot tell it herself, and I find that noble and worthy. It's a small cause, perhaps, the recording and thus saving of one small life in a world full of Nazi-size evil, but sweet Garp gets all riled up about it, and it confirms my suspicion—that all the Lara and lily poems, the retreat into navel-gazing introspection, the logging in of mere ordinary people's lives, doesn't really count; a real and serious writer takes on Real and Serious things, bigger than one's petty self.

But it's just a flurry. His identity, his calling as a writer, is over.

HELEN

Do you miss writing?

GARP

No, not at all. If I do, I'll start again.

I feel betrayed; Garp's definition of himself as a writer is too casually elastic for me, too slippery. Isn't there destiny involved? Where is
his dedication, his passion, his commitment to Art? Doesn't he want
to save the world, join the Pantheon of the Gods? Why doesn't he get
his ass in the chair; he's supposed to be a writer, and a writer writes;
why doesn't he just do his job?

But this line of thinking becomes increasingly uncomfortable to me.
It isn't fair for me to take it out on Garp; I don't have a leg to stand
on here. And, I remind and console myself, he does die young at the
end. Maybe that's what kept him from becoming a real writer, from
fulfilling all that looming, burdensome potential.

I graduated college with my BA in English literature, emphasis: Creative Writing—the lie that appears on my transcripts—and took a
job at a property development company in Westwood for $18,000
a year. I was relieved to have found a job and equally terrified this
was the fence my life was now teetering on. Peep: *I'm a writer*—I still
wanted to assert that at dinner parties, but I knew I had no right. I
was merely one of tens of thousands of English lit grads and Creative
Writing emphasizers, and there was no beach house in sight, no handsome literary lover to dig me a dinner of clams. But two months later
a friend and I sold a screenplay we'd been working on nights and
weekends, and I leapt—stumbled?—off that fence onto another one,
a higher, prettier fence, one that felt more like a pedestal, if you were
willing to look at it the right way.

So, I was a screenwriter. I told myself it counted. I bought an expensive linen vest that looked a bit Edwardian and bohemian writer
glasses; I bought my first computer to replace the IBM Selectric and
process all those screenplay words, a laser printer, a copy of Syd
Field, brass brads and reams of three-hole-punch paper to stack in my
writing space. When my partner and I wrote at my house, I remained
assertively in pajamas and bathrobe. But being a screenwriter isn't
so much a literary enterprise as a social one; it's talking a lot *about*
writing. It's going to pitch meetings and story meetings and talking

to death about plot points and act breaks and character arcs; it's going to screenings and long, overpriced lunches with other screenwriters to piss and moan about development hell. It's meeting your agent or producer for dinner at Spago and trying to feel like you're Jacqueline Bisset at the Algonquin. I told myself I loved it, all of it, and much of the time I did.

My partner and I watched movies about screenwriters. *The Big Picture* made us laugh hysterically but also wince; early in the movie an earnest young screenwriter, fresh from winning an award at film school, eager to make important and powerful movies, is wooed over lunch by a potential agent: [105]

> AGENT
>
> Look, I'm not going to bullshit you . . . I'm going to be straight with you. I don't know you. I don't know your work. But I know that you have *enormous* talent.

It doesn't feel like Sophie's groundless assertion of faith; it's grounds to snicker at them both, and the earnest young screenwriter slowly succumbs to the slick Studio Executive who forces the evolution of his story from a nuanced study of love among a quadrangle of mature adults to a romp about ghost stewardesses in bikinis. (My writing partner and I soon learned that, as satire goes, this was not farfetched.) *Sunset Boulevard* has a gigolo hack screenwriter promising to write a script in exchange for being kept by a delusional and faded movie queen—but the screenwriter never writes, not even in a montage; screenwriting is a party game, a power play, a flirtation.[106] Barton Fink tries to write, in *Barton Fink*, and pity poor Barton Fink for trying; this Clifford Odets–style Real Writer is trapped in a seedy Hollywood hotel room, on a deadline to deliver a fluffy, trivial

---

105 *The Big Picture* (Columbia Pictures, 1989): written by Christopher Guest, Michael McKean, and Michael Varhol; directed by Christopher Guest; with Kevin Bacon and Martin Short

106 *Sunset Boulevard* (Paramount Pictures, 1950): written by Charles Brackett, D. M. Marshman Jr., and Billy Wilder; directed by Billy Wilder; with William Holden and Gloria Swanson

script, watching the wallpaper peel and sweat while slowly losing his writerly mind and his literary pride from having made this deal with the devil.[107]

Sullivan's Travels has a successful writer/director who makes fluffy, trivial movies; he decides he wants to make an important film, something real and serious, and he hits the road in search of true suffering, in order to properly document the human condition.[108] Through a series of zany adventures Sullivan winds up convicted of a petty crime and sentenced to hard time on a chain gang, where he is among, finally, the suffering dregs of humanity. One night these beaten-down, wretched beasts of burden are treated to a fluffy, trivial movie; the poor, suffering men start to laugh; the successful writer/director learns the value of offering the world something fluffy and trivial, how we all need those mindless moments of joy, and he is humbled. My partner and I felt smug because we identified with all these screenwriter anguishes; it meant we were the real thing.

The real thing, as in *screenwriters*, and I had to learn the screenwriter's rules: You force your fine prose into screenplay format (which as a form is more rigid and less organic than a sestina); you don't overwrite description (i.e, leave a lot of white space so the exhausted, overworked reader doing coverage can make it a quick read); you write only what the camera sees, capture the externals, reduce human existence to slug lines (INT. JACK'S BEDROOM—DAY, EXT. MEXICAN RESTAURANT—NIGHT) and make sure characters speak with an eye toward their dialogue margins on the page.

And a screenplay, as a piece of writing, isn't a finished thing—a screenplay is only a phase of a story, on its way to *becoming* its realized existence: a movie. So by definition, it isn't Art; it's one embryonic part in the construction of Art, the crude charcoal sketch, the stumbling choreography, the sculpture's wire armature, the mere tinkering with melodic notes. A screenplay is something the screenwriter creates and nurtures and possesses, briefly, then sends on its way. For

---

107 *Barton Fink* (20th Century Fox, 1991): written and directed by Joel Coen and Ethan Coen; with John Turturro

108 *Sullivan's Travels* (Paramount Pictures, 1942): written and directed by Preston Sturges; with Joel McCrea

other people to turn into whatever kind of thing they want. You wave bye-bye from the door and hope it isn't run over by a bus.

I wrote scripts about characters I told myself not to get attached to, but with whom I always fell, as during a one-night stand, into a passing, passionate love. I wrote sentences I knew I'd wind up cutting in the delivered draft because they slipped into character introspection or an irrelevant linguistic play. I told myself with each assignment that I was going to be a good screenwriter and do whatever the stupid Studio Executive asked, invite in those bikini'd spectral stewardesses, all in order to get those big fat checks (buy a sable coat, or give it to Roosevelt?) and pay for my label as a writer; I'd wind up shrieking in story meetings like a hissing feral cat trying to protect her young, but I'd usually cave in the end and go slinking off, check in hand, final draft delivered with the other.

But if a script is developed in a forest and there is no one there to produce it . . . ? Amazing, how screenwriters can earn a nice living writing those things and never see anything they write live to tell the story. Time after time I turned in scripts to someone who wrote me that check and then locked my writing away forever in the dark drawer of Development Hell. I thought I heard my characters howl in protest. I told myself these characters weren't real, and I swore anew, each time, that I would never fall in love again. I told myself that I was not selling myself, but I worried, late at night, that all those characters I was trafficking in would sneak up on me in the dark and take a razor to my throat.

This was much worse than being a plagiarist.

But it would get me closer to that beach house, I was sure. *Occupation?* I was asked on insurance claim forms, by mail catalogue operators, by people at hipster parties; I wanted to peep *I'm a writer*, but I still couldn't. I'd only be found out. The question became ominous, as if asked each time by an Aryan Border Guard. I could never say it; *I'm a screenwriter* I said instead, filled out, muttered with a sheepish nod, but it didn't satisfy; it confirmed that I was a mere pimp of words.

I thought about Garp. His glove in the gutter, his hovering piano, his creation of stories that come to fruition there, on the page, and that's all they need to do. How at one point, that dazzled me, it felt like more than enough to aspire to in life.

For many years as a kid I slept in a T-shirt that said
ALCATRAZ SWIM TEAM, a souvenir from one of my parents' vacations.
Alcatraz had always intrigued me: Capone and the Birdman, the fog.
The mythic, iconic Rock. I'd seen *Escape from Alcatraz* at least three or
four times. In 1992 I went off to visit friends in San Francisco and took
my first tour of the island and learned how the families of the prison
staff actually lived there, in an Ozzie-and-Harriet kind of family com-
pound. I thought about being a woman or young girl in this most
masculine and foreboding place and was further intrigued. What a
great story. A mother-daughter story, on Alcatraz. I start playing with
it. It will be a screenplay, of course. Sigh. I think about how to structure it in three acts (the climax: a convict escapes and holds the mother
and daughter hostage!) I think about how to pitch it (Chicks on the
Rock!). I think about which stupid Studio Executive might like it. It
takes place, of course, in another era, in a real environment I know
virtually nothing about, and I begin to research it. This absorbs a lot
of time, but I want it to be historically accurate, before the inevitable
arrival of the buxom stewardesses (plane crash on Alcatraz!). I start
dating the imaginary mother and daughter, to listen to their stories,
to live with them on intimate terms, although I know in my gut it will
be only a brief affair, only a matter of months before our relationship
is over and they're handed off to the highest bidder, handed over to
someone else, to be locked away in the bloom of their youth or brain-
washed into other beings.

I stop writing screenplays to sell and my agent stops calling. I
spend my time shopping, spending the money I've stockpiled. I wait
to awaken one morning to find all the work done, to discover those
blank books packed full of a novel. Maybe Garp will creep inside my
head and rewire the circuitry for me; maybe Zhivago will do it for me
while I sleep.

I remember a lesson: Writers must go away to write. Fine; I will try,
again, to be Stingo. I pack up my computer and rent an apartment in

San Francisco on a six-month lease with the last of my screenwriting money. It's a roll of the dice. I set up my *writing space*, spend a few more months hanging out on Alcatraz and sneezing in dusty Bay Area archives and libraries. I walk on the beach looking for Eugene O'Neill or a dreamy guy with a bucket of clams or someone to tell me I *will move mountains*. I fall back on eating cheese and bread and sitting in cafés, holding a variety of blank books and pencils and pens destined to fail me, and drinking far too much red wine. I don't smoke, but I'm tempted to start, if only to maintain the illusion. I hang out in bookstores, but it begins to feel like chastisement: See, all these people wrote *their* books. I don't remember anything I ever might have learned about writing in all those college workshops; I feel I barely remember how to type. I have my four years of accumulated research—this is perhaps worth an honorary degree in the history of Alcatraz, but that's all. I have facts and figures, an idea, an outline, a metaphor, and characters I'm embarrassed to admit I'm hopelessly in love with. And I'm terrified for them, that their life is fully in my unworthy hands. I can't even give them voice.

One morning I sit down at my desk. The bathroom is clean, the fridge is stocked with food. The dog has been walked. One sentence, I tell myself. That's all you have to write. After one sentence, you can go buy a pair of shoes, take the dog for another walk, go to a movie, go back to your lazy-adverb, unproductive waste of a life.

I write my one sentence and hear:

DASH

I don't know what happened, but you better tear that up. Not that it's bad. It's just not good enough.

Nathan calls me *puling*, mocks me as an *artiste*. Jack Nicholson, grinning, wants me to take over his axe and go nuts. Nobodies will line up to not buy everything I ever might write, forget about being translated into Apache. I should be a waitress or a fireman.

And where's my fur hat with the money stashed inside—how am I saving Jews and political prisoners with this sentence? It isn't even a goddamn lily poem; I'll never topple a tsar. Garp was wrong, deluded; he was right to stop. I need to stop now, before I even really begin.

                    DASH
    It's not as if you've written anything before,
    you know. Nobody'll miss you.

He's right, I know he's right.

                    NATHAN
    What's the worst that can happen? I might dis-
    cover you can't write.

I come back to one embarrassingly superficial thing; I told all my friends and family, when I left, that I was going off to write a novel. I've marched off to my room. And here I am, six years old, crouched on my pink organza bedspread and expecting *ease*. Expecting it to get done by magic, by montage. Wishing for a book of children's poems I can steal an *apple/dapple* poem from; I'm crouched in a closet, hiding, too terrified to emerge. Not that anyone cares; nobody'll miss me. This assignment was self-inflicted. But I can't go back empty-handed. My one sentence is lonely, left hanging. It whispers another sentence in my ear, begging me to provide company.

                    JULIA
    Work hard! Take chances! Be very bold!

Blink. I write the second sentence, and then I lose count. Blink. Four months later, I have a stack of three hundred and fifty pages and I can come out now, finally, into the light with a sense of having earned something. I've written my own *apple/dapple* poem. For the first time, I have done my job.

-- -- -- -- -- -- --

I n 2000, the film *Wonder Boys* brings me terror and hope.[109] The writer is back in his bathrobe, a pink chenille one at that. Grady Tripp is a one-hit wonder, a novelist famous for one novel, seven years ago, who is now stranded in academia and mired in a no-end-in-sight second novel (over 2,600 single-spaced pages, typed on a manual typewriter) in which his entire identity is invested; his wife has abandoned him, he's sleeping with the Chancellor of his liberal arts college, he's perpetually stubbled and stoned. It's nice to see Michael Douglas playing authentically pouchy for a change, but I loathe the movie. It hurts to watch. The once-appealing-to-me archetype of the rumpled bathrobe–wearing writer-turned-Creative-Writing-professor has become too painfully relatable. Grady's star student, James, is the cliché of the morose, freaky, suffering writing student (he recites movie-star-suicide facts and figures as a party trick and dismissively announces his brilliant story took him only an hour to write). Grady and James tell each other they're special, that they're unlike the rest of the other teachers/students, but they aren't; they're every annoying writer trope in the book. The movie spins off into self-consciously precious subplots about finding a stolen jacket once worn by Marilyn Monroe, and hiding a dead dog, and whether or not Grady's editor is going to seduce the sensitive James and/or publish his manuscript—as usual, a movie about a writer can't spend too much time showing us the writer writing, or trying to write, because, as I now know, more than thirty seconds of that is so fucking boring you'd want to throw up or yell Fire! in that crowded theatre. Although this cloying, self-conscious wackiness is almost worse.

The movie really hurts to watch, however, because I've become that trope. My first novel, *A Child out of Alcatraz*, was well received and did "nicely." I did it, good, and now I'm supposed to do it again. The pride of that first completed, achieved, *written* book was short-lived; the moment I sat down to write again, I was back on the floor of my closet

---

109   *Wonder Boys* (Paramount Pictures, 2000): screenplay by Steven Kloves, based on the novel by Michael Chabon; directed by Curtis Hanson; with Michael Douglas and Tobey Maguire

in a paralyzed crouch, trying to whip up another *apple/dapple* poem and knowing I couldn't, I could never do that again, it was too impossibly hard. And that first book was so *easy*, I don't even remember the labor of writing—perhaps someone else *did* creep in and write it while I slept, and any day, I'm going to be found out. Grady keeps assuring his editor that his second novel is almost done—his mantralike lament to all obstacles is "I'm trying to finish my novel!"—and I know that song, too. (Again, I can't go into bookstores, the chastisement is back: See, all these people wrote their *second* books . . . .) I know the Grady who freezes up after that beautiful, painless first book and can't seem to do it again; I know the Atlas-like weight of that second book on your shoulders, how it becomes a massive globe that cracks your spine, cripples you into a perpetual hunch. It's hard to rest on laurels turned dry and crisp with age; one touch too many, and they turn to dust.

And I'm supposed to be an academic now, too, the teacher of creative writing students for whom I'm supposed to set an inspiring writerly example. I've sat in those endless fiction workshops and mediated student feedback and personalities and tried to sound knowledgeable about parallel or fragmented structures and narrative arc and the layers of character psychology and putting pressure on the language and unpacking the story and stressing the need for everyone present to be critical yet positive and constructive; I've gone to those interminable faculty cocktail parties and made my dinner of those toothpicked cubes of cheese. I know the outrage you feel when a young student goes all starry-eyed over your (old) book, then offers up a casual and cutting criticism of your current (lesser) work; I know the threat of reading a morose, freaky, suffering student's work and knowing it's superior to yours. I know the awe of watching their hard work, their uncynical investment, their fearless and unabashed commitment. My writerly problem isn't Grady's—he's logorrheic in print, while I can't seem to break one hundred pages of anything—but I identify way too much with the terrifying suspicion of being washed-up, of knowing it's all over. And, while I tell myself that Grady is obviously in his late fifties (although I think Michael Douglas is trying to play forties), and I'm still much younger, this ultimately depresses me—if you're washed up at fifty-five, it's one thing, but if you're washed-up at my age . . . well, that means you have a good thirty or forty years of being washed-up lying ahead of you, a long, pathetic, winding road.

At one point a visiting Famous Writer booms to a packed auditorium:

```
               FAMOUS WRITER
    Everyone has a great idea. But how do you get
    from there to here? What is the bridge from the
    water's edge of inspiration to the far shore of
    accomplishment? It is the faith that your story
    is worth telling . . .
```

at which point Grady passes out. He's lost the sustaining oxygen of faith, the ability to glean any nourishment from the air.

```
               GRADY
    Books. They don't mean anything. Not to anybody.
    Not anymore.
```

He means they don't mean anything to *him*, not anymore, and I'm feeling they don't mean anything to me, either—it *is* all over. I can't *let* the writing mean anything; it's too crushing a weight. But we're both lying; the books and the writing still mean everything to us, and we both know it's too late. We're both already crushed.

But there's also (damn) hope. Grady winds up with the woman he loves, but that isn't it. He gets past feeling threatened by his young student—he applauds wildly on hearing James's manuscript will indeed be published, he paternally passes the Wonder Boy torch—but that isn't it. And he's over feeling he has nothing to offer as a teacher:

```
               GRADY
    Nobody teaches a writer anything. You tell them
    what you know, you tell them to find their own
    voice and stay with it, you tell the ones that
    have it to keep at it, you tell the ones that
```

```
don't have it to keep at it, too, because that's
the only way they're going to get where they're
going. . .
```

but that isn't why.

There's hope because late in the movie, the 2,611 in-progress pages of Grady's second novel (the only copy he has) go flying to heaven, literally; they're snatched up by a ruthless wind and scattered like the weightless leaves of paper they are. (I see Garp and Helen, running to catch those escaping, whirling pages.) I feel panic—this is the ultimate nightmare! The labor of seven years, all those exquisite words, all those perfect sentences, *gone*? Grab those pages, quick, don't let them go!—but Grady just stands there; he just watches. He lets it all go; the burden is released, it floats away like end-of-the-day balloons.

It makes him happy. Perhaps those pages were "lesser"—it doesn't matter. Perhaps they were brilliant—it still doesn't matter. He wrote those words and sentences once; he can write them again. He can write other words and sentences; he's a writer. He goes back to work. (And, regrettably, throws away the bathrobe—that might work as a symbolic gesture, but I refuse to believe it was necessary. The bathrobe is still a legitimate perk.) He is a hero; he is a wonder boy; he is a writer who simply gets back to work. The pressure and promise of that make-it-even-more-glorious second novel—or the third, the fourth, or your first book of essays—is the dark side of the paint job; it's the false lure of the beach house and the sable coat. It's the tease of *You did it once, you don't have to do it again*, and all this can still be yours. It's all about being a Writer, and it doesn't have anything to do with writing. Stop crying about it.

--- --- --- ---

So, I've bought into the cinematic image of the Writer—the abbreviated moments of typing that magically create Art, and both the charmingly furrow-browed struggle and the illusion of ease. So perhaps the movies have soft-soaped me with all that crap. And it's still hard to confess to the emotional investment—it's too scary, you're too easily exposed to Dash's dismissal, to the lash of Nathan's whip, to the banishment to an icy Siberian steppe. But the Real Writer, the Serious Writer, is simply the one who writes. Who keeps writing. Who keeps at it, beyond the montage—for whom the writing *is* the story, not the musical interlude.

And if it's always going to be terrifying, I tell myself, if the faith of having been able to do it *before* so you can surely do it *now* gets wiped out like an Etch A Sketch each and every time you sit down to write, fine. That's just the way it is, so stop crying about it. Or go stand on a rock. Or quit—no one will miss you.

And if you're always going to feel like a fraud, crouched on the floor of your closet among the Mary Janes, no matter how published you get or however many nice reviews, fine. So go put on the lumpy cardigan or linen blouse, if it helps (it does); take a day trip to the beach, stroll the sand and furrow your own brow, go for drinks at the Algonquin the next time you get to New York. Put on some balalaika music and batten the door against wolves. Nothing wrong with keeping a newsreel of those alluring writer images flickering in front of you; go pin them up in the writing space of your mind.

And the writer's job isn't to save the world; it's just to keep the faith, and to write. To be a humbled Sullivan and get back to work. The lily and love poems are indeed revolutionary—they make "just living" worth the fight; the story of your mother's death becomes everyone's story, a touchpoint for the universal experience of grief. And thank God for every moment of mindless joy we can get. And maybe it doesn't even matter if the writing's any good; in the true moment of writing, in the focused, absorbed, committed moment, there are no reviews, no audience, no paint job, no handsome or beautiful lovers fighting over me, no sable coat, no beach house, no being feted, no mountains to move. Who knows if the looming potential even exists, or ever did, or ever will be fulfilled? It doesn't matter. In the moment of the writing, in the warp and weft and forging ahead of it, I'm earning the right to exist on the planet. For just that moment, I'm saving myself.

I hope Julia would approve.

ACKNOWLEDGMENTS

I am enormously grateful to the friends, family, and colleagues who have provided keen-eyed editorial assistance, offered endless and critical feedback, reminisced, brainstormed, shared all those tubs of popcorn, and given me the aisle seat, especially: Bernadette Murphy, Tina-Marie Gauthier, Emily Rapp, Dylan Landis, Cyndi Menegaz, Michelle Nordon, Mary Vincent, Neil Landau, Michelle Henkin, Leslye Kasoff, Barbara DeLucia, Ellen Svaco, Lorie Sears Warnock, Marylee MacDonald, Joe Bogdanovic, Colleen Rooney, and, always, Eloise Klein Healy. And to Dan Smetanka, the wisest, dearest, most true-believing editor ever: Thank you.

I am also grateful to those dreamers of dreams: The screenwriters, novelists, filmmakers, and actors who challenge and inspire us to linger, briefly but essentially, in that luminous space between the imagined story and the real world.